Financial Modeling in Excel®

2nd Edition

by Danielle Stein Fairhurst

A Wiley Brand

Financial Modeling in Excel® For Dummies®, 2nd Edition

Published by: **John Wiley & Sons, Inc.,** 111 River Street, Hoboken, NJ 07030-5774, www.wiley.com

Copyright © 2022 by John Wiley & Sons, Inc., Hoboken, New Jersey

Published simultaneously in Canada

For general information on our other products and services, please contact our Customer Care Department within the U.S. at 877-762-2974, outside the U.S. at 317-572-3993, or fax 317-572-4002. For technical support, please visit https://hub.wiley.com/community/support/dummies.

Wiley publishes in a variety of print and electronic formats and by print-on-demand. Some material included with standard print versions of this book may not be included in e-books or in print-on-demand. If this book refers to media such as a CD or DVD that is not included in the version you purchased, you may download this material at http://booksupport.wiley.com. For more information about Wiley products, visit www.wiley.com.

Library of Congress Control Number: 2021950428

ISBN 978-1-119-84451-8 (pbk); ISBN 978-1-119-84452-5 (ebk); ISBN 978-1-119-84453-2 (ebk)

SKY10031803_120421

Contents at a Glance

Table of Contents

Introduction

I discovered financial modeling in Microsoft Excel when I worked in investment banking in London (as most young Aussies do). Back then, the term *financial modeling* was hardly used, but I was hooked. Since those days, I've devoted my entire career to working in Excel and building models for the purpose of business cases, reports, budgets, and dashboards. I've worked with hundreds of clients in many different countries to help build their models for them or train them on how to build their own. Financial modeling in Excel takes me all over the world (both virtually and in person) and I hope that it brings you the same fun and excitement!

About This Book

I wrote this book based on the experiences I've had with the many insightful people I've trained or worked with over the years. I cover the tools and techniques that are the most commonly needed for building models. This book is aimed at people who already have a smattering of Excel knowledge but want to improve their skills to perform better in their current roles or to get better jobs.

After reading this book, you'll know exactly what a financial modeler does and how to apply the principles of financial modeling to your work. You may not call yourself a "career" financial modeler. Instead, you might think of yourself as a "casual" modeler — maybe it's a side interest for you, or it's just one part of your job. But after reading this book, you may be bitten by the modeling bug and want to pursue a full-time career in this field!

You don't have to read this book from cover to cover — feel free to jump around and read the sections that are of most interest to you! In most cases, I demonstrate the tools and techniques covered by applying them to a simple model — usually what I would expect to be just *part* of a full financial model. In Part 3, you create three full financial models from start to finish. I encourage you to read this book with Excel open and not too far away because you'll want to try out many of the exercises and techniques described in these pages.

Foolish Assumptions

I assume just a few basic things about you. It goes without saying that you're highly intelligent because you recognize the value of having financial modeling skills. But I also assume that you have the following:

>> **A PC with a relatively recent version of Excel installed:** The screenshots and instructions in this book relate to Excel for Microsoft 365 and its capabilities. If you're using a Mac, or a previous version of Excel, you might find some of the instructions slightly different, but you should be able to find your way around.

>> **A working knowledge of Excel and a use for it:** I don't assume that you're an Excel expert, but you should at least know your way around and perhaps have created at least a few basic calculations before.

>> **Some kind of financial background:** You know what a set of financial statements looks like, you know what revenue is, and you know how interest calculations work. Some of the complexities are explained in this book, but I assume that these kinds of basic financial concepts are not entirely new to you.

Icons Used in This Book

This book is jam-packed with tips, tricks, warning, and ways to work smarter, faster, and more accurately.

Anything marked with the Tip icon will make your financial modeling quicker or easier.

If I mark it with the Remember icon, it's really, really important and you should pay special attention.

When you see the Warning icon, you know that I'm trying to save you the pain and agony of making a mistake (one that I've probably made many times myself).

I get very excited when talking or writing about financial modeling, so sometimes I get a little technical on you. Anything marked with the Technical Stuff icon isn't essential to your understanding of the surrounding text.

Beyond the Book

In addition to the material in the print or e-book you're reading right now, this product also comes with some access-anywhere goodies on the web. Check out the free Cheat Sheet for a list of the Excel functions that you absolutely need to know, tips on what to look for when auditing someone else's financial model, and the best keyboard shortcuts for financial modelers. To get this Cheat Sheet, simply go to www.dummies.com and type **Financial Modeling in Excel For Dummies Cheat Sheet** in the Search box.

You can also go to www.dummies.com/go/financialmodelinginexcelfd2e for Excel files you can use to follow along with the exercises and examples in this book, as well as the completed versions of the financial models you build in Part 3.

Where to Go from Here

If you're just getting started and want to find out what all the fuss is about financial modeling, start at Chapter 1 and read on from there. If you're more technical and you want to get into something practical, Part 2 is a great place to start. Have a go at some of the shorter examples before getting started with the longer case studies in Part 3.

If you enjoy this book, I'd like to invite you to connect directly with me online through LinkedIn and other social media platforms. Search for the "Financial Modelling in Excel" LinkedIn group (or go to www.linkedin.com/groups/1724487) to join more than 55,000 other modelers (and counting!) and get involved in the active discussions. You can also subscribe to hear more about the world of financial modeling at www.plumsolutions.com.au/news, and I'd love to meet you at one of my upcoming events, or Financial Modelers' Meetups soon.

Have fun, and happy modeling!

1

Getting Started with Financial Modeling

Explore the practical uses and examples of financial modeling.

Get to know Excel and identify the issues and risks for its use in building financial models.

Document and plan your model's layout and design.

Get important guidelines to follow when building your financial model.

Find your way around an inherited financial model, and audit and check its output for accuracy.

Chapter **1**

Introducing Financial Modeling

The demand for financial modeling skills has increased exponentially in recent years and many job listings for finance positions now include "financial modeling" as a core skill. If you're reading this book, you've probably already discovered how important this skill is, and you know that learning financial modeling will increase your employability in finance or financially focused fields.

In this chapter, I define financial modeling — what it is, who uses it, and why it matters. I also show you some examples of financial models. If you're brand-new to financial modeling, this chapter is a very good place to start.

Defining Financial Modeling

Before you dive into how to use Microsoft Excel to create financial models, you need to know what financial modeling is, who uses financial models, and why financial modeling matters. In this section, I fill you in.

What it is

When I teach a course on basic financial modeling, I always ask my students for their definitions of the term *financial model.* Most of them come up with long-winded descriptions using terms like *forecast* and *cash flow* and *hypothetical outcomes.* But I don't think the definition needs to be that complicated. A *financial model* is a tool (typically built in Excel) that displays possible solutions to a real-world financial problem. And *financial modeling* is the task of creating a financial model.

You may have thought that a financial model was basically just an Excel spreadsheet, but as you probably already know, not every spreadsheet is a financial model. People can and do use Excel for all kinds of purposes. So, what makes a financial model distinct from a garden-variety spreadsheet? In contrast to a basic spreadsheet, a financial model

>> **Is more structured.** A financial model contains a set of variable assumptions — inputs, outputs, calculations, and scenarios. It often includes a set of standard financial forecasts — such as a profit-and-loss statement, a balance sheet, and a cash flow statement — which are based on those assumptions.

>> **Is dynamic.** A financial model contains inputs that, when changed, impact the calculations and, therefore, the results. A financial model always has built-in flexibility to display different outcomes or final calculations based on changing a few key inputs.

>> **Uses relationships between several variables.** When the user changes any of the input assumptions, a chain reaction often occurs. For example, changing the growth rate will change the sales volume; when the sales volume changes, the revenue, sales commissions, and other variable expenses will change.

>> **Shows *forecasts.*** Financial models are almost always looking into the future. Financial modelers often want to know what their financial projections will look like down the road. For example, if you continue growing at the same rate, what will your cash flow be in five years?

>> **Contains *scenarios* (hypothetical outcomes).** Because a model is looking forward instead of backward, a well-built financial model can be easily used to perform scenario and sensitivity analysis. What would happen if interest rates went up? How much can we discount before we start making a loss?

More broadly, a financial model is a structure (usually in Excel) that contains inputs and outputs, and is flexible and dynamic.

Who uses it

Many types of people build and use financial models for different purposes and goals. Financial models are usually built to solve real-world problems, and there are as many different financial models as there are real-world problems to solve. Generally, anyone who uses Excel for the purpose of finance will at some point in their career build a financial model for themselves or others to use; at the very least, they'll use a model someone else created.

WHAT IT TAKES TO BE A FINANCIAL MODELER

Someone working with financial models typically has an undergraduate degree in business, finance, or commerce. Additionally, they likely have at least one of the following postgraduate qualifications:

- An accountancy qualification, such as CA (Certified Accountant), CPA (Certified Public Accountant), CIMA (Chartered Institute of Management Accountants), ACCA (Association of Chartered Certified Accountants), CMA (Certified Management Accountant), or CIA (Certified Internal Auditor)
- A Master of Business Administration (MBA) degree
- A Chartered Financial Analyst (CFA) designation
- A Financial Risk Manager (FRM) designation

Of course, you don't need all those letters after your name to build and work with financial models. I know many skilled modelers who come from backgrounds in IT or engineering, or who don't have any formal qualifications at all. The Financial Modeling Institute (FMI) has set up a formal qualification; three levels of financial modelling qualifications are available. If financial modeling is important for your career, gaining this qualification will be very useful, but it is by no means a requirement. You can also find many training courses in financial modeling.

If you simply want to list financial modeling as a skill on your résumé, a short course is sufficient (backed up by at least a couple of models you've built in the real world). If you're aiming toward a financial modeling career, you'll need formal finance qualifications such as those listed here, as well as intense, practical, hands-on work experience.

Bankers, particularly investment bankers, are heavy users of financial models. Due to the very nature of financial institutions, modeling is part of the culture of the company — the business's core is built on financial models. Banks and financial institutions must comply with current regulatory restrictions, and the tools and controls in place are forever changing and adapting. Because of the risk associated with lending and other financial activities, these institutions have very complex financial modeling systems in place to ensure that the risk is managed effectively. Anyone working in the banking industry should have at least a working knowledge of spreadsheets and financial models.

Outside the banking industry, accountants are big users of financial models. Bankers are often evaluating other companies for credit risk and other measures. An accountant's models, however, are often more inward looking, focusing on internal operations reporting and analysis, project evaluation, pricing, and profitability.

Why it matters

A financial model is designed to depict a real-life situation in numbers in order to help people make better financial decisions.

Wherever there are financial problems or situations in the real world that need solving, analyzing, or translating into a numerical format, financial models help. Sometimes it's just an idea or a concept that needs to be converted into a business case or feasibility proposal. A skilled financial modeler can put substance to the idea by augmenting the details enough to get a working model upon which decisions can be made, investor funds can be gained, or staff can be hired.

For example, financial models can help investors decide which project to put their money into, an executive track which marketing campaigns have the highest return on investment, or a factory production manager decide whether to purchase a new piece of machinery.

Looking at Examples of Financial Models

When you then consider the benefits that a financial model can bring, it's difficult not to get carried away thinking of the application potential of a financial model! When you understand the principles of financial models, you can begin to look at the most common scenarios in which a model would be implemented.

There are a variety of categories of financial models:

>> **Project finance models:** When a large infrastructure project is being assessed for viability, the project finance model helps determine the capital and structure of the project.

>> **Pricing models:** These models are built for the purpose of determining the price that can or should be charged for a product.

>> **Integrated financial statement models (also known as a three-way financial model):** The purpose of this kind of model is to forecast the financial position of the company as a whole.

>> **Valuation models:** Valuation models value assets or businesses for the purpose of joint ventures, refinancing, contract bids, acquisitions, or other kinds of transactions or "deals." (The people who build these kinds of models are often known as *deals modelers.*)

>> **Reporting models:** These models summarize the history of revenue, expenses, or financial statements.

You'll see some overlap between each type of model category. For example, many reporting models also contain integrated financial statements, or a project finance model may be used for valuation purposes, but most models can be classified predominately as one model type. Modelers often specialize in one or two of these model categories.

In this section, I show you some examples of scenarios and places in which these categories of financial models can come in handy, along with the functions and characteristics of each.

Project finance models

Loans and the associated debt repayments are an important part of project finance models, because these projects are normally long term, and lenders need to know whether the project is able to produce enough cash to service the debt. Metrics such as debt service cover ratio (DSCR) are included in the model and can be used as a measure of risk of the project, which may affect the interest rate offered by the lender. At the beginning of the project, the DSCR and other metrics are agreed upon between the lender and borrower such that the ratio must not go below a certain number.

Pricing models

The input to a pricing model is the price, and the output is the profitability. To create a pricing model, an income statement (or profit-and-loss statement) of the business or product should be created first, based on the current price or a price that has been input as a placeholder. At a very high level:

Units × Price = Revenue

Revenue − Expenses = Profit

Of course, this kind of model can be very complex and involve many different tabs and calculations, or it can be quite simple, on a single page. When this structure model is in place, the modeler can perform sensitivity analysis on the price entered using a goal seek (see Chapter 6) or a data table (see Chapter 8).

Integrated financial statement models

Not every financial model needs to contain all three types of financial statements, but many of them do, and those that do are known as integrated financial statement models. You may also hear them referred to as "three-way financial models." The three types of financial statements included in an integrated financial statement model are the following:

>> Income statement, also known as a profit-and-loss (P&L) statement

>> Cash flow statement

>> Balance sheet

From a financial modeling perspective, it's very important that when an integrated financial statement model is built, the financial statements are linked together properly so that if one statement changes, the others change as well. For an example of how to build an integrated financial statement model, turn to Chapter 10.

Valuation models

Building valuation models requires a specialized knowledge of *valuation theory* (using the different techniques of valuing an asset), as well as modeling skills. If you're a casual financial modeler, you probably won't be required to create from scratch a fully functioning valuation model. But you should at least have an idea of what types of valuation financial models are out there.

Here are three common types of valuation financial models you may encounter:

» **Mergers and acquisitions (M&A):** These models are built to simulate the effect of two companies merging or one company taking over the other. M&A models are normally undertaken in a tightly controlled environment. Due to its confidential nature, an M&A model has fewer players than other kinds of models. The project moves quickly because time frames are tight. The few modelers working on an M&A model do so in a concentrated period of time, often working long hours to achieve a complex and detailed model.

» **Leveraged buyout (LBO):** These models are built to facilitate the purchase of a company or asset with large amounts of debt to finance the deal, called a *leveraged buyout.* The entity acquiring the "target" company or asset usually finances the deal with some equity, using the target's assets as security — in the same way that many home loan mortgages work. LBOs are a popular method of acquisition because they allow the entity to make large purchases without committing a lot of cash. Modeling is an important part of the LBO deal because of its complexity and the high stakes involved.

» **Discounted cash flow (DCF):** These models calculate the cash expected to be received from the business or asset a company is considering purchasing, and then discounts that cash flow back into today's dollars to see whether the opportunity is worth pursuing. Valuing the future cash flows expected from an acquisition is the most common modeling method of valuation. Intrinsic to the DCF methodology is the concept of the time value of money — in other words, that cash received today is worth a lot more than the same amount of cash received in future years. For an example of how to calculate DCF, turn to Chapter 11.

Reporting models

Because they look historically at what occurred in the past, some people argue that reporting models are not really financial models at all, but I disagree. The principles, layout, and design that are used to create a reporting model are identical to other financial models. Just because they contain historical rather than projected numbers doesn't mean they should be categorized any differently.

In fact, reporting models are often used to create actual versus budget reports, which often include forecasts and rolling forecasts, which in turn are driven by assumptions and other drivers. Reporting models often start out as a simple income statement report, but end up being transformed into fully integrated financial statement models, pricing models, project finance models, or valuation models.

PUTTING "FINANCIAL MODELING" ON YOUR RÉSUMÉ

When you know exactly what's involved in the modeling process and you have knowledge of financial modeling skills that you've used in the workplace, you're ready to put "financial modeling" on your résumé.

Since the economic crisis of 2008 and the uncertainty created by the COVID-19 pandemic, emphasis on financial modeling has increased. In response, there has been a rise in job descriptions specifying financial modeling as a core competency. If you're applying for a job in finance, employers will no doubt look favorably upon this skill, as long as it rings true with the rest of your résumé. You need to be able to flesh out the tasks in previous positions you've held with examples of what kinds of models you built.

Although short vocational courses in financial modeling (see "What it takes to be a financial modeler," earlier in this chapter) are well respected, what prospective employers really want to see is the *application* of financial modeling techniques in your everyday work.

Just reading this book or taking a financial modeling training course doesn't mean you can add "financial modeling" to your résumé. You need to have actually *used* your modeling skills in the real-world environment. Take every opportunity to use models in your work. If you're not currently employed, find example models online, take them apart, and see how you can improve them.

Whatever you do, don't exaggerate when it comes to the level of experience you have with financial modeling. You may be asked in the interview to back up and discuss in great detail the intricacies of how you created a particular model.

Chapter **2**

Getting Acquainted with Excel

For most people, Microsoft Excel and financial modeling go hand in hand. Given the title of this book, it should come as no surprise to you that I assume you'll be using Excel. In order to build a financial model, you need at least a working knowledge of Excel. So, before jumping into the details of financial modeling, I'm going to introduce you to the tool you'll be using, Microsoft Excel.

Almost every financial model you'll come across will make use of Excel to some extent, but alternatives to Excel do exist, as do add-ins to improve Excel, both of which I cover in this chapter. Finally, I look at some of the issues and risks related to the use of Excel, just so you know what to expect.

Making Sense of the Different Versions of Excel

Over the past few decades, Microsoft has brought out a new version of Excel every couple of years, but the latest subscription model, Excel for Microsoft 365, is planned to have an infinite life. This subscription model is designed to constantly evolve, allowing Microsoft to release features more gradually instead of overwhelming users with lots of huge changes all at once. The subscription model is designed to reduce disruption. Plus, it encourages users to be on the same version, which means fewer compatibility problems.

TECHNICAL
STUFF

In the past, because of the cost of purchasing licenses for each new version of Excel, many businesses delayed the upgrade when a new version was released. This meant that a wide range of versions were being used. In my public training courses, I would often see up to six different versions of Excel being used in the class!

Although Excel 2019 is available, Microsoft is *strongly* encouraging the subscription model. Out of curiosity, I ran a poll in mid-2021 asking about versions on LinkedIn and from 1,400 respondents it seems around 68 percent of people were already using Excel for Microsoft 365, and I would expect this percentage to increase over time. Looking at the new features that are available in Excel for Microsoft 365 but not available in the "latest" stand-alone version of Excel 2019, it's not surprising that the take up of the Microsoft 365 subscription is so high.

WARNING

Some new functions have been introduced in recent versions of Excel. If you build a model that contains these new functions and a user opens it in a previous version of Excel, they'll get a #N/A error. Be cautious using new functions when you're building a financial model, unless you're sure that anyone who needs to use your model will be using the same version of Excel as you.

TIP

If you're not sure whether you've used any functions or features not available in previous versions of Excel, use the Inspect Workbook tool (see Chapter 5) to find out.

And if you're not sure which version of Excel you're using, open Excel and choose File ⇨ Account ⇨ About Excel. At the top of the dialog box that appears, you'll see the version number. If that doesn't work, then you're probably using a very old version; choose Help ⇨ Resources ⇨ About.

A rundown of recent Excel versions

In this section, I walk you through some of the features introduced in recent versions of Excel. A feature that rolled out in 2013, for example, will be available in later versions as well. Although these lists are by no means exhaustive, they are the features you're most likely to use for the purposes of financial modeling and analysis.

REMEMBER

If you have Excel on a Microsoft 365 subscription plan, you get new features as soon as they roll out with each update, instead of having to wait for the next version of Excel.

Excel for Microsoft 365

Although Excel 2019 is currently the latest stand-alone version of Excel, there are some truly major features for which you need to be using Excel for Microsoft 365 because they are not available in Excel 2019 without a Microsoft 365 subscription:

>> **Dynamic arrays** are probably the biggest change to Excel *ever,* and they're particularly relevant for financial modelers. This feature allows the formula to return multiple results to a single formula (see Chapter 6). Dynamic arrays alone are worth upgrading to Microsoft 365!

>> The **XLOOKUP function** replaces the VLOOKUP and HLOOKUP functions (see Chapter 7).

>> The **LET function** assigns names within a formula, which stores your calculations so you don't have to repeat yourself within the formula.

>> The **LAMBDA function** allows you to create your own custom functions.

>> The **STOCKHISTORY function** retrieves historical price data and displays it in multiple cells as an array.

>> **Linked Data types** pull in data from online sources such as Bing and Wolfram. With new artificial intelligence (AI)–powered online data types, a cell can have a region or country value from which more information such as the population, capital city, area, and many more details can be extracted. The first data types supported were Geography, Currencies, and Stocks.

>> **Co-authoring** allows multiple users to edit at the same time if a file is stored in Teams, SharePoint or OneDrive (see Chapter 5). You can also share and collaborate with people outside the organization who don't have a Microsoft 365 subscription.

>> **Threaded comments** is a new style of comment that allows multiple comments to be grouped together as a conversation in a cell.

A few features were first added in Excel 2016:

>> **Map charts** allow you to display data on a map using countries, states, provinces, and even zip codes or postcodes. You can display numbers as a heat map or color coded. Note that these maps use Bing, so your PC needs to be connected to the Internet to create the chart. If you have the right subscription and an Internet connection, you'll see Filled Map appear as an option, as shown in Figure 2-1.

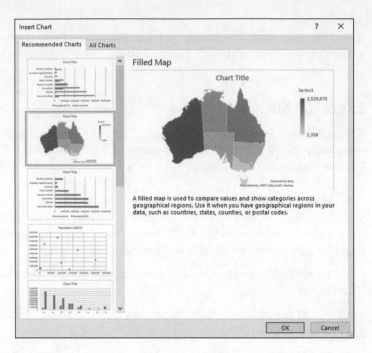

FIGURE 2-1:
A filled map.

>> The following **new functions** are also only available for Microsoft 365 subscribers:

- **TEXTJOIN:** Use this function to link the text in ranges of cells together. This is one of my favorite new functions because you can now string entire *ranges* of cells together, instead of linking them individually as you had to do with the ampersand (&) or the CONCATENATE function.

- **CONCAT:** Use this function to link the text in individual cells together. This was called CONCATENATE in previous versions. You can also use the ampersand (&) instead of CONCAT or CONCATENATE.

- **IFS:** Use this function if you have multiple conditions to include in a single cell. This function makes using a nested IF function much easier.

- **SWITCH:** Use this function to look up a list of values and return a matching result in a single cell.

- **MAXIFS:** Use this function to calculate the maximum value that meets specific criteria.

- **MINIFS:** Use this function to calculate the minimum value that meets specific criteria.

Microsoft Excel 2019

In Excel 2019, the following features were added. None of these are ground-breaking enough to warrant the upgrade from 2016 to 2019, in my opinion:

» **Custom visuals,** such as word clouds, bullet charts, and speedometers.

» **Forms** connected to Excel, so you can have a nice form user interface, with a very easy-to-use tool.

» An improved **Power Query.** Note also the name Power Query was changed to Get & Transform for Excel 2016 but reverted to Power Query with Excel 2019, presumably to fit with the rest of the Power Suite (including Power Pivot, and Power BI).

» **Preferences for PivotTables,** which can now be defined as a default behavior if changing your PivotTable preferences is something you do regularly.

Microsoft Excel 2016

In Excel 2016, the following features were added:

» The **Tell Me What You Want to Do** box was added to the Ribbon. This box is a very user-friendly way of finding your way around Excel.

» The following **new charts** were added: Waterfall, Treemap, Sunburst, Histogram, Box & Whisker, and Funnel. These new charts are a welcome addition to Excel and make it very easy to display the results of your financial model. But remember that if you insert any of these new charts into your model and a user opens it in a previous version of Excel, the charts won't be available — they'll only be able to see a blank white box.

» Power Query was changed to **Get & Transform.** It's on the Data tab on the Ribbon. In prior versions of Excel, Power Query had to be installed as a free downloadable add-in, but Get & Transform comes standard.

» **Forecast Sheet** was added. It's a very powerful way of forecasting using historical data.

Microsoft Excel 2013

In Excel 2013, the following features were added:

» **Flash Fill** was introduced. Flash Fill is a handy tool that picks up on the pattern of what you've entered.

To use Flash Fill, start typing an abbreviated version of your data in the column directly next to it, as shown in Figure 2-2. Based on the pattern of what you've typed, a grayed-out version of suggested text is displayed. Press Enter to accept this data. You can also type the first cell, and then use the shortcut Ctrl+E. If you'd like to try this out for yourself, you can download `File 0201.xlsx` from `www.dummies.com/go/financialmodelinginexcelfd2e`. Open it and select the tab labeled 2-2.

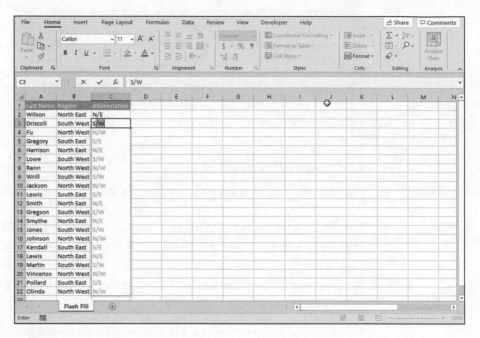

FIGURE 2-2:
Flash Fill.

>> The **Combo Chart** was introduced as a standard chart. Combo Charts display a line chart and a bar chart on two different axes, which is very useful.

>> **Multiple monitors** were made easier to work with because the interface changed so that you can have two separate files open and view them side by side. In the past, you would have had to open a completely new session of Excel to do this, so you couldn't link between files. Whether you link between files or not, having large and/or multiple monitors is definitely recommended for large and complex models!

>> Fifty **new functions** were introduced, enhancing the already abundant function set. Most of the new functions are used for statistics, trigonometry, and engineering, but here are a few that you might find useful for financial modeling:

- **PDURATION:** Use this function to return the number of investment periods required for the invested amount to get to the specific value.

- **IFNA:** Use this function to suppress an #N/A error only.

- **ISFORMULA:** Use this function to return the value TRUE if the cell contains a formula. This function is similar to the ISERROR, ISNUM, and ISTEXT functions.

REMEMBER

Even though these functions might come in handy, they'll return an error if the person opening your model is not using Excel 2013 or later.

Microsoft Excel 2010

At first glance, there were no obvious changes introduced in Excel 2010, but this upgrade was actually deceivingly radical because it was the first version to introduce the Power Suite of tools, now called Modern Excel. Additionally, two other features made an appearance for the first time:

>> **Slicers:** Slicers are a great way of filtering PivotTables.

>> **Sparklines:** Sparklines are tiny charts in a single cell. They're a great way of displaying trends in a small space.

Figure 2-3 shows an example of a PivotTable with a slicer on the left in column A and a series of sparklines in column D. When you select one of the regions shown in the slicer, the data for the PivotTable filters to show only that selection. Additionally, sparklines in column D show the trend over a 12-month period of that line item.

These two features, although not related, work together so that when Africa is selected, for example, the total profit-and-loss numbers for Africa show only in column C, and the 12-month trend for Africa in the sparklines show only in column D. Both slicers and sparklines were particularly useful additions for building dashboards.

REMEMBER

The space in which slicers and sparklines are built will simply show as blank areas if the file is opened in Excel 2007 or earlier.

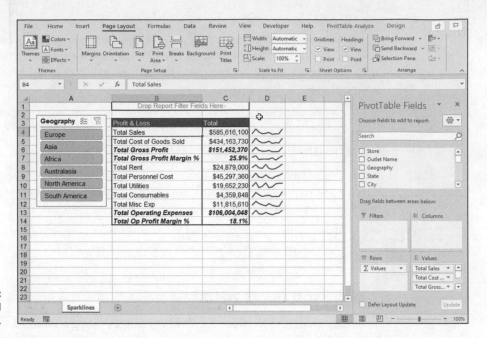

FIGURE 2-3:
Slicer and
sparklines.

Microsoft Excel Online

You can use Excel online through a web browser with Microsoft Excel Online, or Excel for the Web as it's also called. It is completely free, works on any browser, and is particularly useful if you need to share files and collaborate with others. To find out more about sharing and co-authoring, turn to Chapter 5. Microsoft is constantly working to improve the functionality of Excel Online, but a few key features — such as Power Query, VBA, graphics, and icons that you may be used to being able to access through the desktop version of Excel — are missing. Password protection is also not supported and there is a file size limit.

You can also use Excel on iOS and Android devices. Of course, it's not practical to do much work on a model via these apps, but they're handy for viewing or making minor edits when you're on the go. I have no doubt that developments to Excel Online will happen in the near future, but at this stage, it's still a slimmed-down version of Excel. But it's free, which is always a good thing!

WARNING

Microsoft Excel Online is only sufficient for a casual user of Excel, not for a professional financial modeler. You'll probably be able to work through most of the steps in this book using Excel Online but be aware that some key features are missing.

Focusing on file formats

Another thing that you may need to consider when working with different versions of Excel is the file type. Way back in Excel 2007, the file formats were changed from .xls to .xlsx. The .xlsx file format is more secure, faster, and more compact than .xls files. Also, .xls files are also limited to 65,000 rows, which sounds like a lot, but .xlsx files can handle up to a *million* rows.

Although the .xlsx file type has been around for many years, Excel files that have been downloaded from another system are sometimes automatically saved as .xls files. If you have Excel 2007 or later, you can save the file as .xlsx by choosing File ⇨ Save As, and changing the file type from Excel 97–2003 to Excel Workbook.

You might also run into the .xlsm file format. Those files contain macros, which contain executable code. If you're using macros, Excel will prompt you to save the file as .xlsm. And if you accidently save a file with macros in it as .xlsx, all the macros will completely disappear!

TIP

The .xlsb file format is a binary file format and is even more compressed than .xlsx, making the file size even smaller (which means the files open and save much faster than other file types). It has the added advantage of supporting macros. The only disadvantage is that .xlsb files can't be read by Power Query or other databases and software, including other cloud-based spreadsheet programs.

REMEMBER

You should always save your models as .xlsx file types, or .xlsb if file size becomes an issue.

Defining Modern Excel

Any version of Excel released from Excel 2010 onward is referred to as *Modern Excel* because it introduced the groundbreaking Power Suite, which consists of Power Pivot, Power Query, and Power BI. The introduction of these tools was the most exciting thing to happen in the Excel world since the PivotTable.

Table 2-1 offers a summary of the features of Modern Excel.

WARNING

None of these tools is, at the time of writing, available in Excel for Mac, although some steps have been taken toward functionality for Power Query on the Mac. At this stage, you can edit, import, and refresh several different data sources, but the integration is still limited. So, if you use the Modern Excel Power Suite, be sure your model doesn't need to run on a Mac.

TABLE 2-1   Modern Excel Power Suite

Tool	What It Does	Programming Language	Relevant Version
Power Pivot	Pulls much larger quantities of data than can be handled in standard Excel from different sources and stores it in a highly compressed format. Users can create relationships, perform complex calculations, and display output from different tables into a single-view PivotTable.	DAX	First introduced as an add-in to Excel 2010; native to Excel for Microsoft 365
Power Query	Extracts data from various sources. The user can cleanse and format the data and save this procedure; the procedure can then be repeatedly performed each time the data is refreshed.	M	First introduced as an add-in to Excel 2010; native to Microsoft 365
Power BI	A cloud-based, self-service analytics tool with which you can create dashboards, reports, and visualizations. You can access the functionality of Power Pivot and Power Query within Power BI.	DAX for Power Pivot and M for Power Query functionality	Desktop version first made available in 2015. Note that Power BI is the only tool mentioned that does not sit within Excel.

The self-service BI space, in particular, is growing rapidly, and there are many other pieces of software that can perform similar tasks. In my opinion, these Modern Excel tools are the way to go for handling and visualizing data for the following reasons:

>> **Low cost:** Power BI Pro (with larger data capacity and enhanced sharing capabilities over standard Power BI) comes with a small monthly cost, but the other tools are included with your Microsoft 365 subscription license.

>> **Familiarity:** Because they're part of Excel, and mostly use the familiar Excel interface, existing Excel users can get the hang of it more quickly than completely new software — although Power Pivot can take some time to figure out.

>> **Integration:** It's very easy to convince the boss to implement these tools because they're already part of Excel.

At first, many financial modelers I know didn't see these new tools as being relevant to them. Sure, they are data analysis tools as opposed to modeling tools, but modelers spend a lot of time extracting, updating, and manipulating data. Power Query, in particular, is a useful tool for performing these tasks more quickly and efficiently.

You should consider using Power Pivot or Power Query for the data in your model if any of the following is true:

>> The data your model is using contains many thousands of rows and your model is starting to slow down, especially when you add formulas.

>> You use PivotTables or tables extensively.

>> Your data needs to be sourced from multiple locations.

TIP

The powerhouse behind Power Pivot is the *data model,* which stores the tables and their relationships inside the workbook. One of the many useful things about the data model is that it stores the data very efficiently, and you can have *millions* of rows of data that you'd never be able to store and use in an ordinary Excel file.

The disadvantage of using Power Pivot is that, although you don't need to be a BI specialist to view and edit reports, learning how to build models with Power Pivot is not particularly straightforward, even for advanced Excel users. You can get started on these tools with some free YouTube videos.

As a modeler, you'll be using Excel all day every day, and you need to keep up to date with all the changes, including the new tools of Modern Excel, because Microsoft releases new updates regularly. Throughout this book, I recommend the use of these tools to access, retrieve, or update the data for your model, or to display the outputs, but in terms of building your financial model, I'll stick with plain vanilla Excel.

For more information on some of the tools in Modern Excel, check out *Microsoft Excel Power Pivot & Power Query For Dummies* by Michael Alexander (Wiley).

Recognizing the Dangers of Using Excel

Financial modelers, like anyone working extensively with Excel, are very aware of the inherent risks involved. According to a study by Ray Panko, who is a leading authority on spreadsheet practices, close to 90 percent of spreadsheets contain errors.

Some managers treat models as though they are able to produce the answer to all their business decisions and solve all their business problems. It's frightening to see the blind faith that many managers have in their financial models.

After reading this book, you should have a good idea of the importance of financial modeling in businesses today. The reliance on Excel-based financial models is so entrenched within the culture of many organizations, and the practice of handing "legacy models" over to junior staff who don't understand how the models work is a widespread practice. Models that have been used over and over for many years are passed on and reused. As a consultant, I've seen this time and again — the user doesn't understand how the model works, but they're "fairly confident" it's giving them the correct results.

Considering the importance of spreadsheets in business, the risk of error is not one to be taken lightly. The European Spreadsheet Risk Group (EuSpRIG) was set up in 1999 purely for the purpose of addressing issues of spreadsheet integrity. They research and report on spreadsheet horror stories, which contain the latest spreadsheet-related errors reported in the media and how they could have been avoided. The disastrous consequences of uncontrolled use of spreadsheets are always disturbing, and make for somewhat gruesome reading.

I'm always slightly terrified when people say that they're going to go ahead with a multimillion-dollar project "because of the results of the financial model." It's very easy to get a formula wrong, or for the input assumptions to be just a few basis points out, all of which may well have a material impact on the output. Tweaking the input assumptions by just a few dollars either way can have a huge impact on cash flow, profitability, and the downright viability of a project!

We know that both formula and logic errors are very easy to make and prevalent in corporate financial models. As a financial modeler, you should be vigilantly looking for errors *as you build the model*. For strategies for reducing error in your models, turn to Chapter 13.

Although the major dangers of using Excel relate to its susceptibility to errors, the related issues of capacity and lack of discipline also warrant a mention. In this section, I take a closer look at each of these issues.

Capacity

Prior to Excel 2007, the maximum number of rows that Excel could handle was 65,000. That may seem like a lot, especially if you're just getting started with Excel, but it's *nowhere near* enough. The average Excel user would regularly run out of rows and have to resort to using Microsoft Access or keeping data in multiple workbooks to store the data. My, how things have changed!

From Excel 2007 onward, the number of rows was increased to over a million, which seemed like a big improvement at the time. In this age of big data, though, it's still very easy to run out of rows, especially when you start running a few formulas down the column. Realistically, anything more than half a million rows becomes very slow using ordinary Excel.

TECHNICAL STUFF

I still classify the lack of capacity of Excel as a danger because, despite all the new capabilities of Modern Excel (such as the data model), they're still being developed and few people are using them to their full capacity yet. To deal with the size limitations of Excel when working with large amounts of data, people are still cutting the data into various chunks, importing and exporting from other databases to avoid having to store data, and deleting archived data, all of which are dangerous practices because they're prone to error and are unbelievably time-consuming.

Lack of discipline

Excel is a highly flexible tool. You can pretty much do *anything* in Excel, but it doesn't mean that you should! One of the reasons I love it so much is the lack of boundaries or restrictions. Most software forces you to use it in a certain way, but Excel allows you to type anything into any cell.

Now, as wonderful as it is to be without boundaries, it's also incredibly dangerous and somewhat alarming. You know just how much damage can be done with an incorrect financial model, and the fact that there are no checks and balances — except what you as the modeler put into it — is a terrifying prospect.

Many of the best practices of financial modeling, such as those laid out in Chapter 4, have been created for the purpose of contending with this lack of discipline in financial models. Error checks, formatting, and rules about model layout, design, and structure are all designed to put some boundaries around a model, which, without them, becomes a dangerous tool in the wrong hands.

Errors

The possibility of error in a model is the number-one thing that keeps a financial modeler awake at night. As a modeler, you must have a healthy respect for spreadsheets and their susceptibility to error.

Imagine you're working on an exciting new project. You've provided a financial model that's being used for a project or key function of your business. It looks fantastic. People are fired up; money is being spent. But weeks or months into the project, the numbers suddenly aren't adding up. Why is the project so far over budget? On review, you suddenly realize there has been an error in your original calculations. Yikes! Your credibility and confidence in your work are being questioned, leading to some uncomfortable moments during meetings (not to mention, concern over your future at the company).

What form can these errors take? Generally, modeling errors can be grouped into three broad categories: formula errors, assumptions or input errors, and logic errors.

Formula errors

Formula errors are the easiest errors to make and relatively easy to spot, but they're horribly embarrassing when they're discovered. These kinds of "mechanical" errors are also the easiest to avoid by self-checking and correction. Chapter 13 covers some techniques you should employ while building your model to reduce the possibility of formula errors.

A common formula error is simply picking up the wrong cell in the formula — for example, linking to cell B98, which contains 6, instead of cell B97, which contains 0.6. This error initially might seem quite minor, but let's say your initial investment was $100,000. Through your modeling, you work out that there is 60 percent profit margin, but due to this error, you predict $600,000 profit instead of $60,000. Oops!

Assumptions or input errors

Your model's formulas may be calculating perfectly, but assumptions in financial models are a textbook case of "garbage in, garbage out." If the assumptions you've used as inputs are incorrect, the model will also be incorrect.

When it comes to input errors there are two main types to consider:

» **Data input:** Data input errors can easily occur if you're updating operating costs, for example, on a week-to-week basis. If these costs aren't linked correctly or refreshed regularly, you can get an incomplete or inaccurate picture of the process. Sometimes linking this information to a separate, automatically generated file and using some of the new Modern Excel tools such as Get & Transform (formerly called Power Query) can automate and expedite this process. Also, be sure to confirm who is responsible for updating the spreadsheet and make sure any changes to the process or update schedule don't affect your model.

» **User input:** User input errors occur more frequently when you're less familiar with the product or project you're modeling. For example, when it comes to the salary costs of a program, you may factor in the benefits that an employee will receive and assume it will be 5 percent of their salary, which is a fairly standard across-the-board assumption. However, because you're new to the organization, you may fail to take into account other factors that affect the employee's benefits, such as an increase in the cost of delivering the dental and medical program that the company prides itself on. Suddenly, this drives the cost to 12.5 percent of salary, completely blowing out all the staff costs you've so carefully calculated.

REMEMBER

If you're making assumptions, you need to record them, consider them, and lay them out carefully in your model. (See Chapter 4 for more information about assumptions documentation.) It's also a good idea to confirm these inputs with the key stakeholders.

The old saying "Too many cooks spoil the broth" most certainly applies to *building* a financial model. Unless you have a strict, collaborative set of standards that will ensure that the model is laid out and assumptions are entered consistently, you'll achieve the best result by having only one modeler working to build the model. When it comes to *using* the model, however, anyone should be able to use a well-built model. If you're worried about people messing up your calculations or entering inputs incorrectly, make sure your instructions and documentation explain how to use the model. Also, apply data validations or cell protection to the model to restrict changes the user can make.

Logic errors

Errors in the model's logic are probably the most difficult to spot, because you can have the assumptions, inputs, and formulas all working perfectly, but the logic and methodology — the way the model is built — can still be incorrect. You must capture the logic and ensure that the builder's approach is clear. Otherwise, if you lose the key person who built the model, confusion can ensue.

For example, in Figure 2-4, the model shows the percentage of the investor's funds that have been loaned. The percentage has been calculated by dividing the *investment balance* (the current investment plus the new investment) by the *portfolio balance* (the current loans plus the new loans minus the loans expired).

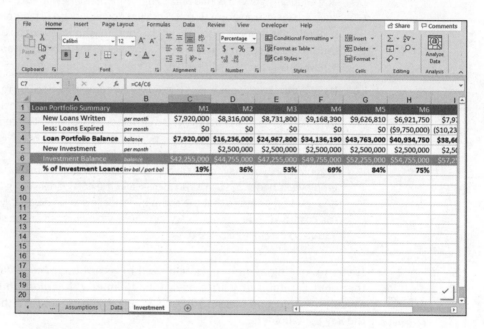

FIGURE 2-4: Calculating investment portfolio ratios.

Hold on a second. Do you calculate it based on the number of loans written or the cumulative balance? You can see how the way the ratio has been calculated can cause confusion for those not familiar with this model. It's important to document how you're calculating it. You might also easily confuse monthly amounts with cumulative balance; you can see that this is clearly documented in column B.

Looking at Alternatives and Supplements to Excel

Excel is often called the "Swiss Army knife of software" or the "second-best solution" because you can do practically anything in Excel, but it's not *always* the best tool for the job. You can write a letter in Excel for example, but Word is a much better tool for that purpose. You can keep your company accounts in Excel, but a purpose-built general ledger system will deliver a much better result.

Desktop spreadsheets are so popular because they're easy to use to communicate ideas and strategies in an understandable business model. Working in an analytic role, the spreadsheet actually becomes part of the way people think about business issues, relationships, and different scenarios they want to explore — if Excel as a tool shapes the very way you consider your approach, this doesn't exactly encourage creativity. The spreadsheet tool actually becomes a part of the process of the analysis and decision making, so you'll sometimes hear people say, "Let's get this into Excel and see what it looks like!"

So, what are the other options available? Instead of assuming that Excel is the best tool for financial modeling, you should be aware of the alternatives, as well as some of the add-ins that supplement Excel specifically for the purpose of financial modeling. Following is a list of some of the alternatives and supplements to Excel. Keep in mind that this isn't a comprehensive list, and I'm not endorsing any of these products. These are just options worth your consideration:

>> **Data extraction and analysis:** Alteryx, KNIME, SAS, Tableau, and Oracle-based tools are no doubt far more robust and secure than Excel solutions that pull data from other systems into Excel manually such as macros or Power Query in Excel. These kinds of enterprise-grade solutions are purpose-built for the extraction and analysis of data and are a good long-term solution, but they're often difficult to use and take a long time to implement due to lack of familiarity.

>> **Planning and performance management:** Anaplan, Causal, Tagetik, and Visyond are alternative cloud-based options designed to replace spreadsheets altogether. These tools offer powerful capabilities that support analysts in forward planning and making confident decisions based on data rather than spending their time correcting errors.

>> **Excel add-ins for model building:** Modano is a modular content management and sharing platform for Excel, enabling pieces of spreadsheets to be reused, shared, and linked to save time and reduce risk. Its main application is financial modeling, but it can be used to modularize any spreadsheet. Instead of replacing Excel, Modano improves Excel and combats some of its inefficiencies and shortcomings. Modano replaces BPM, an older Excel add-in that systemized the implementation and review of spreadsheet best practices.

Another modular model-building tool is Openbox, in which you design the model and logic using natural language and by dragging and dropping components within the model, the software automatically builds the Excel model upon request. It also has a preview function, which allows you to preview parts of the model before it's built.

Both Modano and Openbox have libraries of content that are available to access, edit, and use as required.

>> **Excel add-ins for auditing:** Checkbox, Excel Analyzer, OAK, Spreadsheet Advantage, Spreadsheet Detective, Spreadsheet Professional, and XL Compare are Excel add-ins that can help develop and review financial models. They interrogate a spreadsheet in extreme detail to help identify where you might have an error. The software produces key statistics on any spreadsheet, such as the number of unique formulas, where the formulas can be found across each sheet, and the relationships between sheets. It also produces a map of each cell to indicate whether that cell is a text, number, new, or consistent formula.

>> **Dashboards and data visualization:** After you've finished building your financial model, you may want to display the results in a chart or dashboard. This can be done on the front sheet of an Excel workbook, in Microsoft Power BI, or using one of hundreds of other purpose-built data visualization and dashboarding tools. One such tool is Modeler, which can transform your model into an app with no coding, using just Excel and PowerPoint. The most popular non-Microsoft tools at the moment are QlickView and Tableau, but this area is growing rapidly. Turn to Chapter 9 for more information about how to present your model output using standard Excel tools.

>> **Budgeting and forecasting:** Many of the models you'll build are for the purpose of budgeting and forecasting — and then reporting on those budgets and forecasts. Most major general ledger systems have additional modules built specifically for the purpose of budgeting, forecasting, and reporting. These tools provide a much easier, quicker method of creating budgets and forecasts that is far more robust and less error-prone than using Excel templates. Hundreds of budgeting and forecasting tools are available; some of the most popular are Adaptive Insights, Board, Oracle (JD Edwards), and TM1 (Cognos).

» **Power BI Apps Source (add-ins):** Following the inaugural Financial Modelling Innovation Awards in 2020 the winner emerged: ValQ. ValQ is scenario modeling software inside Power BI within the Microsoft AppSource platform. This low/no-code software (requiring no DAX) means that the ability to run scenarios easily within Power BI will rapidly accelerate financial modeling capabilities inside what is typically an analytics and visualization tool. No doubt more entrants into this space will emerge over time.

THE CASE FOR EXCEL

So, why do we still use Excel, even though a "better" solution might exist? Here are some of the reasons:

- **Every business already has Excel installed.** Your company doesn't have to purchase extra licenses or pay for expensive consultants to install it.

- **Little training is needed.** Most users have some familiarity with Excel, which means other people will be able to edit, change, and understand your Excel model.

- **Excel is very flexible.** You can build almost anything you can imagine in Excel (within size limitations, of course).

- **Excel "talks" to other systems very well.** With Excel, you can report, model, and contrast virtually any data, from any source, all in one report.

- **Most important, Excel is commonly used across all industries, countries, and organizations.** This means that the Excel skills you already have, and the skills you'll hone by reading this book, are highly transferrable. You can use those skills in other jobs at other companies no matter where your career takes you. Sure, there are thousands of other pieces of software that you can learn, but I believe that for a career in finance, *one of the best things you can do for your career is to improve your Excel skills.*

Of course, I can't predict the future, but it's difficult to imagine a world where Excel is not the dominant finance software.

Chapter **3**

Planning and Designing Your Financial Model

Planning and design can sometimes be the most difficult part of building a financial model — especially for those of us whose skills are more technical and numerical than visual. When building your model, you need to pay close attention to the design layout and ensure that it's clear, coherent, and logically structured. Even a very simple model can become complex if poorly designed, and a well-designed model will be so logical that it will simply speak for itself.

TIP

Before jumping in and starting to build the model, take a moment to think about what your model needs to achieve — this will help with the design build.

Identifying the Problem That Your Financial Model Needs to Solve

A financial model is usually built in order to answer a question or to solve a problem. For example, the question "Should I purchase this new asset?" can result in a model containing cash flow analysis, which compares the cash flow if the asset is purchased versus if it is not purchased. "How much should I pay for this new asset?" is an entirely different question, and the answer will be a single number or a range of possible numbers.

REMEMBER

You need to identify the problem *before* beginning the model-building process.

For example, if the model you're building is for the purpose of making a decision, you need to build at least two scenarios — one with the existing business and one including the new venture — as well as a comparison between them. Modelers sometimes call this a "do nothing" versus as "do something" scenario. So the model will consist of three components:

>> "Do nothing" scenario

>> "Do something" scenario

>> Scenario comparison

In the example shown in Figure 3-1, a small bus company has serviced two bus routes for many years. The financial model shows 12 months of historical data and has forecast the next 12 months. Due to a change in demographics and a new train line servicing the area, ticket sales for the northern route have been declining consistently, and the company expects this trend to continue. If the company does nothing, as shown, the profits will more than halve over a two-year period.

TIP

You can download a sample copy of this model in File 0302.xlsx at www. dummies.com/go/financialmodelinginexcelfd2e.

You start building this model by creating the three tabs and determining that the comparison sheet should contain a comparison between the two scenarios. Then you design the "do nothing" scenario and then look at how different the numbers are if the company adds a new bus line.

TIP

Keeping models consistent is important. For this reason, the "do nothing" scenario contains an extra blank row in each block of data, which is where the new western route can be inserted. The Total Profit line is shown in row 27 of both scenario pages, which makes the model easier to follow, and less prone to error when linking the charts and summary page to the outputs.

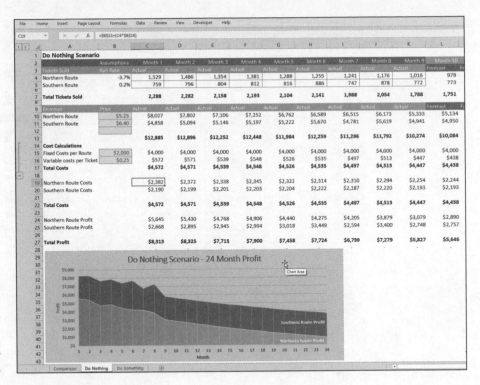

FIGURE 3-1:
"Do nothing"
scenario

Because this model is quite small, you don't need separate input and assumptions sheets, as you do with larger models. The inputs and assumptions are listed within the scenario sheets themselves.

If the company decides to put on a new route to service the western regions, you can replace some of the lost sales from the northern routes with the new service. In the "do something" scenario shown in Figure 3-2, you can see that although not all the lost profitability has been recouped, the bus company is still viable.

REMEMBER

When using a financial model to make a decision, you need to look at the *difference* between the two scenarios. If you only look at the "do something" scenario in isolation, it doesn't look particularly appealing.

Figure 3-3 compares the two scenarios to help decide on a course of action. You can see from the comparison sheet that the best course of action would be to "do something" — assuming, of course, that these are the only options available to us.

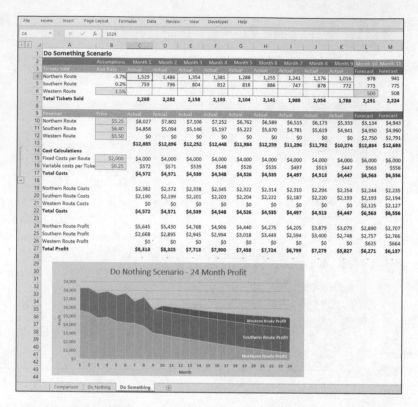

FIGURE 3-2:
"Do something"
scenario.

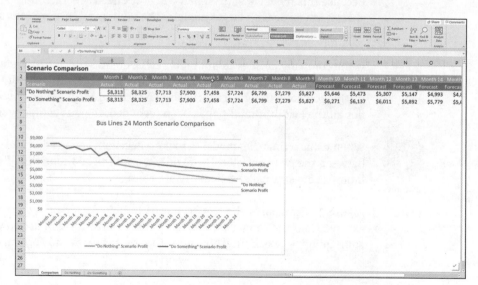

FIGURE 3-3:
Comparison
between
scenarios.

Designing How the Problem's Answer Will Look

When you've identified the problem that needs to be solved, it's very tempting to dive straight in and begin the model-building process, but it's a good idea to stop for a moment to plan the model and determine how the output will look. When it comes to building a financial model, you want to start with the end in mind.

Start by creating a mockup design of the output page. You can do this in Excel, or by simply sketching it on a whiteboard or paper. It can be difficult to visualize what the output will look like until you have the data in it. Modelers aren't often the most artistic types, but you should have at least some idea of the elements that need to be on the output page.

For example, for a business case, let's say you want to show the net present value (NPV), internal rate of return (IRR), and payback period. To do this, you need cash flow, so the key elements will be revenue and expenses, from which you can derive profitability, and then the NPV, IRR, and payback. You can flesh out the outputs page something like the design shown in Figure 3-4.

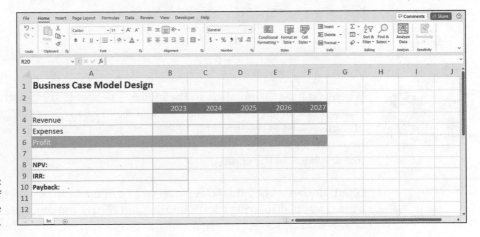

FIGURE 3-4:
Initial design of business case output page.

Then, having completed the financial model, you decide to include some scenario analysis, as well as the customer numbers. The final output page ends up as shown in Figure 3-5. For more information about displaying data visually, see Chapter 9.

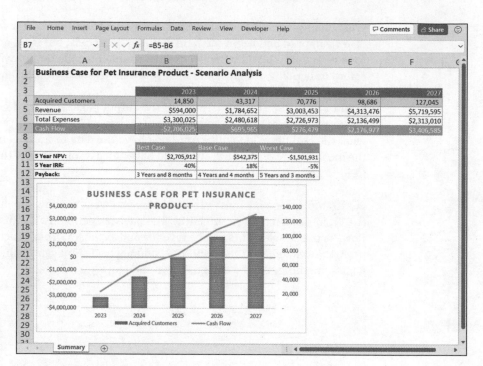

FIGURE 3-5: Completed business case output page.

TIP

When you have the numbers in the model, you should try to include at least one chart. If you're not sure how the data will look visually, you can highlight a range of numbers, go to the Insert tab of the Ribbon, and in the Charts section, press the Recommended Charts button. This gives you a preview of what the data will look like displayed in the chart.

Often, the output of a financial model will be in the form of a dashboard, which is a great way of displaying a lot of information clearly and concisely. Building dashboards in Excel has become so popular in recent years that I run dedicated training courses on dashboard reporting, which are particularly popular with financial modelers who need to display the output of their financial models. Figure 3-6 shows a sample output of a financial model such as the financial statements model built in Chapter 10. You can download a sample copy of this model in `File 0303. xlsx` at `www.dummies.com/go/financialmodelinginexcelfd2e`.

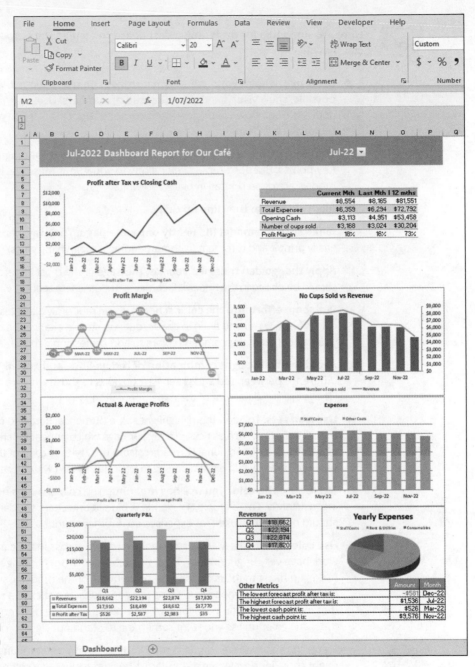

FIGURE 3-6:
Dashboard output of a financial model.

TIP

Here are some tips for designing a dashboard to display the output of your financial model:

>> **Don't overwhelm your users with numbers on a dashboard.** Wherever possible, show visuals and charts instead of numbers. Use data labels or a data table (as shown in the lower-left corner of Figure 3-6) if you want to show numbers on a chart.

>> **Use contrasting techniques, such as color, bold, and shading to highlight key points.** But don't rely on color alone to show your message, because models are often printed in black and white.

>> **Align objects so they line up tidily.**

>> **Make sure the model fits neatly onto one page.** That way, people can easily print it and refer to it (without needing a magnifying glass).

>> **Apply the "golden triangle."** Your key message or the most important information should be placed in the upper-left corner — this is where readers will look first.

>> **Put some effort into the color scheme.** Excel randomly allocates standard colors (usually red and blue) to charts, but you should change the colors to match your model theme or company colors to add professional "polish" to your model.

>> **Avoid the traffic light combination of red, yellow, and green.** The difference between red and green isn't obvious to those who are color blind. (That's around 8 percent of the male population!)

>> **Use icon sets.** To apply them, highlight some numerical data and choose one of the sets of icons, such as ticks, crosses, or flags which appear when you click on Icon Sets under Conditional Formatting from the Styles section of the Ribbon. This will automatically add extra meaning to your dashboard without relying on color.

>> **Make sure the color you use has meaning.** The colors should not be reused inconsistently. For example, if revenue is blue in one chart, the same blue should not then be used for expenses on another chart.

>> **Use color sparingly.** Many legacy models I come across in my consultancy work have very bright rainbow colors, which (aside from blinding the user) make it difficult to focus on the key components of the model. Using some color to make your model appealing is a good idea, but stick to a single color that matches your company logo (or your mood) and use different shades of the same color unless you want something to stand out significantly.

TIP

Some companies have standard color coding, but if your company doesn't, you might consider developing a standard. Consider including a color code key on the cover page. The use of predefined styles found on the Home tab can make color coding very quick and easy. Many companies have their predefined color coding loaded as style templates, which ensures consistency in color coding in financial models. Here are some commonly used color codes that are supported by the built-in styles in Excel that you may consider adopting in your company:

- Blue font and beige background for input cells

- Pink or gray for error checks

- Green or orange for external links

TIP

To match the logo of your company, find out the RGB color code and use this code to apply the exact same colors to your model's headings, totals, or charts. Considering that *millions* of different colors are available in Excel, it's almost impossible to pick the correct one by eye.

FINDING AN RGB COLOR

If you want to find the exact RGB or Hex color code that's been used in your company logo or the image you'd like to insert in the model, it isn't yet possible to find it directly in Excel (although this could change soon because this is a highly requested feature). In the meantime, there is a workaround using PowerPoint's Color Picker instead. Find the color code by following these steps:

1. **Open Microsoft PowerPoint, and insert the image that contains the color you want.**

2. **Right-click the background and select Format Background.**

   A dialog box appears to the right, as shown in the nearby figure.

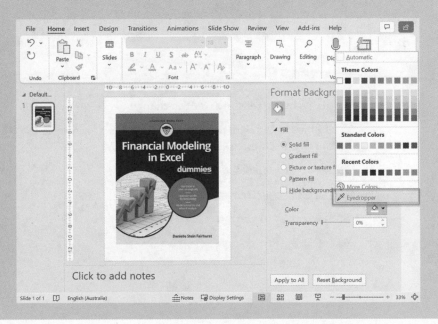

(continued)

(continued)

3. **Select the Eyedropper tool, hover the Eyedropper over the color you want to re-create, and click when you've found the right color.**

4. **Go back to Font Color, and select More Colors.**

   The amount of red, green, and blue (RGB) is shown. When I click anywhere within the yellow area in the image, I get the exact RGB color code that the designer originally used to create the image (Red = 255, Green = 241, Blue =0), as shown in the nearby figure. Alternatively, you can use the Hex color code instead, which in this case is #FFF100.

   When you have the RGB color, you can use the color in your Excel model.

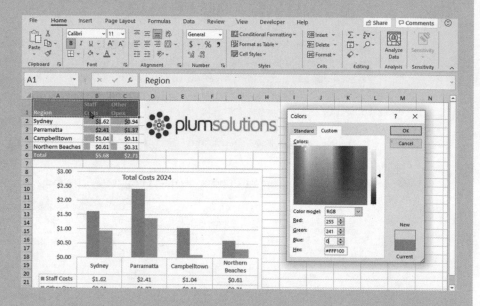

5. **Highlight the cells you want to change.**

6. **On the Home tab of the Ribbon, click the arrow next to the Fill Color button in the Font section.**

7. **Select More Colors at the bottom.**

   The Color dialog box appears.

8. **Select the Custom tab.**

9. **Select the RGB colors as shown here.**

Gathering Data to Put in Your Model

A financial model is only as good as its inputs or source data, and a large part of the modeler's job is often collecting, interpreting, analyzing, and even manipulating or extrapolating the data to go into the model. In many cases, as much time can be spent collecting data as is spent actually building the model, so if you can collect the data in the correct format in the first place, this can save you a lot of time.

TIP

You often have to obtain data you need to build the model from other people or external sources, which can be a frustrating and time-consuming process. Here are some guidelines that can make the data–gathering process easier:

>> Let other parties know well in advance what information you need and its purpose.

>> Give them a due date that is realistic for them and fits your time frame.

>> Design the input sheets in your model so that the data can be pasted directly in.

>> Use dummy data in the meantime if you need to so that you can continue building the model while waiting for the information to come in.

>> Allow enough time to check the quality and reliability of the information that has been submitted.

DETERMINING THE TIME SERIES FOR YOUR MODEL'S DATA

Most financial models include a time-series element. The majority of models you're likely to see will be either on a monthly, quarterly, or annual basis. It's important to get the correct time-series unit right from the start, because it's much easier to summarize a monthly model up to a full year than it is to split an annual model down to its monthly components. For an example of modeling time series, turn to Chapter 12.

Before you start gathering data to include in your model, be sure that you're clear about what level of detail you'll need the data to be in. For example, you could be building an annual model for your company's fiscal year, which goes from October 1 to September 30, but the survey data you've collected and want to include is for the period January 1 to December 31. If you've got access to the raw data on a monthly basis, you'll be able to manipulate the data so that it's accurate; otherwise, you'll need to extrapolate.

>> Make sure people know what you expect in terms of data quality. Does it need to be 100 percent accurate or is an estimate okay? Normally, model input data is simply taken at face value, and the source is documented in the assumptions. If an estimate is used, be sure to document it as such.

>> Be specific about what format you need the data in. Giving them a template to complete can prevent misunderstandings. For example, instead of a request like "Please provide information on key customer accounts," which might yield a list of 500 customers and their addresses, a template like the one shown in Figure 3-7 would give better results.

TIP

Consider using protection to prevent incorrect entry, such as restricting inputs to either a "yes" or a "no," as shown in column F of Figure 3-7. For instructions on how to use data validations, see the section on "Restricting user data entry" in Chapter 6. If you'd like to try this out for yourself, you can download File 0301.xlsx from www.dummies.com/go/financialmodelinginexcelfd2e. Open it and select the tab labeled 3-7.

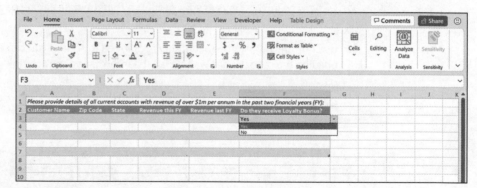

FIGURE 3-7:
Information request template.

Documenting the Limitations of Your Model

If other people are going to be using your model, be sure to explain the assumptions you made in building the model, especially if the person who is going to be using your model is not an experienced modeler. Users tend to put blind faith in the outcome of the model, which can be dangerous. Instead of taking the model results as gospel, the user should simply use them as a guide.

Models are only a construct that reflects reality; they are *not* reality. You can make this clear to users of the model by using language such as "Based on our forecasts . . ." or "Assuming trends continue. . . ."

In the example of the decision analysis model for the bus company case study (see the section "Identifying the Problem That Your Financial Model Needs to Solve," earlier in this chapter), the builder of this model might say, "We're going to lose half of our profit over the next 12 months," which is not incorrect, but it would be more accurate to say, "Based on current forecasts, we're going to lose half of our profit over the next 12 months unless we take action" and then show the inputs and assumptions used. For example, the modeler is assuming the following:

» **Five hundred tickets will be sold in the first month of operation.**

» **Ticket sales will increase by 1.5 percent per month after the first month.**

» **There is no cannibalization between the routes.** Often, when launching a new product, some existing customers switch to the new product. Because the new route is servicing a new area, the modeler doesn't expect any cannibalization and hasn't included it in this model.

Considering the Layout and Design of Your Model

The problem that needs to be solved and the output required often influence the layout and design of the model. So, it's not a bad idea to spend some time thinking about the layout before you get started. Not only do the layout and structure of the model relate to the logic and functionality, but they can also influence the look and feel of the model's interface and how users navigate through the model.

When you're building a model for the first time, you may have trouble knowing where to begin. The key elements of a financial model are

» Inputs or source data

» Assumptions documentation

» Calculations

» Outputs

STEPS TO BUILDING A MODEL

Here are seven steps to follow when starting to build a financial model:

1. **Design the high-level structure.**

   You won't know *exactly* what the layout of the model will be until you actually start building the calculations, but you should have some idea of the tabs. Start by assembling the data you have so far into the broad categories described in the "Defining inputs, calculations, and output blocks" section later in this chapter.

2. **Design outputs — summaries, charts, and reports.**

   Because you already know the problem that your financial model needs to solve, you should have an idea of what that answer might look like. For example, if you're making a decision about investing in a new product, the output might be the resulting cash flow and an NPV. By thinking about the output of your model early on in the process, you'll be more focused and will ensure that all your calculations work toward the desired end result.

3. **Design inputs.**

   Set up where the inputs and source data will go. Even if you don't have all the information yet, set it up so that it can be dropped in at a later date. This can help you make sure that you ask for or gather the data in the right format, as well as design the model correctly. For example, do we need data for the calendar year or the financial year? Will you need to use the same assumption for every month/year or it is going to change?

4. **Start calculating.**

   Start with a tab labeled "workings" or "calculations," but keep in mind that this will probably expand as the model grows. Link the formulas to your inputs, but break larger problems into smaller ones and don't try to attempt too much at once. You might begin by thinking that all expenses can go on one tab, but if depreciation, for example, begins getting rather complicated, you might decide that depreciation needs a tab of its own.

5. **Connect outputs.**

   Link your calculations to the outputs page. Charts are a great way of visualizing and presenting the output of your model. As you're building the outputs, test at every stage to make sure that the model makes sense, and adjust as necessary.

6. **Add scenarios.**

   When the model is working correctly, you can add sensitivities and scenario analysis. See Chapter 8 for information about how to build scenarios into your model. If you've designed the model well in the first place, adding scenarios is a fairly straightforward process.

7. Assumptions documentation.

Most of these steps are sequential, but assumptions documentation should never be left right to the end. Do it as you go!

Throughout the model-building process, be sure to test, check, and validate as you go. For more information on key rules to follow when building a model, turn to Chapter 4.

When starting to build your model, start by laying out each of these elements in four separate tabs and think about what will go in each section. Separate each of these elements clearly. Although every model should contain these elements, not every financial model is structured in the same way. Unless a model is very small — like the bus company case study earlier in this chapter — there should be a dedicated tab for each major component of the model.

Structuring your model: What goes where

When designing the layout of a model, most experienced modelers follow these rules:

>> **Separate inputs, calculations, and results, where possible.** Clearly label which sections of the model contain inputs, calculations, and results. You can put them on separate worksheets or separate places on one worksheet, but make sure that the user knows exactly what each section is for. Color coding can help with ensuring that each section is clearly defined.

>> **Use each column for the same purpose.** This is particularly important when building models involving time series. For example, in a time-series model, knowing that labels are in column B, unit data in column C, constant values in column D, and calculations in column E, makes it much easier when editing a formula manually.

>> **Use one formula per row or column.** This forms the basis of the best-practice principle whereby formulas are kept consistent using absolute, relative, and mixed referencing, as described in greater detail in Chapter 4. Keep formulas consistent when in a block of data, and never change a formula halfway through.

>> **Refer to the left and above.** The model should read logically, like a book, meaning that it should be read from left to right and top to bottom. Calculations, inputs, and outputs should flow logically to avoid circular referencing. Be aware that there are times when left-to-right or top-to-bottom data flow can conflict somewhat with ease of use and presentation, so use common sense when designing the layout. By following this practice, you can

avoid having calculations link all over the sheet, which makes it harder to check and update. Excel will also calculate more quickly if you build formulas in this way because it calculates left to right, and top to bottom, so not only does it make your model easier to follow, it will calculate more efficiently.

» **Use multiple worksheets.** Avoid the temptation to put everything on one sheet. Especially when blocks of calculations are the same, use separate sheets for those that must be repeated to avoid the need to scroll across the screen.

» **Include documentation sheets.** A documentation sheet where assumptions and source data are clearly laid out is a critical part of any financial model. A cover sheet should not be confused with an assumptions sheet. A model can never have too much documentation!

Defining inputs, calculations, and output blocks

Typically, modelers work from back to front when building their models. The *output*, or the part they want the viewer or user to see, is at the front, calculations are in the middle, and source data and assumptions are at the back. Like the executive summary, a board paper, or another report, the first few pages should contain what casual viewers need to see at a glance. If they need further information, they can dig deeper into the model.

Here are some guidelines of what might be included on each tab in your model:

» **Cover sheet:** Although not always included, the cover sheet contains many details about the model. Of course, the cover sheet is not much use unless you keep it up to date. If you decide to include a cover sheet, you may add details such as the following:

- A log of changes and updates to the model with date, author, change details, and their impact on the output of the model, which can help with version control

- The purpose of the model and how it is intended to be used going forward

- Who originally wrote the model and who to contact with questions

- Table of contents

- Instructions on how to use the model

- Disclaimers as to the limitations of the model, legal liability, and caveats

- Global or key assumptions integral to the use of the model

In my experience, cover sheets and instruction pages are rarely used. If you decide not to include a cover sheet, make sure that the model contains explicit instructions regarding operation, purpose, assumptions, source data, and disclaimers.

>> **Input sheet:** This is the only place where hard-coded data should be entered. There may be one or more input sheets if there are large amounts of data, but the input data should be laid out in logical blocks.

>> **Output, summary, and scenario sheets:** These present the final outcomes. They may also contain scenario drop-down boxes or user entry fields that allow the users of the model to generate their own outputs. This section might also contain a dashboard.

>> **Calculation or workings sheets:** Split the calculation sheets logically and then, within each sheet, set them up consistently. If the calculations become long and confusing, it makes sense to split them into logical sections. For example, they can be split by type of service, customers, financial tables, geographical location, or business segments. If calculation sheets are split, ensure that the layout and formatting are as consistent as possible across all sheets.

>> **Error check sheet:** This sheet contains links to all error checks in the model. Error checks should be performed in the calculation section, but a summary of all error checks in one location means that once the model is in use, the modelers can quickly check to see if any of the error checks have been triggered.

Determining your audience

Who will be viewing or using your model in the future? If it's for only your own use, you should still follow good model design but there's no need to spend a lot of time on the formatting to make it look cool. You should still add assumptions and source documentation for your own reference even if you know that no one will ever look at it.

No matter who you think is going to use your model, you should always adhere to the rules outlined in Chapter 4.

There are a few types of people who can comprise your model audience:

>> **Professional modelers:** If your model is for a large-scale investment or if money is being lent based on the outcome of your model, you can expect that professional modelers are going to want to "look under the hood" of your model to take it apart and audit it. You can greatly reduce the cost of an audit

by using consistent formulas to reduce the number of unique formulas in the model (see Chapter 4). Do not hide sheets or attempt to protect parts of the model — it will only frustrate the professional modeler who will want to see how your numbers were calculated.

>> **Occasional modelers:** Some models will be used by people for whom looking at models is only part of their job — you yourself perhaps fall into this category. They know their way around Excel but aren't really interested in understanding the intricacies of the entire model. They just want to make sure it's working properly because they need to rely on the numbers and perhaps they need to use it by changing some of its numbers from time to time. When building a model for the occasional modeler, you want to make the model as easy to follow as possible. Keep it streamlined, and don't clutter the output pages with unnecessary detail. Move any detailed and less important assumptions to the back so that they can be referred to only if necessary.

>> **Nonmodelers:** Sometimes your model will be viewed or used by members of the board, salespeople, or marketing folks for whom modeling or using Excel is not part of their everyday lives. For example, you might be producing a sales dashboard report that is produced every week and the user simply needs to change the drop-down box to look at a different product or region. You want to make the output pages as simple to use and as appealing as possible for a nonuser of Excel. For some ideas on dashboard design and using color, see "Designing How the Problem's Answer Will Look" earlier in this chapter. The user is unlikely to want to take the model apart and look into the formulas, so to simplify the way the model looks, you might consider hiding the calculation sheets and perhaps even the data sheets — with or without a password.

TIP

Password protection should only be used as a deterrent to prevent nosy colleagues. It's not a security system and should not be relied upon as such. Search the web for "Excel password remover," and you'll find plenty of software available that can remove the password.

In conclusion, planning and designing a financial model is a critical part of the model build. It takes a unique mixture of logic, clarity of thought, and graphic layout skills by the financial modeler to build a well-designed model, and this often proves to be difficult to implement in practice. Model design can sometimes be the most difficult part of building a financial model and it is, in my experience, one of the most difficult aspects to teach and learn. Learning how to build a well-designed model comes with experience. But a faster way to develop design skills is to critically assess other models you come across, taking note of what works and what doesn't, and then applying it to your own models.

IN THIS CHAPTER

» **Documenting assumptions**

» **Creating dynamic formulas using links**

» **Entering data once**

» **Modeling with consistent formulas**

» **Building error checks**

» **Formatting and labeling your models**

Chapter 4

Building a Financial Model by the Rulebook

Because Excel is such a wonderfully flexible and universal tool, you can pretty much do anything with it — but that doesn't mean you should! A key danger of using Excel is lack of discipline, leading to errors. When building a financial model in Excel, you're unlikely to encounter the limitations and boundaries imposed by other, less flexible software, so there are certain rules you should follow to avoid these issues. In this chapter, I fill you in on some key rules you should follow when building a financial model.

Document Your Assumptions

The term "garbage in, garbage out" is never truer than in relation to financial modeling. You can have the most beautifully laid-out financial model with perfect formatting, a great design, and fabulous-looking charts and scenario tables, but if the inputs are not trusted, the model is effectively useless and no one will use the outputs. Important decisions are made based on the outputs of financial models, so listing the assumptions that have gone into the model is critical.

WARNING

Documentation of assumptions is certainly not the most exciting part of financial modeling, so you may be tempted to leave it to the end. Don't fall into this trap! When you're done building your model, you won't remember the source or reasoning for the assumptions. Document as you go. Whenever you make a structural change or even a minor change to one of the inputs, document it, even if it seems unimportant at the time.

TIP

List assumptions on a separate page, and label them clearly, so that they can be easily identified and referenced at a glance. For a small model, you may decide to mix source data and assumptions together. In a large model, you may separate them with as much detail as is possible or practical. For a detailed model, you may list every assumption on a dedicated sheet and then summarize the important ones on a separate sheet. Think about the level of detail in your model, and let that guide the detail of your documentation of assumptions.

Still not convinced that documenting assumptions is important? How's this for persuasion: When you move to another role or you are away (hopefully, on vacation!), and something goes wrong with the model, who do you think they're going to blame? You guessed it! Think of documenting assumptions as covering your butt. Your model needs to be able to speak for you when you aren't around to explain or defend your work. The documentation of assumptions should explain your thought process and potentially also why the model is built the way it is. That way, if there are any questions as to the structure of the model, the approach to certain formulas or the assumptions, they can be easily explained by the model itself.

REMEMBER

A model is only as good as the accuracy of the assumptions. You need to mitigate your liability by documenting your assumptions thoroughly and adding caveats where necessary.

TIP

Here are some commonly used methods for including documentation in a model:

>> **In-cell comments:** There are three different methods of creating in-cell comments:

- **Notes:** The most common method of creating an in-cell comment is to simply insert a note (previously referred to as a comment) within the cell, which is indicated by a red triangle in the upper-right corner of the cell, as shown in Figure 4-1.

  To create a note, right-click the cell and select New Note, or use the short cut Shift+F2. To make a change to an existing note, right-click the cell with the note and select Edit Note, or again use the shortcut Shift+F2. Similarly, to delete a note, right-click the cell and select Delete Note, or use the shortcut Shift+F2, press Esc, and then press Delete.

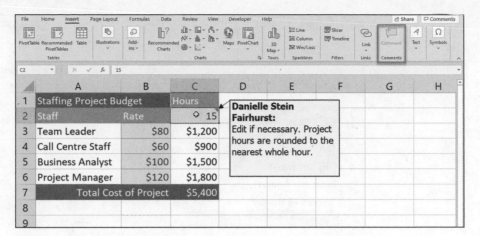

FIGURE 4-1:
Red triangle
notes.

If you want to try the examples out for yourself, you can download `File 0401.xlsx` at `www.dummies.com/go/financialmodelinginexcelfd2e` and select the tab labeled 4-1.

- **Threaded comments:** Comments have changed in Excel for Microsoft 365. You can now have conversations within the cell, as shown in Figure 4-2, which is extremely useful for validating the inputs in a financial model. To create a Comment, right-click the cell and select New Comment to start a conversation, and then click Post when you've finished typing. You can resolve the thread when the conversation is complete.

- **Data validation input message:** Another, less common method of creating an in-cell comment is to use the Input Message functionality that is part of Data Validation. These types of messages are in some ways more discreet, because the cell won't have any indication there is a message (like the red triangle in the corner of cells which contain notes), and you don't see the note until you actually click the cell, as shown in Figure 4-3.

- This sort of in-cell comment is especially useful for creating little instructions and warnings regarding input data to users, because they'll see the Input Message as soon as they select the cell.

- To create a data validation input message, click the cell and then, in the Data Tools section of the Data tab of the Ribbon, click the Data Validation button and the Data Validation dialog box appears. Select the Input Message tab, and type the message you want to appear. This message will appear only when the cell is selected.

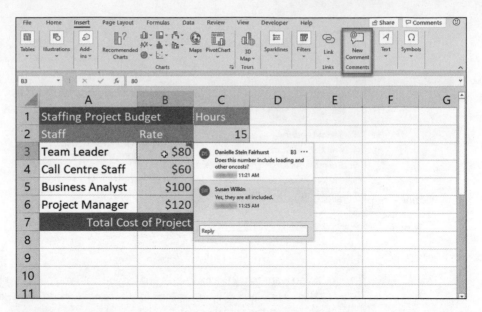

FIGURE 4-2:
Threaded comments.

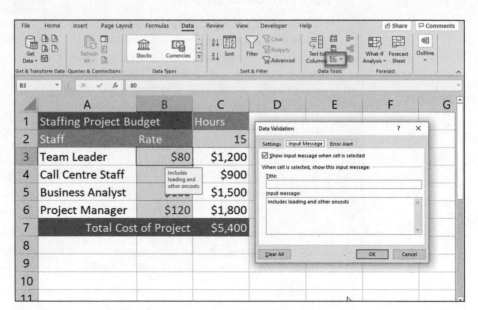

FIGURE 4-3:
Data validation input messages.

Documentation of assumptions using in-cell comments is most appropriate for specific information relating to only one cell or range, because they can be viewed only in a single cell. In-cell comments are useful for communicating details to another modeler about specific calculation details, because the comments are shown only on-screen and won't show when printed unless you change the settings. More wide-ranging, generic assumptions should be documented using other methods.

Of the two types of in-cell comments, my personal preference is the data validation input message, because they're neater and cleaner looking. Remember, though, that if the cell isn't selected, the comment won't be viewed, so make sure that the comment is only cell-specific. More important, general assumptions and comments should use plain text or another method of documentation.

» **Hyperlinks:** There are two different types of hyperlinks that are useful for documenting assumptions and source data in financial modeling:

- **Cell and file hyperlinks:** You can create hyperlinks to sources or other reference files and other sections of a model. Cell and file hyperlinks can aid in navigation of a long and complex model. They're especially helpful for new users to find their way around the model.

  To insert this kind of hyperlink, on the Insert tab, select the Hyperlink icon from the Links section. On the left side, select Place in This Document. Then select the sheet and cell reference or named range of the hyperlink source. You can change the Text to Display at the top to display something like Go to Calculations instead of Calculations!B147, for example. Similarly, you can insert a hyperlink to another file for source referencing.

- **URL hyperlinks:** Hyperlinks can also be used to refer to relevant websites directly from your spreadsheet. For example, if the interest rate you assume in your financial model came from a central bank's website, you can simply copy the URL into a cell in your model. Note that if you're using Get & Transform (formerly called Power Query) you can link data straight from external data sources, including websites, directly into your spreadsheet, which can be quickly updated without having to manually open the website.

  TIP

  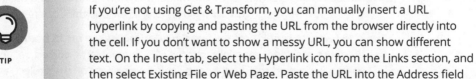

  If you're not using Get & Transform, you can manually insert a URL hyperlink by copying and pasting the URL from the browser directly into the cell. If you don't want to show a messy URL, you can show different text. On the Insert tab, select the Hyperlink icon from the Links section, and then select Existing File or Web Page. Paste the URL into the Address field at the bottom, and change the Text to Display at the top.

>> **Hard-coded text:** This method of assumptions documentation is not very sophisticated, but as with many things in financial modeling, the simple solution is often best. As you can see in Figure 4-4, the assumption has been simply typed into the cell below the calculation table. There is no danger here that a modeler or user might overlook this assumption, whether it's being viewed on the computer or in a printout.

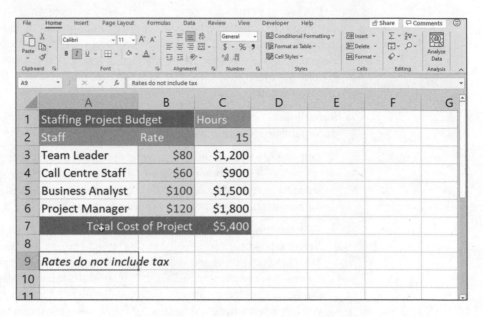

FIGURE 4-4:
Hard-coded text.

>> **Linked dynamic text:** Documenting assumptions liberally within your model is very important, but it's very difficult to keep the documentation up to date when your model is dynamic and inputs are continually changing. For example, in the project costings model shown in Figure 4-5, you want to make sure that the person using the model understands that only 15 hours has been entered into the model, so you want to put the commentary below "Calculations based on 15 hours of billable time spent." This seems fairly obvious in this example, but if the model was more complex, and the inputs were on a different page, it would be useful to include this comment.

If you were to simply type the text **Calculations based on 15 hours of billable time spent** manually into cell A10, this would be correct . . . until someone changes the number of billable hours spent on the project, and then the text would quickly become out-of-date. There is a very high risk in this case that you could distribute the model with incorrect assumption documentation.

Instead of typing in the hard-coded value of 15, you can convert the text to a dynamic formula using an ampersand (&), as shown in Figure 4-5. If this formula is used, it will automatically change if the value in C2 changes:

```
="Calculations based on "&C2&" hours of billable time spent."
```

Download File 0401.xlsx at www.dummies.com/go/financialmodelinginexcelfd2e and select the tab labeled 4-5 to try this out for yourself. Change the value 15 in cell C2 to another value, such as 20, and you'll see that text changes from "Calculations based on 15 hours of billable time spent" to "Calculations based on 20 hours of billable time spent."

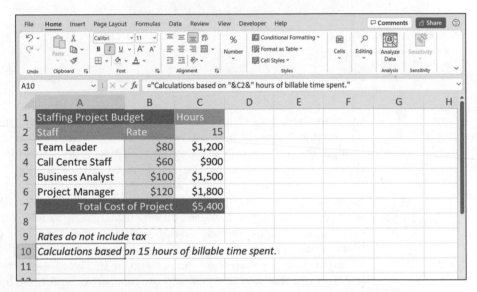

FIGURE 4-5: Linked dynamic text.

Create Dynamic Formulas Using Links

In financial modeling, you need to understand the difference between linked and hard-coded numbers. A *linked number* will automatically change when the source data changes. In Figure 4-6, cell C3 contains the formula =B3*$C$2. This means that if, say, the number of hours spent on the project in cell C3 changes from 15 to 20, the cost of the team leader will change from $1,200 to $1,600. If you want to try this out for yourself, you can download File 0401.xlsx at www.dummies.com/go/financialmodelinginexcelfd2e and select the tab labeled 4-6.

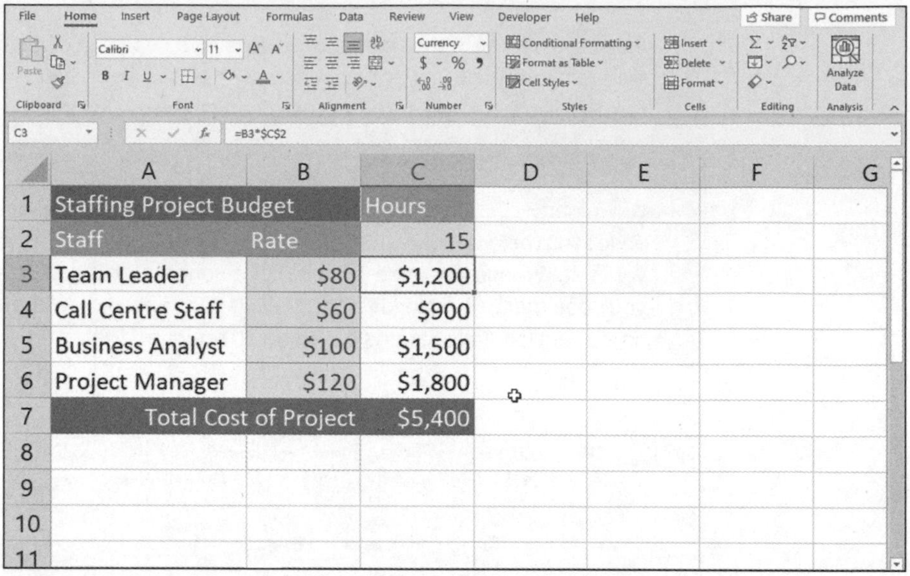

FIGURE 4-6:
Formulas versus
hard-coded
numbers.

In comparison, cells C2 and cells B3 to B6 contain *hard-coded numbers*. These are simply typed directly into the cell and won't change unless a user manually changes them. These cells can also be called *input cells* because if a user or modeler changes them, it will change the model output calculations.

TIP

Format cells containing hard-coded numbers differently so that it's obvious to the user which cells can be changed and which cannot. By formatting input cells differently, it's a signal to your user or another modeler that this is a hard-coded input variable that is designed to change if necessary. Excel has helpfully provided an Input style on the Home tab, as shown in Figure 4-7. There is no hard-and-fast rule that says that you *must* use this particular format, but it's important that you do use a consistent format throughout your model so that the user can see at a glance which cells should be changed, and which should not.

This process of linking calculation cells to input cells is an important concept in financial modeling. Always link as much as possible so that when the model inputs change, the outputs also change. *The only hard-coding should be input cells.* To find out more about linking between cells, sheets, and external files, see Chapter 6.

REMEMBER

By linking, you can trace source data back through the links, making your model auditable, traceable, and easy to validate. If you got the input from somewhere, you should document where it came from wherever possible, because that will help with auditing and validation, and give your model credibility.

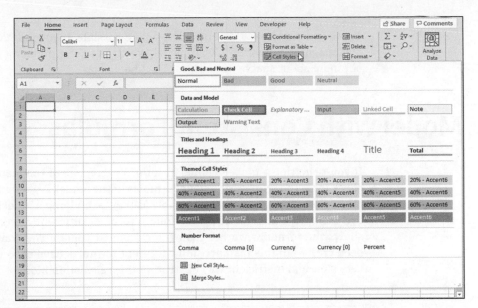

FIGURE 4-7:
Input style on the Home tab.

Only Enter Data Once

When entering data, you should document where it came from if possible, and then link to it with formulas. This may sound obvious but be careful never to enter the same value twice — enter it once as a source and always reference that one cell.

During a long and complex model build, it's very easy to forget that you've entered certain assumptions or inputs, and then enter them again in a different part of the model. For example, in my intermediate online financial modeling course, we build a business case from start to finish, during which we use inflation multiple times within the model, both for indexing salaries, as well as increasing the revenue charged to the customers. Because we've entered the inflation in a single cell on the assumptions page, and then referred to it multiple times throughout the model, any fluctuation in the rate of inflation can be quickly and easily applied throughout the model.

WARNING

Never type a value within a formula. A calculation such as =453*24 should not appear in a financial model. Similarly, a statement such as =IF(H$6<=$E7,0,157000) should have a link to a cell with the value 157000, instead of having the 157000 typed in the formula. The only exceptions to this rule are those things that are standard or commonly accepted values that will not change, such as 24 hours in a day, 7 days in a week, or 12 months in a year. In fact, some hard-core modelers even say that you should put the value 12 in a separate cell, and then link to that cell as an assumption that there are 12 months in the year, but I think that's taking it a bit far!

Try to link directly to the source data where possible. If you link to a link, this creates spaghetti links within your model, which can cause problems later on. To find out more about spaghetti links, turn to Chapter 14.

Model with Consistent Formulas

If you're getting a model audited by a third party, one of the many things they'll check for is the number of unique formulas in the model. A good modeler will create as few unique formulas as possible as they're building a model. In the following example, I'm calculating portfolio returns of different amounts. Figure 4-8 shows the formulas, rather than the calculated values. The way this block has been created in this instance, nine different formulas have been used, which is a very slow and inefficient way of creating this calculation block.

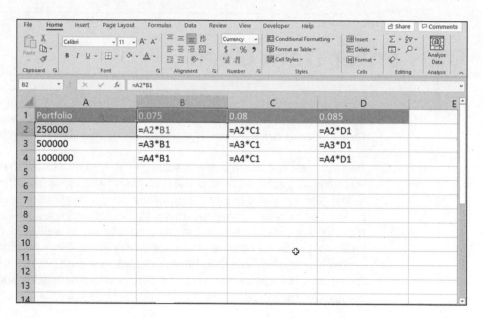

FIGURE 4-8:
Calculating portfolio returns using nine unique formulas.

Download File 0401.xlsx at www.dummies.com/go/financialmodelinginexcel fd2e and select the tab labeled 4-8 or simply open Excel, re-create this example and try it out for yourself. You'll see that creating the formulas shown in Figure 4-8 is a slow and tedious process.

TECHNICAL STUFF

If the formulas aren't all showing when you download and open this file, click the Show Formulas button in the Auditing group on the Formulas tab in the Ribbon. Or, you can use the Ctrl+` shortcut (the ` symbol can be found to the left of the 1 on most keyboards, under the ~ sign).

The task is made much simpler by merely including a few dollar signs in the formula in cell B2 and then copying. Using one single formula and then copying it across and down the calculation block, as shown in Figure 4-9, is much quicker and less prone to error.

	A	B	C	D
1	Portfolio	0.075	0.08	0.085
2	250000	=$A2*B$1	=$A2*C$1	=$A2*D$1
3	500000	=$A3*B$1	=$A3*C$1	=$A3*D$1
4	1000000	=$A4*B$1	=$A4*C$1	=$A4*D$1
5				
6				
7				
8				
9				
10				
11				
12				
13				
14				

FIGURE 4-9: Calculating portfolio returns using one single formula.

TIP

Using mixed referencing within the formula — by putting a dollar sign before the row or column to be anchored — is a far more efficient way of modeling. For more information about how to use relative, absolute, and mixed cell referencing, and for step-by-step instructions for completing this example, see Chapter 6.

REMEMBER

This concept of building your models with consistent formulas wherever possible saves time, avoids error, and is much easier to audit. And it's a key component of good financial modeling. If you only pick up one modeling technique from this book, this is it!

Modelers should strive for consistency of formulas within models for all the reasons I outline in this section, but consistency, in general, is something to aim for in all aspects of the model build. Use consistent colors and formatting, consistent labels, and even consistent layouts. If sheets are similar, work on the sheet until you're completely happy with the layout, and then copy the sheet. This way, the design, formatting, and layout will be identical. Then when you need to update it, group the sheets to make global changes. Have columns and rows matching on multiple sheets — for example, on calculation sheets, if January's calculations start in column F, then January should always start in column F on every calculation sheet.

Build in Error Checks

Even if you've only just started modeling, you're probably well aware how easy it is to make a mistake in a financial model! There are three ways to prevent errors in a financial model:

>> **Avoid making the mistake in the first place.** In this book, I describe several techniques that you can employ to avoid making mistakes in the first place, such as being consistent with your formulas.

>> **Check the model for errors.** Despite your best efforts, errors will almost inevitably slip through, so check, double-check, and have someone else check your model after it's complete.

>> **Include error checks.** As you're building the model, include error checks that prevent inadvertent errors from slipping into the model due to incorrect entries, calculations, or user error.

For more examples of different types of commonly made mistakes, and some ways to avoid making these errors in your models, see Chapter 13. This section focuses on the first two points: techniques for model building to reduce error, as well as ways to check the model for errors.

Error checks are a critical part of a well-built financial model so that the user or modeler can see at a glance if the formulas are calculating correctly. For example, when creating management reports, check that the sum of each individual department's report adds to the company-wide total. This can be done by inserting a simple IF function, among other methods.

In the example shown in Figure 4-10, a capital budget has been built with estimated spend dates in column E. In the capital spend schedule shown in columns F through K, the spend gets spread out over the six-month period that has been modeled. The modeler knows that the total capital spend amount of $124,700 shown in cell D17 should be the same as the total capital schedule amount shown in cell L17, and if the two amounts do not equal each other, then the model is not calculating properly. So the error-checking cell E1 contains the very simple formula =L17-D17. However, as I explain later in this section, that isn't actually the best way to check.

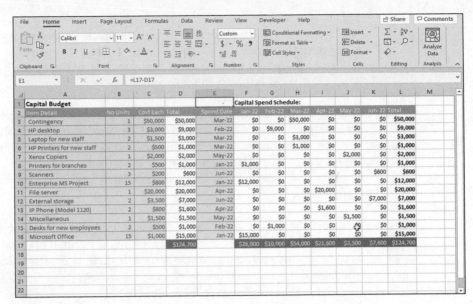

Cell reference: E1 = =L17-D17

Capital Budget					Capital Spend Schedule:						
Item Detail	No Units	Cost Each	Total	Spend Date	Jan-22	Feb-22	Mar-22	Apr-22	May-22	Jun-22	Total
Contingency	1	$50,000	$50,000	Mar-22	$0	$0	$50,000	$0	$0	$0	$50,000
HP desktop	3	$3,000	$9,000	Feb-22	$0	$9,000	$0	$0	$0	$0	$9,000
Laptop for new staff	2	$1,500	$3,000	Mar-22	$0	$0	$3,000	$0	$0	$0	$3,000
HP Printers for new staff	2	$500	$1,000	Mar-22	$0	$0	$1,000	$0	$0	$0	$1,000
Xerox Copiers	1	$2,000	$2,000	May-22	$0	$0	$0	$0	$2,000	$0	$2,000
Printers for branches	2	$500	$1,000	Jan-22	$1,000	$0	$0	$0	$0	$0	$1,000
Scanners	3	$200	$600	Jun-22	$0	$0	$0	$0	$0	$600	$600
Enterprise MS Project	15	$800	$12,000	Jan-22	$12,000	$0	$0	$0	$0	$0	$12,000
File server	1	$20,000	$20,000	Apr-22	$0	$0	$0	$20,000	$0	$0	$20,000
External storage	2	$3,500	$7,000	Jun-22	$0	$0	$0	$0	$0	$7,000	$7,000
IP Phone (Model 1120)	2	$800	$1,600	Apr-22	$0	$0	$0	$1,600	$0	$0	$1,600
Miscellaneous	1	$1,500	$1,500	May-22	$0	$0	$0	$0	$1,500	$0	$1,500
Desks for new employees	2	$500	$1,000	Feb-22	$0	$1,000	$0	$0	$0	$0	$1,000
Microsoft Office	15	$1,000	$15,000	Jan-22	$15,000	$0	$0	$0	$0	$0	$15,000
			$124,700		$28,000	$10,000	$54,000	$21,600	$3,500	$7,600	$124,700

FIGURE 4-10:
A simple error
check.

In Figure 4-11, you can see that a user has entered an incorrect value in cell E4. Feb-23 is not a valid entry because the capital spend schedule only allows for dates during 2022. This means that the financial model shown in Figure 4-10 is incorrect — the user has entered $124,700 worth of capital expenditure into the model, but only $115,700 has been allocated across the year. The number showing in cell E1 ($9,000) alerts the user to the fact that there is a problem. Download File 0401.xlsx at www.dummies.com/go/financialmodelinginexcelfd2e and select the tabs labeled 4-10 and 4-11 to try triggering this error check for yourself.

Capital Budget				(9,000)	Capital Spend Schedule:						
Item Detail	No Units	Cost Each	Total	Spend Date	Jan-22	Feb-22	Mar-22	Apr-22	May-22	Jun-22	Total
Contingency	1	$50,000	$50,000	Mar-22	$0	$0	$50,000	$0	$0	$0	$50,000
HP desktop	3	$3,000	$9,000	Feb-23	$0	$0	$0	$0	$0	$0	$0
Laptop for new staff	2	$1,500	$3,000	Mar-22	$0	$0	$3,000	$0	$0	$0	$3,000
HP Printers for new staff	2	$500	$1,000	Mar-22	$0	$0	$1,000	$0	$0	$0	$1,000
Xerox Copiers	2	$2,000	$2,000	May-22	$0	$0	$0	$0	$2,000	$0	$2,000
Printers for branches	2	$500	$1,000	Jan-22	$1,000	$0	$0	$0	$0	$0	$1,000
Scanners	3	$200	$600	Jun-22	$0	$0	$0	$0	$0	$600	$600
Enterprise MS Project	15	$800	$12,000	Jan-22	$12,000	$0	$0	$0	$0	$0	$12,000
File server	1	$20,000	$20,000	Apr-22	$0	$0	$0	$20,000	$0	$0	$20,000
External storage	2	$3,500	$7,000	Jun-22	$0	$0	$0	$0	$0	$7,000	$7,000
IP Phone (Model 1120)	2	$800	$1,600	Apr-22	$0	$0	$0	$1,600	$0	$0	$1,600
Miscellaneous	1	$1,500	$1,500	May-22	$0	$0	$0	$0	$1,500	$0	$1,500
Desks for new employees	2	$500	$1,000	Feb-22	$0	$1,000	$0	$0	$0	$0	$1,000
Microsoft Office	15	$1,000	$15,000	Jan-22	$15,000	$0	$0	$0	$0	$0	$15,000
			$124,700		$28,000	$1,000	$54,000	$21,600	$3,500	$7,600	$115,700

FIGURE 4-11:
An error check
triggered.

This error check is very simple and quite discreet. To make it more obvious, you may prefer to include the description "error check" next to the error-checking cell in cell D1, which would make it more obvious to the user what has happened when the error check is triggered.

The error check shown in Figure 4-10 is my preferred method of error checking, because it's so simple and quick to build. Because it returns a value in the case of an error, it may be a little too discreet for your tastes — it doesn't necessarily alert the user immediately that an error had been made. However, it's certainly quick and easy to follow and, for this reason, a fairly common error check favored by many modelers.

TIP

If you use this kind of error check, format it using the Comma style (found on the Home tab in the Numbers group) and remove the decimal place and format it with a red font. This way, the zero won't show if there is no error, and a red number will show if there is an error.

Alternatively, you may prefer the other error-checking formula such as =D17=R17, which will return the value TRUE if they are the same or FALSE if they aren't.

However, either method can potentially provide a false indication of an error, as shown in the following section.

Allowing tolerance for error

=IF(D17<>R17,"error",0) is a superior error check, but every now and then it can return a false error result, even though the values appear to be the same. (See Chapter 7 for how to use an IF statement in a formula like this.) This "bug" is caused by the fact that Excel carries calculations to 14 decimal places. After that, Excel truncates the value, which can cause minute discrepancies, which will cause the formula to report an error when the difference is as small as 0.00000000000001 off. To avoid the potential for false error checks, use one of the following methods:

>> **Test the absolute value of the difference against a nonzero tolerance.**
For instance =IF(ABS(D17–R17)>1,"error",0) will allow the values to differ by 1 before reporting an error. You should use Excel's ABS function, which will take the absolute value of the result, so it doesn't matter if it's a positive or negative difference.

>> **Test whether the rounded value of the difference is nonzero using a formula such as** =IF(ROUND(D17–R17,0)=0,0,"error") instead.

There are many variations of this formula. Some modelers prefer to show the word *OK* if the numbers are right, and *Check* if they aren't.

Applying conditional formatting to an error check

To make the error check even more prominent to the user, consider using conditional formatting that makes the cell have a red highlight if the error check has been triggered. On the Home tab of the Ribbon, in the Styles group, click the Conditional Formatting button. Then hover the mouse over Highlight Cells Rule and select Equal To (see Figure 4-12).

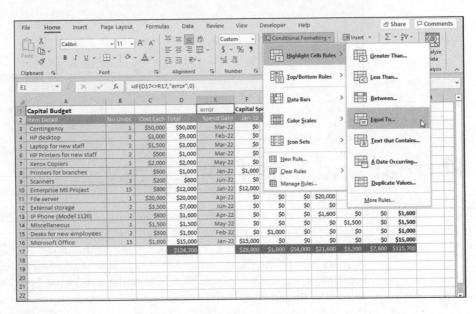

FIGURE 4-12: Applying conditional formatting to an error check.

When the Equal To dialog box appears, as shown in Figure 4-13, type the word **error** into the Format Cells That Are Equal To box and click OK. By default, it will turn the cell to Light Red Fill with Dark Red Text, but you can change this in the drop-down box.

WARNING

Be careful. If you just change your error check formula to return a different alert, such as "Err" or "Check," the conditional formatting rule won't be triggered. You'll also need to change the conditional formatting rule to check for the new word.

Conditional formatting is commonly applied in error checks because it makes the error check more prominent when it's triggered. This obviously makes it more likely the user will realize there is an error in the financial model and solve it before using the model's outputs. However, conditional formatting isn't limited to error checks — it can be useful whenever you want to draw a user's attention such as to the highest and/or lowest values in a range or some unusual result in a set of calculations.

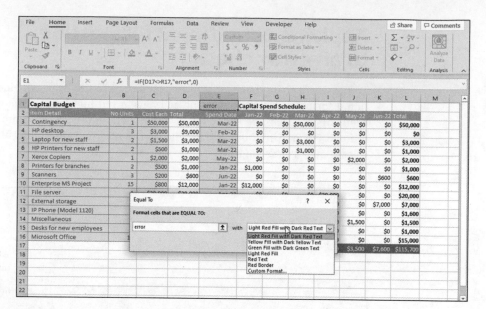

FIGURE 4-13:
Editing the
conditional
formatting color.

Format and Label for Clarity

Applying appropriate formatting and labeling to financial models is sometimes neglected by even experienced financial modelers. You need to include as many descriptions and instructions as possible within the model to make it absolutely obvious how to use the model and how the calculations work. Don't assume that someone using the model will be able to understand what they're supposed to do to update, use, or modify the model.

Here are some simple formatting rules to consider:

REMEMBER

>> **Format input cells differently from calculation cells.** (See "Create Dynamic Formulas Using Links," earlier in this chapter.)

>> **Use symbols for currency.** If the currency is dollars, format 5000 as $5,000 for example, or if it's in euros, format it as €5,000.

>> **Include units or currencies in column and row headings.** Where possible, each column or row should contain only one type of unit or currency.

- **»** **Use commas for thousands.** This makes your model easier to read and prevents mistakes and misinterpretations.

- **»** **Include a dedicated units column.** Make sure the units denoted by the amounts in that column are entered into that column's heading (for example, "MWh," "Liters," or "Headcount").

- **»** **Reserve a column for constants that apply to all years, months, or days.** For example, if growth rate is 5%, have that in column D, and then link all calculations to column D.

- **»** **Label your data clearly.** It sounds simple, but mixing units (for example, mixing apples and oranges, or miles and kilometers) is a common source of error in financial modeling, and good formatting and labeling will avoid this.

- **»** **If you round figures, show this clearly at the top of the column with a descriptive heading.** For example, make the column heading "Revenue rounded to nearest $'000" to avoid confusion and misinterpretation.

Chapter **5**

Using Someone Else's Financial Model

As a consultant, my favorite scenario occurs when a client comes to me and asks me to build a new model *from scratch*. This situation does happen every now and then, but it's very rare. Normally, clients have a financial model that isn't working properly, or they need to update their model from last year, or they need to change the layout or design of their model. Being able to create my own models from scratch every time would be nice, but it's rarely practical. Instead, most of the time, like most modelers, I'm working with inherited models — models I've had to take over from someone else.

When you inherit a model, not only do you inherit the inputs, assumptions, and calculations the original modeler has entered, but you also inherit their *mistakes.* Using someone else's model involves taking responsibility for someone else's work, sometimes from people you've never even met! If you're going to be taking responsibility for someone else's model, you need to take it over and make it your own. You need to take responsibility for the workings of this model, and you have to be confident that the model is working correctly.

In this chapter, you explore some ways of checking, auditing, validating, and, if necessary, correcting other people's models so that you can be confident in the models' results.

Considering Templates for Building a Financial Model

Models are often inherited in the form of templates. Dealing with a model built from a template is quite a different prospect than using a model that has been purpose-built for the job. In this section, I start by taking a look at why a modeler would use templates in the first place. Then I steer you in another direction and tell you why.

Why templates can be appealing

If you describe yourself as a "casual" financial modeler, your usual job might be something else entirely, but part of your professional and personal life means that you need to create a budget or financial statements, or maybe just do some pricing calculations. If this is you, you're probably looking for an easy way to create a quick financial model that gives you the results you need. Starting to build a full financial model entirely from the ground up, especially when you have no idea where to begin, can be rather daunting. Using a template is a very appealing option because it requires a much lower initial investment of time and money than building a model yourself.

WARNING

If the business or situation you're trying to model is *extremely* simple and/or your business is *exactly* the same as every other business, you'll be fine with a template. However, most templates are really just a nicely formatted spreadsheet. There is a bit more to building a robust, responsive, and accurate financial model than plugging a few numbers into a spreadsheet.

If you're looking for a shortcut to building a financial model, keep in mind what a fully functional, dynamic model does that a basic spreadsheet does not. For more information about differentiating a model from a spreadsheet, turn to Chapter 1.

What's wrong with using templates

When you're first starting out, a template may be a good way to get going. But think of a template as a car with no engine — it looks great on the surface, but there's no performance! Here are a few important features you *won't* have when you use a template:

>> **Financial models need drivers:** What makes a really good financial model is its ability to take the business model and represent it financially. Revenues and expenses don't just happen — something occurs that makes that revenue

or expense become a reality. Drivers are absolutely critical in creating a financial model that is flexible and scalable. For example, if you were to achieve 10 percent market penetration, and your product was priced at $5, your revenue would be, say, $100,000 per month. Many templates simply show a hard-coded value of $100,000 for revenue, but in your model, you need to know exactly what had to happen in order for revenue to be calculated at $100,000.

Of course, the beauty of this method not only means that investors or other users can trace back to see how the revenue is calculated, but you can also run scenarios and sensitivity analyses on these inputs. What if penetration were 12 percent? What if you decreased the pricing by 10 percent? This sort of analysis is virtually impossible with a simple input of $100,000 for revenue.

>> **Customized inputs:** A fill-in-the-blanks template has to suit everyone, so in order to meet the requirements of virtually any business model, the inputs must be kept generic (Revenue Item 1, Revenue Item 2, and so on). Of course, you can change the titles of these line items, but what if you have different lines of businesses that need to be separated?

Here's another example: "Office Rent" — a line item often found in a template — may not apply to your company. Maybe you bought your building, have a mortgage (a liability, not an expense), and need a way to factor in the mortgage pay down and interest portion of each payment. An experienced financial modeler would have no problem working this into a customized forecast. If you're using a template, you'll have a hard time getting the template to meet your needs. Plus, you'll probably spend more time manipulating the template to meet your needs than you would've spent just building it from scratch.

>> **Scalability:** Just like that cheap one-size-fits-all shirt you bought from the market, your model will probably never fit properly. It's pretty much guaranteed that whatever number of inputs the template designer has chosen won't be exactly what you need. Inserting or deleting rows may seem simple, but any Excel modeler knows how deadly that can be. Before you know it, you've ended up with a model full of dreaded #REF! errors. To avoid this, the template designer likely created a large number of unnecessary rows and columns just in case you need them. Most templates contain a huge amount of redundant information and unnecessary complexity, which is confusing, takes up memory, and is simply poor modeling practice.

>> **Specialized functionality:** The standard financial reports have always been the balance sheet, cash flow statement, and income statement, but there are many additional reports that might be useful to *your* business but not necessarily to others. Unfortunately, you won't find anything beyond standard, minimum functionality in a template.

You're not very likely to have much more than very basic scenario analysis functionality built into a template. For example, it would be nice to be able to change a few inputs and do a scenario analysis to find out how increasing market penetration by 10 percent affects the bottom line. A good scenario analysis tool built into a financial model is really what makes a model useful, because you can easily see what changing not just one variable but multiple variables does to the company.

Templates are great for very surface-level projecting, or "back of the envelope" calculations where a high level of precision is not required. But if you're serious about your modeling, you'll want it done correctly and as accurately as possible. Finding a template that will meet your specific needs is nearly impossible. Between the work you'll do adjusting it and the frustration you'll experience using it, you'll wish you'd just built the model from scratch!

Why you should build your own model

Imagine you are working on the due diligence for a potential acquisition by your company of a smaller one. Someone else created a model to project the financials but has since left the company, and you're responsible for the financial model now. Your investor asks why your sales projections increase so sharply when the expenses do not. The answer — "because that's what the financial model says" — is simply not good enough. If you're responsible for the model, you need to be familiar enough to able to answer a question like that — perhaps not off the top of your head, but you should be able to understand the drivers of the model to provide a timely and insightful answer to these kinds of questions. Blindly accepting the output of a model is foolish and extremely dangerous.

Learning from other people's models is often helpful, but it's rarely efficient to build a model using their templates. Trying to change things becomes difficult when a formula doesn't change in the way you expect it to, and a nuance will come back to haunt you because you didn't understand the financial model to begin with. You may think that a template will help you save time, but in the long run, it will end up costing you more time and lead to potential error. Although building your own model can be time-consuming, you'll no doubt be far more comfortable with the results. Not only will you be able to vouch for the accuracy of the calculations, but during the model-building process you'll improve your modeling and Excel skills and your understanding of the business.

HAVING SOMEONE ELSE BUILD A MODEL FOR YOU

You can always hire a consultant to build a financial model for you. If you decide to take this route, my advice is to work closely with the modeler and make sure they understand the problem properly before they begin to build the model. As they're building, ask lots of questions and make sure you understand exactly what they've done and why they've done it. Don't just blindly accept any of the outputs. Test the model rigorously throughout the process. **Remember:** You're going to be the one using the model and taking responsibility for its outputs in the future, and it's your job on the line if the model doesn't reflect the situation accurately. Make sure you can make changes to the model yourself so that you don't have to call the consultant back every time you need a simple edit.

REMEMBER

Never trust someone else's work, or take the outputs of their model at face value. When inheriting a model, your choices are to start over and build your own model from the ground up or validate and verify the existing model to the extent that you're comfortable to take responsibility for the calculations. Starting over to build your own model from scratch is inefficient and a waste of resources. Unless the model is in extremely poor shape, it's usually far more efficient to use what you already have — but leave no cell untouched during the process of validation and verification.

Inheriting a File: What to Check For

When you're inheriting someone else's model, the best-case scenario is a model handover meeting where you can sit down with the person who built it and they can take you through all the various moving parts. Unfortunately, this kind of meeting is rarely practical. Usually, the original modeler is unavailable and you're thrown in the deep end, having to figure out how the model works on your own. A good modeler will have built the model in such a way that it can speak for itself, without the need for additional explanation. It will flow logically and have good documentation, labels, and instructions that make it easy to navigate and figure out how to use. Any model *you* build in the future will contain these features, but the model you inherit may or may not include them.

In the absence of any training or handover documentation, when you first start using someone else's model, there are a few things to look for when you first open up the file.

Meeting a model for the first time

When you open a financial model someone else has given you for the first time, take some time to get acquainted with it. If you're planning to make this model your own, and take responsibility for its outputs, you're going to be spending quite a bit of time together. Familiarize yourself with the layout and how it's built. In particular, pay attention to the following:

» **Formatting:** Get used to the formatting, and decide whether you're happy with the formats they've used, particularly the color scheme, and decide if you want to change it. Are all formulas and hard-coded values formatted differently? Does it match your company colors?

» **Formulas:** Take a look at the formulas. Are they consistent? Do they contain any hard coding? A good way to see all the formulas at once is to select Show Formulas on the Formula Auditing section on the Formulas tab on the Ribbon, or just press Ctrl+`. For more information on formula auditing, see the "Using Audit Tools to Find and Correct Errors" section later in this chapter.

» **Workbook calculations:** Most of the time, calculations happen automatically, so that when you change something in the model, the formulas change as well. Sometimes, however, when a file is very large, or a modeler likes to control the changes manually, the calculation has been set to manual instead of automatic. I've spent many happy hours auditing a formula, wondering why the numbers aren't changing, only to discover that there was nothing wrong with the formula at all — the automatic calculation was simply turned off!

To check this setting, choose File ➪ Options. In the Options dialog box, select the Formulas section and check that the calculation options at the top of the dialog box have been set to automatic instead of manual. Alternatively, a quicker way to access these settings is from the Calculation section of the Formulas tab on the Ribbon. Select the Calculation Options button and you can switch between manual and automatic calculation from the drop-down options that appear. If you see "Calculate" in the status bar in the lower-left corner of the screen, you know that the workbook is set to manual calculation.

» **Error checking:** An easy way to see at a glance whether there are any Excel errors in a sheet is to press the Error Checking button in the Formula Auditing section of the Formulas tab of the Ribbon. This will look across the entire sheet and alert you to any Excel error values that you should be aware of. See Chapter 13 for more information on what kind of errors you might encounter and how to handle them.

>> **Named ranges:** Many models contain named ranges, which is not a problem, but they often harbor errors due to redundant names and external links. Review the named ranges in the Name Manager, which is on the Formulas tab of the Ribbon, and delete any named ranges that contain errors or links to external files, or that are not being used. For more information about the use of named ranges in a financial model, see Chapter 6.

Figure 5-1 shows an example of a model showing multiple error values in the Name Manager.

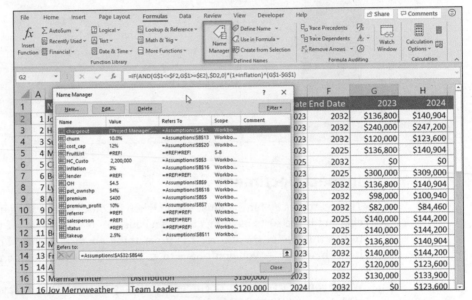

FIGURE 5-1: The Name Manager showing multiple named ranges containing error values.

Inspecting the workbook

Excel has a fantastic tool called Inspect Workbook that's a great way of getting to know the hidden features of your model and identifying potentially problematic features that would otherwise be very difficult to find.

To use Inspect Workbook, press File. On the Info tab, click the Check for Issues button, as shown in Figure 5-2.

The text under Inspect Workbook will tell you immediately the potential issues you should know about. Then under the Check for Issues button, there are three options to choose from: Inspect Document, Check Accessibility, and Check Compatibility.

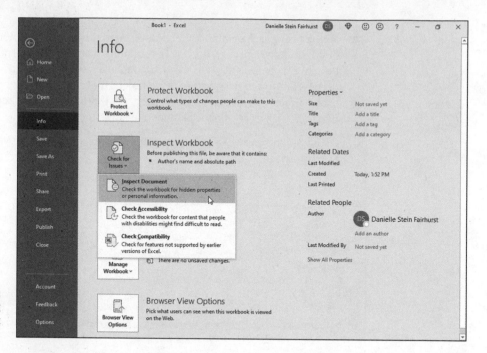

FIGURE 5-2:
Accessing
the Inspect
Workbook tool.

Inspect Document

This feature is by far the most useful when it comes to checking inherited files. It checks for the sorts of things that can cause problems for you if you're planning to use this file in the future. The great thing about it is that it checks all these items in one go — you don't have to go in and check each item one at a time.

When you select Inspect Document, you may be prompted to save the file. If so, click Yes, and the Document Inspector dialog box (shown in Figure 5-3) appears. This dialog box lists all the things the Document Inspector can check for. Leave all the check boxes selected, and click Inspect.

After you've clicked Inspect, any potential issues will be flagged, as shown in Figure 5-4. Scroll down the list and take a look at anything that has been flagged. You can decide whether you'd like to remove the features from the workbook here and now, or ignore them and come back to it later.

WARNING

The Inspect Workbook feature is great for *identifying* problem-causing features in your model but it's not very helpful for *resolving* them. It provides a summary of all the items the tool has found, and it gives you the option to remove these immediately from the workbook. This is not a good idea. Instead of simply stripping a whole lot of features (and accompanying data) from your model, take the time to understand what each of the features is, think about why the modeler might have included them in the model, and whether you need them going forward.

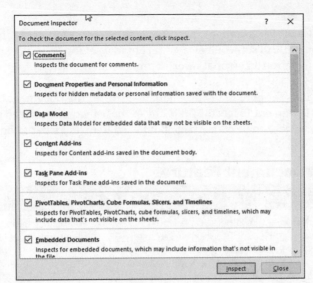

FIGURE 5-3:
The Document
Inspector
dialog box.

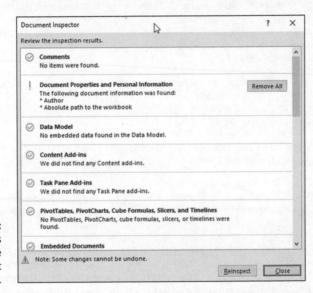

FIGURE 5-4:
Potential issues
flagged in the
Document
Inspector.

For example, the tool may discover that there are hidden sheets in the file. If so, it gives you the option to delete those sheets immediately without looking at them. The sheets probably contain important information, and your formulas may link to cells in those hidden sheets, so accepting the recommendations of the Document Inspector will very likely cause more problems than it solves.

WARNING

If you *do* remove features through the Document Inspector, there is no Undo option. Make sure you save a copy of the file first, just in case!

TIP

Another use of the Document Inspector is to remove additional information before passing on a file to someone else — sort of like selling your old cellphone on eBay and making sure all personal information is removed first.

Table 5-1 lists the potentially problematic features the Document Inspector checks for. If the Document Inspector finds any of these features, refer to this table to find out why you need to be concerned about each item and what to do about them.

TABLE 5-1   **Inspect Document Features**

Feature	Why It Matters	What to Do about It
Comments	Quickly find any comments a previous author has included. This might include any instructions or documentation about model inputs or assumptions on how it has been calculated that you need to know.	Read any instructions another modeler may have left for you.
Document properties and personal information	Every file contains "metadata" such as the name of the author, last saved data, and file path and so on, which is all useful information, especially when you don't know where the model has been.	See who built the model originally, see when it was last saved, and make sure you're using the latest version.
Data model	If you've used the data model (which is possible if you've used Power Query or multiple PivotTables), it will check for embedded data not visible on the sheets.	Take note if these exist.
Content add-ins	Unless you know specifically what the add-in is doing, you should remove it.	The easiest way to remove it is to allow the Document Inspector to remove it.
Task pane add-ins	Unless you know specifically what the add-in is doing, you should remove it.	The easiest way to remove it is to allow the Document Inspector to remove it.
PivotTables, PivotCharts, cube formulas, slicers, and timelines	If you've inherited a model, you might not realize that the model contains PivotTables and related features. This is important because PivotTables don't refresh automatically the way formulas do.	Be sure to refresh any PivotTables, make sure they're still accurate, and ensure that any slicers or timelines still work properly. Remove them if no longer needed.
Embedded documents	Someone may have embedded files within the document. It's an unusual practice, but if they're there, you probably want to know about it.	Open the embedded document to see if it contains information you need.

Feature	Why It Matters	What to Do about It
Macros, forms, and ActiveX controls	These contain executable code, and if they're contained in the model, you'll want to know about it. I don't advocate the use of these tools unless absolutely necessary. Keeping models as simple as possible is important, and these tools are quite difficult for the casual modeler to use.	Find out what these tools are doing in the model, and remove them if no longer necessary. The code might be critical for model functionality so you should get an expert who knows VBA (the macro coding language) to take a look before you remove it. Saving the file in XLSX format instead of XLSM will remove any executable code.
Links to other files	These are dangerous because if the source file changes, the data can change in your model without your realizing it.	To see if links exist in your model, select Edit Links from the Connections section of the Data tab in the Ribbon. The Edit Links dialog box will display a list of all external links in the file. If links exist, check to see if they're accurate and still necessary. If not, remove them by selecting the link in the Edit Links dialog box, and pressing Break Link. This will quickly convert all cells containing external links to their hard-coded values throughout the model.
Real Time Data (RTD) functions	The RTD functions will refresh data automatically from real-time data servers into Excel, such as stock prices.	Locate them by searching for RTD within the sheets' formulas. Review the accuracy of the formula and delete if no longer necessary.
Excel surveys	Someone may have created an online survey that feeds into your model. The questions may be entered in Excel Online, but not visible in the workbook. If a survey is there, you'll want to know that's where your data is coming from.	Test the form and make sure it's still working. Remove the survey functionality if it's no longer needed. The easiest way to remove this is to allow the Document Inspector to remove it.
Defined scenarios	Scenario Manager may have been used on this model, and all the scenario information may be stored in the scenario and may not be visible on the sheet.	Select Scenario Manager from the What-if Analysis button on the Forecast section of the Data tab. You can view the scenarios separately, or click Summary to see a summary of all the inputs and outputs that have been saved in the Scenario Manager. If scenarios are needed, consider using an alternative method of scenario analysis (see Chapter 8 for more information on scenarios).

(continued)

TABLE 5-1 *(continued)*

Feature	Why It Matters	What to Do about It
Active filters	If filters have been activated, some data is not visible on the sheet. This can cause problems when using formulas or copying and pasting. For example, you might add up a list of items, not realizing that a filter has been applied and that you aren't looking at the entire list.	The filters won't cause you any problems unless they're applied, so there is no need to remove them entirely. Clear the filters by selecting Clear from the Sort & Filter section on the Data tab. This way you can apply the filters in future if needed.
Custom worksheet properties	Someone may have customized the worksheet properties. Unless you know specifically why they've done it, you should remove it.	The easiest way to remove custom worksheet properties is to allow the Document Inspector to remove them.
Hidden names	If hidden names exist in your model, they're unlikely to be of much use to you. Unless you know specifically why someone has used them, you should remove them.	You can't manually remove hidden names without using VBA, so the easiest way to remove them is to allow the Document Inspector to remove them.
Ink	Someone may have used digital ink to annotate the workbook.	Take a look and see if the annotations contain important information.
Long External References	External links with file paths that are longer than 218 characters can cause errors when you save.	To find the external files being referenced, select Edit Links from the Connections section of the Data tab on the Ribbon. Remove the reference or edit the file path to make it shorter.
Custom XML data	Unless you know specifically why this is in your model, you should remove it.	The easiest way to remove this is to allow the Document Inspector to remove it.
Headers and footers	Headers and footers are easily missed because they don't show up in the soft copy unless you print or print preview.	Choose File ⇨ Print to see a print preview. Look for headers and footers and check whether they contain any important information. Click Page Setup toward the bottom of the page to change them.

Feature	Why It Matters	What to Do about It
Hidden rows and columns	Hidden rows and columns are very common and are the cause of one of the most common errors in financial modeling. Not realizing that hidden rows are in the model and might be inadvertently included or not included in sum totals is extremely dangerous. You definitely want to know if hidden rows or columns are contained in the model.	Highlight the row or column before and after the hidden one, right-click, and choose Unhide to unhide them. It's okay to hide rows and columns to tidy up the model and not show everything you don't need to see, but it's better practice to use grouping instead. To apply grouping, select the entire row or column you want to hide, and select Group from the Outline section of the Data tab.
Hidden worksheets	Hidden worksheets are less dangerous than hidden rows or columns, but if you're taking over a model, you'll want to know exactly what's on the hidden sheets.	Right-click one of the sheet tabs at the bottom and choose Unhide. You'll need to unhide each hidden sheet separately.
Invisible content	Invisible content is usually caused by users copying and pasting data from a website and inadvertently including invisible objects with it. Removing invisible content is highly unlikely to cause a problem.	To find objects, you can use Go To Special (Ctrl+G) and select objects, but the easiest way to remove them is to allow the Document Inspector to do so.

Check Accessibility

This option checks to see whether people with disabilities might have trouble accessing any of the features of the file. For example, all visuals and tables should have alternative text to help people who can't see the screen understand the image.

Check Compatibility

This option checks whether the file uses new tools available in this version of Excel that aren't available in previous versions of Excel (see Chapter 2).

TECHNICAL STUFF

If you're not planning to share the file with anyone using previous versions of Excel, you can leave any new features in, but if you aren't sure what version of Excel your users may have, you may want to consider replacing them with tools that are available in prior versions. Refer to Chapter 2 for a list of features and their version compatibility.

Using Audit Tools to Find and Correct Errors

When inheriting a model, there are several factors to come to grips with: the layout, design, formatting, assumptions, and formulas. Of all these, following the formula calculations is the most difficult, and verifying and validating formulas can be very time-consuming. The fastest way to understand a formula when you see it for the first time is to go into Edit mode. Double-click a cell, or select it and press F2. If the formula's source inputs are on the same page, they'll show visually where the source data is coming from that feeds the cell calculation, as shown in Figure 5-5. The color codes are helpful; each range in the formula will be the same color as the highlight source data that feeds it. If you'd like to try this out for yourself, download `File 0501.xlsx` from www.dummies.com/go/financial modelinginexcelfd2e. Open it and select the tab labeled 5-5.

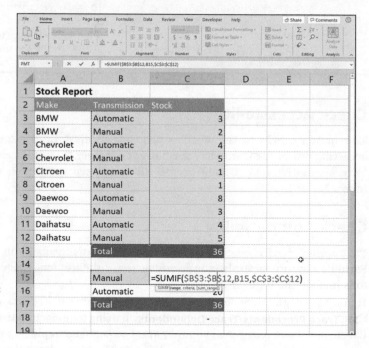

FIGURE 5-5:
Using Edit mode to see formula inputs.

TIP

When you're in Edit mode and you decide that you need to change the range the formula is referring to, you can use the mouse to click and drag the colored lines to reference a different cell. For example, in Figure 5-5 if you want the range B3:B12 to be A3:A12 instead, click the colored line showing between the A and B column and drag it so that the cell reference is column A instead of column B.

On the Formulas tab in the Ribbon, there is a formula auditing section that contains a number of tools that you'll find useful when trying to understand someone else's financial model. Just remember that using these audit tools in Excel is not the same as performing a formal financial model audit.

TECHNICAL STUFF

A formal *financial model audit* is a very detailed process in which a model auditing team takes the model apart and checks it meticulously for errors. If the bank is lending you money based on the results of the financial model, one of the conditions of the loan might be that the model be audited to make sure that the results can be relied upon. Getting a model professionally audited can be an extremely expensive undertaking, but it's really the only way to ensure that there are no errors. Note that a financial model audit is sometimes called a *model review* to differentiate it from a *financial audit.*

Of course, creating your own financial model is a lot more interesting than checking someone else's. But Excel's audit tools make checking someone else's model somewhat easier. Formula errors are the most common type of error in financial models, and the audit tools exist almost solely for the purpose of finding these formula errors.

Checking a model for accuracy

The formula auditing tools can help get to the root of what's causing the error in a cell through tracing relationships among cells within your worksheet. These tools will help you find the source of an error, but they'll also, more importantly, help you find an error you didn't know was there. By tracing the relationships, formula auditing lets you test formulas to see the *precedents* (cells that directly supply the formulas) and the *dependents* (the cells that depend on the results of the formulas). Excel also offers a way to visually reverse any potential sources of an error in the formula of any particular cell.

The formula auditing tools can be found in the command buttons located in the Formula Auditing group on the Formulas tab of the Ribbon. These command buttons include the following:

>> **Trace Precedents/Trace Dependents:** In trying to understand a model, you'll spend the majority of your time working through the formulas and making sure you understand exactly how each output has been calculated. Trace Precedents and Trace Dependents are good places to start when you're trying to see where the cell links are coming from and going to. These tools are helpful to identify the linkages that exist between the cells and display the relationships visually with blue tracer line arrows.

To use Trace Precedents, start with an output cell that contains a formula you want to understand, such as the formula in cell G26 in Figure 5-6. Select the cell and click the Trace Precedents button in the Formula Auditing section of the Formulas tab. This displays blue tracer line arrows, which show which cells G26 depends on.

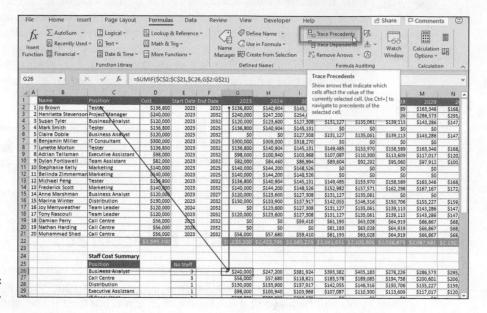

FIGURE 5-6:
Trace Precedents.

Using the same cell, you can see which cells, in turn, depend upon G26 by using Trace Dependents, as shown in Figure 5-7.

TIP

Click the Trace Precedents or Trace Dependents button again, and it goes further and shows the precedent of the precedent, or the dependent of the dependent.

If the source data is located on another sheet, instead of the blue tracer line arrow, a black dotted line appears with the worksheet icon, as shown in Figure 5-8.

Cells that are the cause of errors will show as red tracer arrows instead of blue. When the cell links to external files, the source file must be open so that the Formula Auditing tool can trace these dependencies.

TIP

The tracer lines disappear when the file is saved. You can manually remove them by clicking Remove Arrows under the Trace Dependents button on the Ribbon. Make sure you remove the arrows before printing the sheet; otherwise, they'll show up in the printed document.

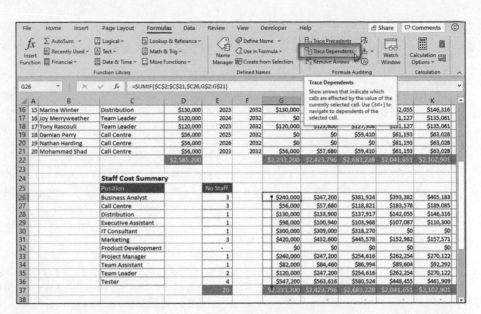

FIGURE 5-7:
Trace Dependents.

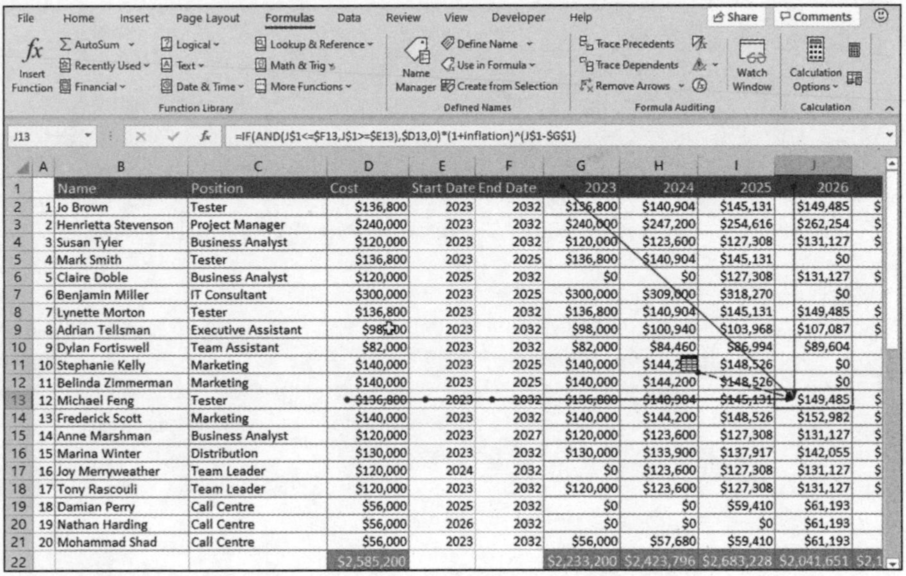

FIGURE 5-8:
The black dotted line indicates a link to an off-sheet source.

TIP

You can also jump to precedent cells by using these shortcuts:

- Ctrl+[to jump to and highlight precedent cells

- Ctrl+] to jump to and highlight dependent cells

- Ctrl+G or F5 and then Enter to return to the previous cell

DEALING WITH REDUNDANT ASSUMPTIONS

A common problem in financial models, particularly "legacy models" that have been around for a long time and have been passed on from one staff member to another, is that inputs and assumptions may exist that aren't actually being used in the model's calculations. Redundant assumptions can happen when modelers need to use source information that is already in the spreadsheet and re-create it without realizing that they're entering a duplicate set of assumptions or data. Often, as a model evolves, parts of the model calculations are deleted, but the assumptions that fed into those calculations remain, despite the fact that they're no longer needed. Using the Trace Dependents formula auditing tool is the easiest way to see whether any formulas are linking to an input cell. This tool will allow you to trace forward and backward throughout the model.

One technique you can use to remove redundant cells is to color-code all the input assumption and calculation cells. Then go to the model outputs and trace back the formulas, using trace precedents and trace dependents. As each input assumption is validated, change the color of the input cells back to their original color. At the end of the process, if any cells are still colored, you'll know that they're redundant and they can be deleted.

When removing redundant inputs from a model, delete entire rows or columns by right-clicking and selecting Delete Row or Delete Column instead of selecting the cell and pressing Delete. This way, if the deletion had been linking to a formula, you see an error. Clearing cells simply changes the value to zero, which won't necessarily return an error and can cause undetected errors to remain in the model.

Formula auditing doesn't always show up if certain tools such as data tables, array formulas, and the INDIRECT and OFFSET are relying on that cell. For this reason, make sure you save before deleting any redundant assumptions in your model and check the output of the model for #REF! or other errors before continuing. If removing the cells has caused an error, you can simply undo or close without saving to revert to the version of the file prior to the changes.

Making sense of the formulas

Of the tools that are contained within the Formula Auditing section of the Formulas section on the Ribbon, Trace Precedents and Trace Dependents are likely to be of most use to you. There are a few other tools, however, which also warrant a mention.

>> **Evaluate Formula:** Another way of checking formulas is to actually take them apart using the Evaluate Formula tool. This tool is most useful with long and complex nested formulas because it evaluates each part of the formula separately in the current cell that you're in, as shown in Figure 5-9.

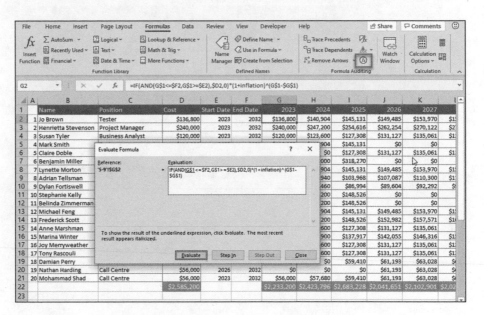

TIP

You can also evaluate a partial formula manually by selecting a part of the formula and pressing F9. You have to select an entire section of the formula that makes sense in its own right; for example, in a nested formula such as =IF(D3=0,0,IF(E3<$F$1,-E3/D3,0)) shown in Figure 5-10, you can select this portion of the formula: E3<$F$1. If you then press F9, the result of that portion of the formula alone will be displayed as a value, which in this case is FALSE. You can see that the statement being evaluated is false, so the "value if true" part of the formula will be the result of the statement, rather than the "value if false." (For more information on using IF statements, see Chapter 7.)

>> **Error-checking tools:** If you make a mistake — or what Excel thinks is a mistake — a green triangle will appear in the upper-left corner of the cell. This happens if you omit adjacent cells, such as the error that is shown in Figure 5-11, or if you enter an input as text that looks like it should be a number.

In this instance, Excel provides a very helpful notification that the formula in cell B8 does not include the entire range above it, which is highly likely to be an error. This menu gives you various options to help correct the error.

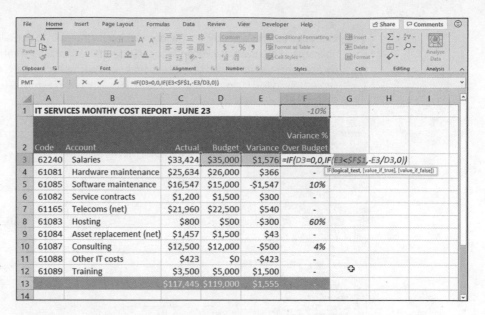

FIGURE 5-10:
Auditing part of the formula manually.

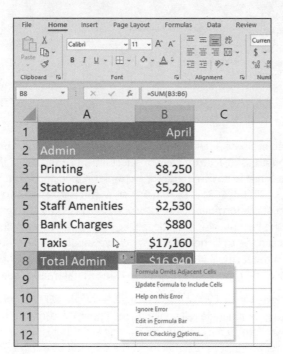

FIGURE 5-11:
Error checking.

This error-checking feature adheres to a number of rules that Excel uses to correct errors, or what it defines as errors, such as inconsistent formulas, cells omitted from a formula, or numbers entered as text. Cells that contravene these rules will trigger the error-checking feature and be marked with a green indicator.

Although this error-checking feature is often helpful, many modelers find it irritating, so you can turn it off or edit its rules by selecting the Error Checking Options at the bottom of the menu shown in Figure 5-11. The Excel Options box, shown in Figure 5-12, appears. There, you can turn off the error checking entirely by unchecking the Enable Background Error Checking option or change the errors it alerts you to by changing the options in the Error Checking Rules section at the bottom of the dialog box.

Another part of Excel's error-checking feature can be accessed via the Error Checking or Trace Error options, also in the Formula Auditing section on the Formulas tab in the Ribbon. As shown in Figure 5-13, the error-checking option will find any Excel errors on the sheet, and then the Trace Error tool will apply Trace Precedents to find the source of the error.

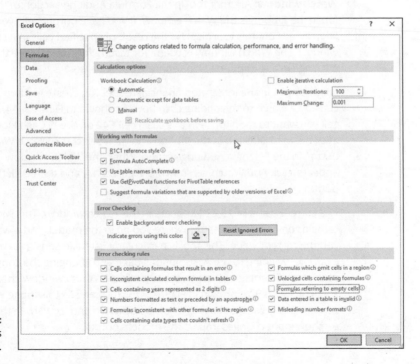

FIGURE 5-12: The Excel Options dialog box.

FIGURE 5-13:
The Error Checking tool.

>> **Watch window:** Another tool in the Formula Auditing section of the Formulas tab in the Ribbon is the Watch window. If you have output cells you'd like to keep an eye on, this tool displays the result of specified cells in a separate window. The Watch window is useful for testing formulas to see the impact of a change in assumptions on a separate cell or cells.

For example, in the integrated financial model you create in Chapter 10, you can add a watch to the ending cash flow. As shown in Figure 5-14, select the cell you want to monitor — in this case, cell C42 on the IS Cash Flow sheet. Click the Formulas tab in the Ribbon and then select the Watch Window button in the Formula Auditing section. When the Watch Window dialog box appears, click Add Watch, as shown in Figure 5-14, and then click the Add button.

The current value of $5,297 appears in the Watch window. This window remains on-screen no matter where you go in the model, and always shows you the current value. This tool is particularly useful in sensitivity analysis. For example, by going to the Assumptions page and changing the consumables cost from 45 cents to 50 cents, the value in the Watch window changes from $5,297 to $5,223, as shown in Figure 5-15. You can see this in the Watch window easily without having to jump backward and forward in the model to see how input changes impact the model's outputs.

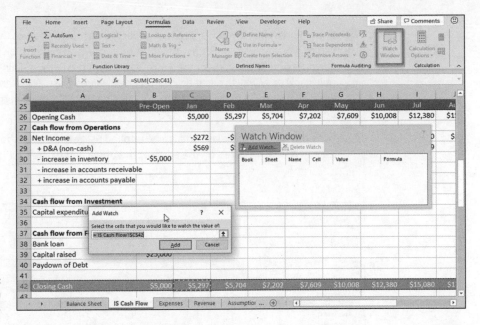

FIGURE 5-14:
The Watch window.

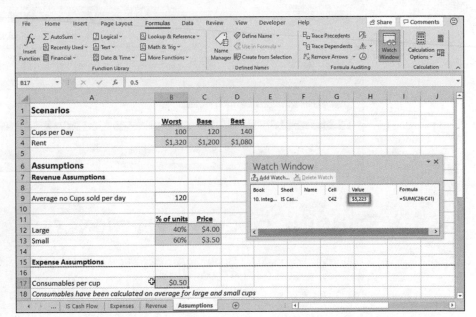

FIGURE 5-15:
Using the Watch window to monitor the impact of changes in inputs to ending cash flow.

>> **Show Formulas:** If you want to look at all the formulas and not the resulting values, you can use the Show Formulas option, which can also be found in the Formula Auditing section of the Formulas tab on the Ribbon. This is also a very quick and easy way to see if any hard-coded values exist. For example, in Figure 5-16, you can see that there are hard-coded /12 values in rows 18 and 19.

Note that Show Formulas can also be applied using the Ctrl+` shortcut. (Note that ` is usually located on the ~ key at the upper-left of the keyboard.)

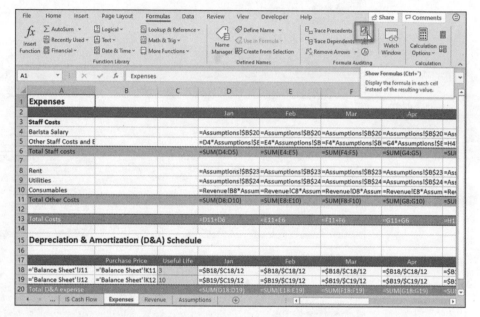

FIGURE 5-16: Using Show Formulas to uncover hard-coded values.

FINDING CIRCULAR REFERENCES

If you inadvertently link a formula to itself somehow, this will cause a *circular reference*, which is a form of error because Excel doesn't know how to calculate it. For more information on what causes circular references and how to correct them, turn to Chapter 14.

If you know that circular references are causing problems in your model, the Error Checking tool has a quick way to find all the offending circular references in the model. Under the Error Checking drop-down arrow in the Formula Auditing section of the Formulas tab on the Ribbon, as shown at the top of Figure 5-13, under the Trace Error you see a Circular References option. If circular references exist in your model, the Circular References icon will no longer be grayed out.

SHARING YOUR WORK

When you've spent a lot of time building a financial model, you take pride in your work and want to "own" the entire model. Your instinct might be to keep the model to yourself, and not let anyone mess things up. This approach doesn't work very well in a corporate environment, however. Modeling should be a collaborative, team effort. You should build models in such a way that others can understand, edit, use, and interpret the results.

This book is focused on making you a good financial modeler — one who knows how to build a financial model that others can easily follow. As a model user, however, you don't always know where the model has come from and whether the model builder has built the model well. The tools outlined in this chapter enable you to take apart, validate, and verify models you've inherited so that you can use them with confidence.

Sharing and Version Control

Financial models are made to share, but the greatest challenge for collaboration between financial modeling teams has always been version control. Picking up a model a colleague has been working on and realizing after several days of effort that it wasn't the latest version is disastrous and can lead to many hours of frustration and rework.

The Shared Workbook feature in Excel, which has been available for many years, was unreliable and fraught with feature limitations. Shared Workbook has been replaced with co-authoring in Excel for Microsoft 365, and it promises to be more useful for financial modelers.

To enable co-authoring, select Share in the upper-right corner, add the email address of who you'd like to share with, and choose a cloud location. Note that the recipient doesn't need to be inside your organization. They can work on your file using Excel for the web, or if they have a version of Excel that supports co-authoring, they can edit the document in their desktop app. Turn to Chapter 2 for more information on Excel for the web.

Co-authoring in Microsoft 365 allows users to:

» Colleagues can immediately see the exact area that's being edited in real time.

» Co-authoring in Microsoft 365 comes with a chat component that makes it possible for colleague or coworkers to chat with each other without leaving the document they're working on.

» Users can co-author across multiple devices such as a mobile device or laptop simultaneously.

» Auto-save is enabled automatically, which is critical if you have multiple people working on the same file. Be aware, though, that you'll need to turn this off if you're planning to make test edits and then close without saving.

2

Diving Deep into Excel

Select and apply Excel's most relevant modeling tools and techniques.

Discover the many functions and formulas useful for building a financial model.

Examine and perform different techniques for building scenarios and sensitivity analysis into your financial model.

Explore methods for displaying and presenting the output from your financial models.

IN THIS CHAPTER

» **Introducing cell referencing**

» **Applying named ranges**

» **Dealing with links and the potential errors they can cause**

» **Improving your modeling skills with shortcuts**

» **Restricting user entry with data validations**

» **Working out a break-even point with goal seek**

Chapter **6**

Excel Tools and Techniques for Financial Modeling

When you're using Excel for the purpose of financial modeling, much of the emphasis is on selecting the right function to include in the formulas to calculate the results of the model. Besides functions, a number of tools and techniques are also useful to include in your models. Chapter 7 focuses on Excel formulas. This chapter looks at some of the other practical tools and techniques commonly used in financial modeling in Excel.

Referencing Cells

In Chapter 1, I explain why not every spreadsheet built in Excel is a financial model. In order to be able to call your spreadsheet a financial model, it must contain formulas. And in order to build formulas, you need to reference cells. It follows therefore that as a financial modeler, you must understand how to reference cells in Excel.

An Excel worksheet is made up of over a million rows and more than 16,000 columns. Each of these cells is referred to like the coordinates of a map, and the cell references are what you use to build the formula. For example, in Figure 6-1, the cost of $450 has been entered in cell B2. So, if you want to use that value in another cell, you would use the cell reference =B2.

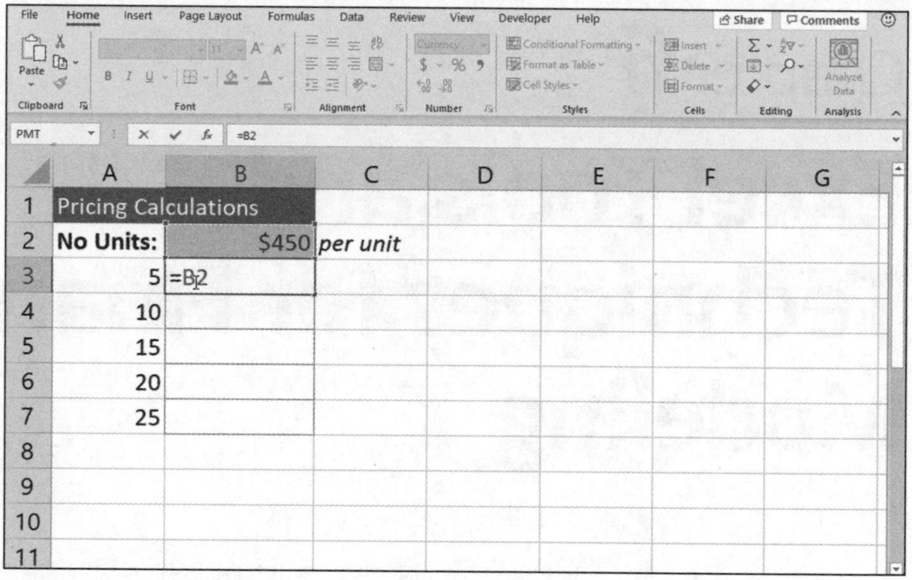

FIGURE 6-1:
Cell referencing.

You can download File 0601.xlsx at www.dummies.com/go/financial modelinginexcelfd2e.

This kind of reference is called a *relative cell reference,* and it's the default way that Excel treats the reference when you first link to a cell. There are three types of cell references, however, and the way you choose to reference a cell will depend on how you want your formula to change when you copy it to other cells:

» **Relative cell reference:** Both the column letter and the row number change relative to where the formula is copied. A relative cell reference is simply a cell name, such as B2.

» **Absolute cell reference:** The column letter and row number of a cell name are preceded by dollar signs, such as $B$2, to indicate that the cell reference should not change when copied.

» **Mixed cell reference:** Either the column letter or row number is preceded by a dollar sign to indicate which of these is to remain unchanged when copied. Both $B2 and B$2 are examples of mixed cell references.

Understanding the difference between relative, absolute, and mixed cell referencing is important when it comes to efficiently building your financial models and maintaining formula consistency. Formula consistency is critical for best practice in financial modeling (and in any other sort of analysis using Excel). In order to have consistent formulas across and down the block of data, you need to understand how cell referencing works. Although cell referencing is a very basic feature of Excel that is taught in introductory Excel courses, it's surprising how many modelers don't recognize its importance.

REMEMBER

The dollar sign in cell referencing tells Excel how to treat your references when you copy the cell. If there is a dollar sign in front of a row number or column letter, the row or column does not change when you copy it. Otherwise, it does change. So an absolute reference will not change its cell reference when you copy it, whereas a relative reference will change.

I walk you through each of these types of cell referencing in greater detail in the following sections.

Relative cell referencing

Relative cell referencing is the default in Excel. For example, Figure 6-2 calculates the total price by referring to values in cells B2 and A3. The asterisk is used to multiply the numbers in the two cells.

TIP

Although you can manually type out a cell reference, this may introduce hard-to-detect typing errors. To avoid this problem, enter your cell reference by typing the formula up to the point of the cell reference and then select the cell with the value to be used in your formula. You can do this by clicking the cell with your mouse or using the arrow keys on your keyboard. When you select a cell, Excel automatically places the cell name in your formula.

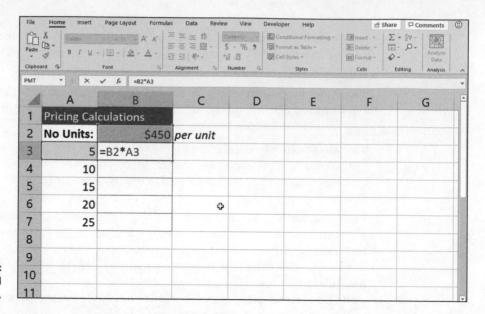

FIGURE 6-2:
Relative cell referencing.

When you copy a formula with relative references to the cell below, the row numbers of the references adjust accordingly. In the same way, when you copy the formula to the next cell over, the column letters change. For example, when the formula in cell B3 is copied down the range, the references automatically change, as shown in Figure 6-3, and the results will be wrong!

To get the correct result using relative references, you'd need to re-create the formula five times instead of copying it down, as shown in Figure 6-4.

Although this does give the correct results, it's not the fastest and easiest way of building this formula. There are several reasons why this solution is not recommended:

>> It takes a lot longer to build.

>> The formula is prone to error because you're far more likely to accidentally pick up the wrong cell.

>> Updating it will mean having to update each and every formula in the range.

>> It's more difficult for someone else to follow and, hence, more difficult to audit.

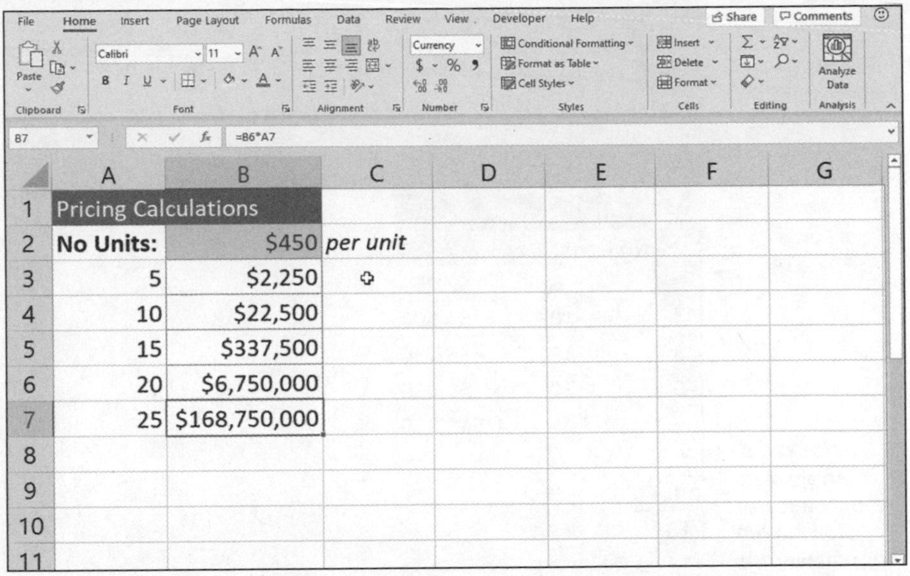

FIGURE 6-3:
A relative reference copied down (incorrect and not recommended).

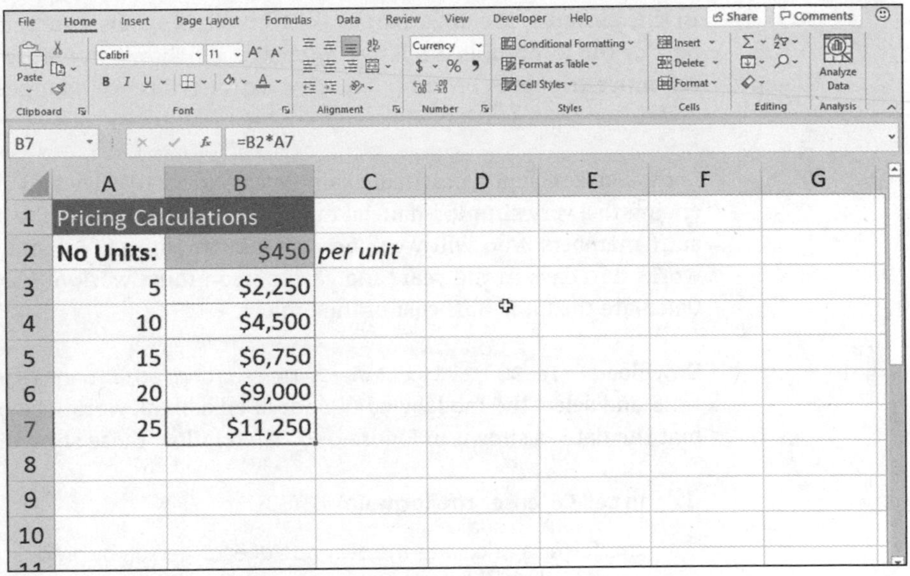

FIGURE 6-4:
A relative reference built separately (mathematically correct but not recommended).

Absolute cell referencing

A much better solution would be to use the formula =$B$2*A3 and then copy the formula down the range, as shown in Figure 6-5. Putting one dollar sign before the column letter and another before the row number in the cell reference anchors the reference when it's copied. This is called an *absolute reference*.

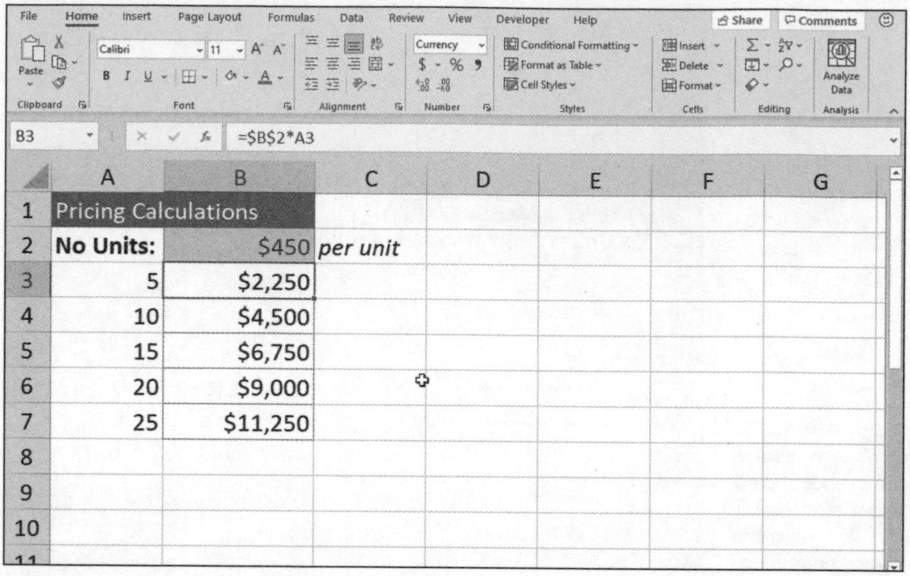

FIGURE 6-5:
An absolute reference copied down (recommended).

In this example, the $B$2 part of the formula is an absolute reference, and the A3 part of the formula is a relative reference. As shown in Figure 6-5, the absolute reference remains constant, but the relative reference changes when it's copied down.

Let's take a look at a practical example and apply relative and absolute cell referencing to a very simple financial model. You've been given the annual salaries for staff members who will work on a particular project. Assume that each person works 260 days in the year, and each person must work 60 days on this project. Calculate the total staff cost of the project.

Download File 0601.xlsx at www.dummies.com/go/financialmodelinginexcel fd2e and select the tab labeled 6-6, or open a blank workbook and enter and format the data as shown in Figure 6-6. Then follow these steps:

1. **In cell C6, enter the formula** =B6/B3.

This formula calculates the daily rate of each person by dividing their annual salary by the number of days they work per year. The formula result is $923.08.

2. **Press F4 to apply absolute referencing.**

The formula changes to =B6/$B$3.

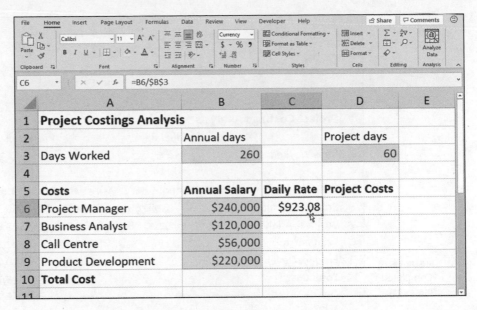

FIGURE 6-6:
Calculating daily staff rate using absolute referencing.

	A	B	C	D	E
1	**Project Costings Analysis**				
2		Annual days		Project days	
3	Days Worked	260		60	
4					
5	**Costs**	**Annual Salary**	**Daily Rate**	**Project Costs**	
6	Project Manager	$240,000	$923.08		
7	Business Analyst	$120,000			
8	Call Centre	$56,000			
9	Product Development	$220,000			
10	**Total Cost**				
11					

C6 = B6/$B$3

3. **Copy this formula down the column.**

   Now you need to calculate what those project costs are based on the daily rate by multiplying the number of project days by the daily rate.

4. **In cell D6, enter the formula** =C6*D3.

5. **When you copy it down, you want the project days reference to remain constant, so press F4 to fix this reference.**

   The formula is =$D$3*C6 with the resulting value of $55,385.

6. **Copy this formula down the column.**

7. **In cell D10, enter the formula** =SUM(D6:D9).

   The result $146,769, which is the total project cost.

8. **Compare your results to Figure 6-7.**

   You can perform some sensitivity analysis by changing the number of project days in cell D3 from 60 to 65. Change the cost for the business analyst in cell B7 from $120,000 to $150,000. Observe the effect it has on the project costs.

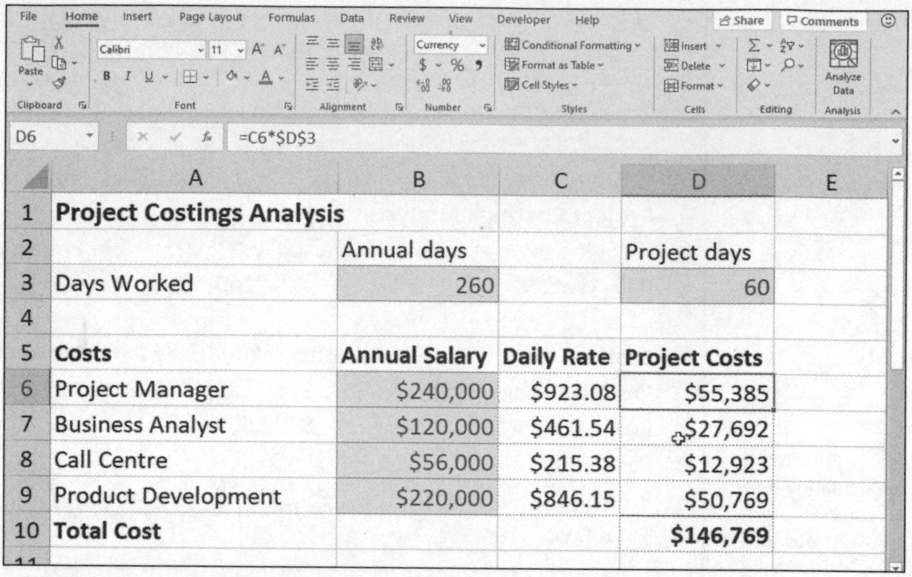

FIGURE 6-7:
Completed
project costs.

Mixed cell referencing

Mixed cell referencing is a combination of relative and absolute referencing; one part of the reference is absolute, and the other is relative. When you add a dollar sign before the row, the row remains anchored when the cell is copied; when you add a dollar sign before the column, the column remains anchored when the cell is copied.

For example, if you create the reference =B2 in a cell, and then copy that reference down, it will change to B3. If you add some anchoring, here are the results in each case:

Cell	Copies as Cell
=B2	=B3
=$B$2	=$B$2
=B$2	=B$2
=$B2	=$B3

The dollar sign anchors a row number or column letter when you copy it. You can anchor both the column and the row (absolute referencing), or you can anchor one or the other (mixed referencing).

Mixed cell referencing is a concept critical to good financial modeling practice, so it's important for a financial modeler to understand this fundamental concept. Used effectively, mixed cell references make your model

>> Faster to build and more efficient

>> Less prone to error

>> Quicker, easier, and cheaper to audit

TIP

The easiest way to quickly add absolute and mixed cell referencing is to press F4 immediately after adding the reference to the formula. This keyboard shortcut cycles through combinations of relative and absolute referencing. You can repeatedly press F4 after entering the cell name in a formula to cycle through the mixed references. For example, type **=B2** and then press F4 to display =$B$2. Press F4 again to display =B$2. Press F4 again to display =$B2. And press F4 again to display =B2.

Let's look at a practical example of how to use mixed cell referencing. In the following example, you want to calculate how much you'd receive in interest under three different portfolio amounts and three different interest rates. The most efficient way to perform this calculation is to create a single formula with appropriate references and then copy that formula to other cells. You need to create a formula that multiplies the interest amount in row 1 and the borrowing amount in column A.

REMEMBER

Instead of creating nine different formulas, you're creating only *one single formula* using mixed cell referencing, which you can then copy across, saving you time and reducing the possibility of error.

Follow these steps:

1. **Download** File 0601.xlsx **from** www.dummies.com/go/financial modelinginexcelfd2e **and select the tab labeled 6-8 or create a blank workbook and enter and format the data as shown in Figure 6-8.**

2. **In cell B2, type** = **and then select cell A2 by clicking it or pressing the left-arrow key.**

3. **Press F4 three times to display the mixed reference $A2.**

4. **Type *, select cell B1, and this time press F4 twice to display the mixed reference B$1.**

REMEMBER

To anchor the row, put the dollar sign before the row. To anchor the column, put the dollar sign before the column.

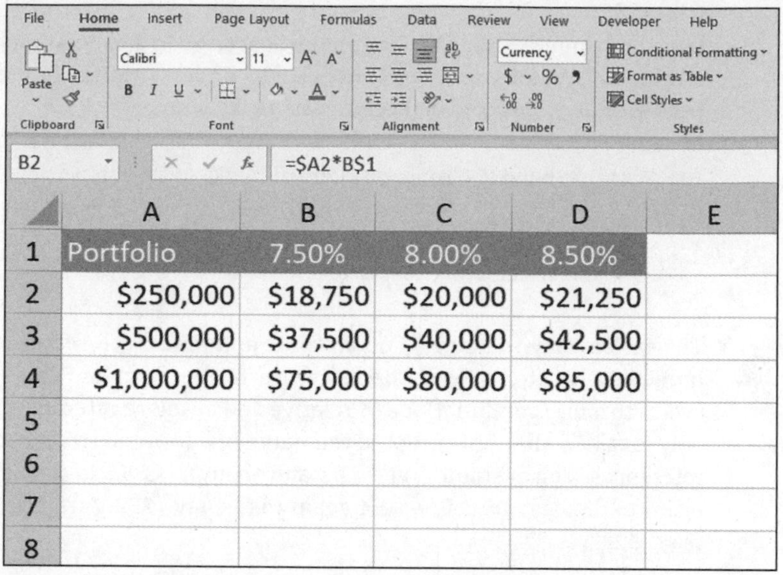

![Excel screenshot showing the ribbon, formula bar with =$A2*B$1 for cell B2, and a worksheet table]

Formula bar: B2 — =$A2*B$1

	A	B	C	D	E
1	Portfolio	7.50%	8.00%	8.50%	
2	$250,000	$18,750	$20,000	$21,250	
3	$500,000	$37,500	$40,000	$42,500	
4	$1,000,000	$75,000	$80,000	$85,000	
5					
6					
7					
8					

FIGURE 6-8:
Mixed cell
referencing.

5. **Press Enter to show the formula** =$A2*B$1 **in cell B2.**

   The result is $18,750 as shown in Figure 6-8.

6. **Select cell B2 and copy it across and down the rest of the block of data.**

   Copying and pasting can be done in several different ways. Choose the option that suits you best:

   - Go to the lower-right corner of cell B2 and select the fill handle with the mouse. Drag it across to cell D2 and release the mouse. Then drag down to row 4.

   - Copy cell B2 with the shortcut Ctrl+C, and select the entire block either with the mouse or by holding down the Shift key together with the right arrow and down arrow. Press Enter to paste.

   - Highlight the entire block of data either with the mouse or by holding down the Shift key together with the right arrow and down arrow. Use the shortcuts Ctrl+R and Ctrl+D to copy right and copy down.

7. **Review the results.**

   Note how your carefully crafted formula generates data for the entire block of cells. Compare your worksheet to the one shown in Figure 6-8.

TIP

Maintaining consistency of formulas is a fundamental technique of financial modeling that will save you and anyone else using your model a lot of unnecessary time in building, checking, and auditing the calculations.

When formulas make calculations based on data stored in your spreadsheet, use cell references wherever possible, instead of typing the actual data. Typing numbers into formulas is called *hard-coding,* and it should be avoided unless the numbers are source data — and, if so, documented as such. This rule is also important to follow when building your models because it makes them much easier to update, both for you and others using your models. If you've used cell references instead of hard-coded the numbers into the formula, and you change a value in a cell referenced by a formula, the formula automatically recalculates.

Naming Ranges

Many financial modelers like to include named ranges in their models. Named ranges are just a way of naming a cell, or a range of cells, to use it in a formula, instead of using cell references.

In Figure 6-5 earlier in this chapter, I used an absolute reference to anchor the formula to the consistent price of $450. This cell is called B2, and it won't change. However, I can also change the name of it to something else, such as "price." That's what a named range is.

Understanding why you may want to use a named range

You don't have to include named ranges in a financial model, and some of the best financial models don't use them at all. Those who haven't used them before sometimes struggle to see the benefits of including them in financial models. Most of the time, named ranges aren't really necessary, but there are a few reasons why you should consider using them in a financial model:

>> **Named ranges can make your formulas easier to follow.** A formula containing lots of cell references can be confusing to look at and difficult to edit. But if the cell references are replaced by a range name, it becomes much easier to understand. For example, the formula =SUM(B3:B24)-SUM(F3:F13) can be expressed as =SUM(Revenue)-SUM(Expenses) to calculate profit.

>> **Named ranges don't need absolute referencing.** By default, a named range is an absolute reference, so you don't need to add any in.

>> **Using named ranges is ideal when you're linking to external files.** When the cell reference in the source file changes (such as when someone inserts a row), the formula linking to it will automatically update, even if the file is closed when the update is made.

>> **If you decide to use macros in your model, you should use named ranges when referring to cell references in the Visual Basic code.** As with external links, this practice is more robust than using cell references.

TIP

In general, named ranges just make your life easier as a modeler. They make your formulas neat and tidy, easier to read and follow. You aren't *required* to use named ranges in your model, but you should know what they are and how to edit them if you come across named ranges in someone else's model.

Creating a named range

To create a named range, follow these steps:

1. Select cell B2.

2. In the Name box in the upper-left corner (see Figure 6-9), type over the name and call it something else, like Price.

   Note that the name you type must not contain any spaces or special characters. For instance, if you want to call it "Year 1 Price," you need to name it "Year1Price" or "Year1_Price" or something along those lines.

3. Press Enter.

FIGURE 6-9:
The Name box.

110   PART 2 Diving Deep into Excel

Named ranges don't necessarily need to be confined to a single cell; you can also create named ranges for an entire range of cells, and these can be used in formulas. Simply highlight the range instead of a single cell, and type over the name.

Finding and using named ranges

Clicking the drop-down arrow next to the Name box shows all the defined names in the workbook, as shown in Figure 6-10.

Clicking the name in the drop-down box will take you directly to select that cell or range of cells included in the named range automatically. It doesn't matter what sheet you're in when you select the name. This can make finding your way around the named ranges in a model much faster. You can also press Ctrl+G to bring up a dialog box with all the names, or press F3 to paste names.

After you've created a range name, you can use that name in a formula instead of cell references. In the example shown in Figure 6-11, you can create the named range Price for cell B2 and the named range Units for the range A3:A7. In cell B3, you can use the formula =Price*Units to calculate the price, and then copy it down the column, as shown in Figure 6-11.

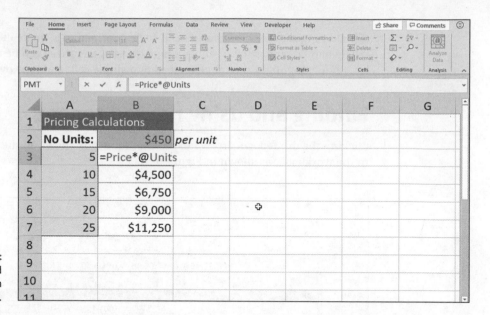

FIGURE 6-11:
Using named ranges in a formula.

TECHNICAL STUFF

You might notice an @ symbol suddenly appear in front of the Units name. This means that Units refers to a range of cells but that the formula refers to this row only.

You can use a named range in a formula in several different ways:

>> Simply type **=price** in a cell.

>> Type **=** and then select cell B2 with the mouse to pick up the name of the cell.

>> Press F3 and then double-click the name to paste it into a cell.

>> Select the Formulas tab on the Ribbon and, in the Defined Names section, select the name you want to use from the Use in Formula drop-down list.

TIP

If you're planning to use named ranges in your model, create them *first*, before you build your formulas. Otherwise, you'll need to go back and rebuild your formulas to include the named ranges.

A cell does not need to be an input field in order to assign a name to it, although it often is in financial models. The cell can also contain a formula as well as a hard-coded input value.

WARNING

Named ranges can be useful, but you don't want to have too many. They can be confusing, especially if you haven't been consistent in your naming methodology. It's also quite easy to accidentally name the same cell twice. So in order to keep names neat and tidy, be sure to use the Name Manager to edit or delete any named ranges that are no longer being used. Note that copying sheets into a model can copy named ranges, which can also contain errors as well as external links you're not aware of. This can slow down the file, so it's a good idea to look through the Name Manager every now and then to tidy it up.

Editing or deleting a named range

You can manage all the named ranges you've created in the Name Manager, which can be found in the Defined Names section on the Formulas tab on the Ribbon. It's easy to create a named range and forget it's there, so try to keep your names tidy. If you need to remove a named range or find that you've accidentally named the wrong cell, you can add, edit, or delete existing named ranges in the Name Manager.

Dynamic Ranges

As mentioned in Chapter 2, Microsoft 365 has many ground-breaking new features, and one of the most relevant for financial modelers is the introduction of dynamic array formulas, also called dynamic ranges. These types of formulas treat the entire range as one rather than individual cells.

Several new functions were introduced to work with dynamic ranges, and one that modelers may find useful is the UNIQUE function. In the past, if you wanted to create a list of unique values, you had to make a copy of the data and use the Remove Duplicates tool found on the Data tab.

To use the UNIQUE function, type =**UNIQUE(** and then highlight the range containing duplicates (see Figure 6-12), and press Enter. A unique list of values appears. Try changing one of the values to something else (for example, change cell A5 to Testing Leader), and your dynamic array will automatically expand to include the new value.

TIP

You can tell a dynamic array formula because a faint blue line will appear around the range, as shown in Figure 6-12.

WARNING

Because dynamic array formulas automatically expand and contract or "spill" based on the source data, be sure to allow plenty of space below a dynamic range. If a cell contains data blocking the range, the array formula won't be able to spill properly, so you may see a #SPILL error. Clear the cells below the formula to fix the error.

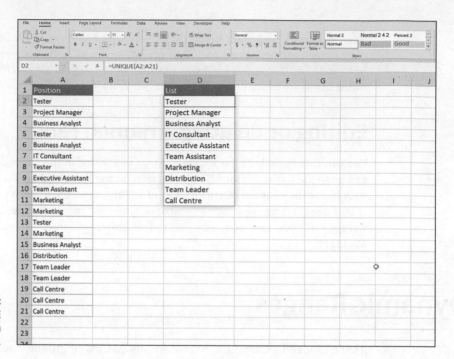

FIGURE 6-12:
Using a UNIQUE function as a dynamic array.

TECHNICAL STUFF

Other functions that work as dynamic arrays you may like to try include the FILTER, SEQUENCE, SORT, SORTBY, XLOOKUP, and XMATCH functions.

Linking in Excel

As discussed in Chapter 1, the *definition* of financial modeling is that when the inputs change, the outputs change as well. Linking in Excel is what makes this happen. If you're just typing numbers into formulas, such as =453*12, that's not financial modeling. You need to create a formula that links to a cell or cells so that when the cell changes, the result of your formula will change as well.

There are two types of links in Excel: *internal links* (links within the model) and *external links* (links to other files). So far, in this chapter, I've been performing links on the same page. Almost every financial model involves multiple pages, though, so it's almost always necessary to link to other sheets within the same file.

Internal links

In this section, you have some simple profit-and-loss calculations, and you're going to create a summary report by linking between sheets. Follow these steps:

1. **Download** `File 0602.xlsx` **from** `www.dummies.com/go/financial modelinginexcelfd2e` **and select the tab labeled IS.**

   A completed version is also available in `File 0603.xlsx`, which you can download and use to compare your work.

2. **On the IS worksheet, select the cell C4 and calculate the sales revenue by entering the formula** =F3*F4.

   The calculated result is $29,502.

3. **Go to cell C19 and calculate the manufacturing cost by entering the formula** =F19*F3.

   The calculated result is $7,152.

4. **Go to cell C20 and calculate the sales commission by entering the formula** =F20*C4.

   The calculated result is $1,475.

5. **Excel will sometimes put additional decimal places automatically, so change the number formatting to currency with no decimal places if necessary.**

   You can do this by pressing the Decrease Decimal icon in the Number section of the Home tab of the Ribbon.

6. **Check that the profit margin is calculating correctly.**

   The calculated result in cell C25 is 20%.

7. **Compare your results to Figure 6-13.**

   Now you have your detailed P&L and you can create a summary on the first worksheet (Summary) using links.

8. **On the Summary worksheet, select cell B5.**

9. **Link through the fixed costs by entering the formula** ='IS'!C15.

   Do *not* type this out. Instead, click cell B5, type **=** and select the next tab using the mouse. Click cell C15 on the IS tab using the mouse, and press Enter.

10. **Similarly, select cell B6 on the Summary worksheet and link through the variable costs by adding the formula** ='IS'!C21.

11. **Go to cell B4, and link through the sales revenue by adding the formula** ='IS'!C4.

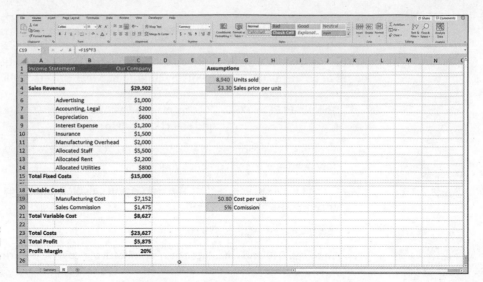

FIGURE 6-13:
The completed income statement.

12. **Compare your results to Figure 6-14.**

A good layout for a financial model is to have assumptions together on a single page, usually at the back. Let's move the assumptions to a separate sheet at the back of the model. Don't worry — this is a lot easier than it sounds!

13. **Insert a new sheet by clicking the plus sign behind the last tab.**

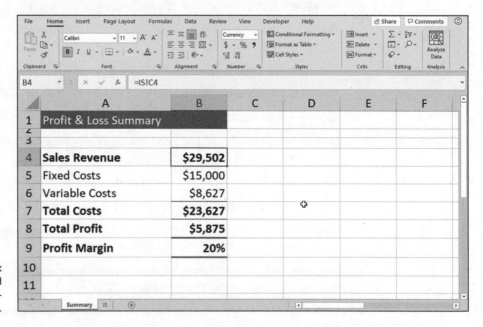

FIGURE 6-14:
The completed income statement summary.

14. Double-click the tab name, and change Sheet1 to Assumptions.

15. Go back to the IS worksheet and highlight the area of the sheet that contains the assumptions (cells F1:G20).

16. Press Ctrl+X to cut the data onto the Clipboard.

17. Go to the Assumptions worksheet, select cell A1, and press Ctrl+V or press Enter to paste the data to the new sheet.

TIP

When you have data on the Clipboard, pressing Enter will paste the data and remove it from the Clipboard. Pressing Ctrl+V will leave the data on the Clipboard in case you want to paste it again. Either technique will work in this case.

WARNING

The formulas in this model work in exactly the same way as they did before we moved the assumptions to the new sheet. It's important that you used *cut* and paste here, not *copy* and paste, or the links would not have worked properly.

18. Go back to the Assumptions worksheet and tidy it up. Remove the blank rows 5 through 18 by highlighting the rows, right-clicking, and pressing Delete.

Now you have a simple but tidy model. It links, it's clear, it's straightforward, and it's easy for someone else to understand.

External links

So far, I've only been looking at creating links from one cell to another, either on the same sheet or on a different sheet within the same file. Sometimes, however, the data you want to link to exists in another file, so you need to link from *one file to another.* These are called *external links.* They're created in a very similar way to internal links; simply type = and then select the cell in the file you want to link to, and press Enter. Working with external links isn't as straightforward as working with internal links, however, so it does require a lot more care.

External links can be the cause of many problems, such as broken links, incorrect data, and error messages. Your model will be much simpler if you can avoid external links, but if you decide to include them, you should do so with caution. Most problems happen when users

>> Change filenames or move the file to another location.

>> Change the source file sheet name when the file linking to it is closed.

>> Insert rows or columns in the source file when the file linking to it is closed.

>> Email files that contain links.

Improving external links with named ranges

One of the main issues with linking to external files is that if users insert or delete rows or columns in the source file, or change tab names, this causes errors in the files that are linking to it. If you're lucky, it will show a #REF! error, which you can easily find and correct. If you're not so lucky, it will show a value that *looks* as though it is correct, but is in fact completely wrong.

Imagine that you want to use an interest rate in your financial model, which is being generated in another model. This interest rate frequently changes, so you decide to create a link, rather than hard-coding the number. This will save you time having to update it every time. You create a link from your financial model to another source file, using the following link:

='G:\My Drive\Plum Solutions\Consulting Clients\Transactions\Files\[Interest Calculations.xlsx]Sept'!$D$23

If both files are open at the same time, and you insert a row in the Interest Calculations.xlsx file, the link will automatically update from $D$23 to $D$24. However, if your file is closed, your model will not update. This means that the next time you open it, your model will be picking up the wrong cell!

The way around this issue is to create a named range in the source file (for example, the word *interest*), and then if that cell moves in the source file, the cell will still retain its name, and the formula in your model will still be correct. See the section on "Creating a named range" earlier in this chapter for how to do this:

```
='G:\My Drive\Plum Solutions\Consulting Clients\Transactions\Files\[Interest
    Calculations.xlsx]Sept'!interest)
```

The next time your model tries to update the link, it will look for the name interest, rather than $D$23, and the integrity of the link will be maintained. This is why using named ranges when dealing with external links is considered best practice: It's a much more robust way of linking files together.

WARNING

Don't use formulas in external links. When linking to an external file, use a simple, direct formula such as ='G:\My Drive\Plum Solutions\Consulting Clients\Transactions\Files\Interest Calculations.xlsx'!interest. Using more complex formulas, such as SUMIF, can mean that the links show errors unless the files are both open at the same time.

Finding and editing external links

In the Connections group on the Data tab, click Edit Links. The Edit Links dialog box, shown in Figure 6-15, appears. Click the Change Source button to tell your model the new location of the file it has been linked to.

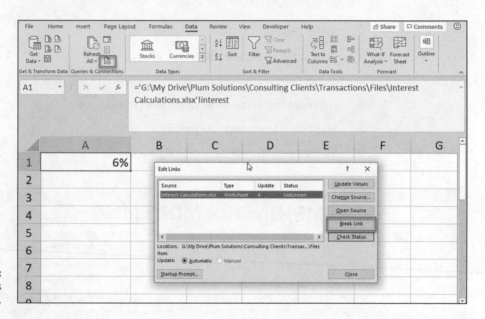

FIGURE 6-15: The Edit Links dialog box.

TIP

Another handy use for Edit Links is to break all links in a file. If you're emailing a file, it isn't recommended that you leave links in it. You can paste the cell values one by one, but breaking links will convert every single formula in the entire file to their hard-coded values. Click Edit Links, and you'll be able to select the external files and click the Break Links button.

WARNING

Sometimes your model will have links that simply won't break! These "phantom links" are most commonly the result of links contained in named ranges. Deleting the names that contain external links from the Name Manager will remove them from your file. If that doesn't work, other possible reasons can be links in conditional formatting, charts, objects, or PivotTables.

Using Shortcuts

If you're spending a lot of time modeling in Excel, you can save yourself a lot of time by learning some keyboard shortcuts. For example, when copying and pasting a cell, you can follow this process:

1. Select the cell.

2. Right-click with the mouse.

3. Select Copy from the contextual menu.

4. Highlight the destination range with the mouse.

5. Right-click again with the mouse.

6. Select Paste from the contextual menu.

CHAMPIONSHIP MODELING

Speed and accuracy in financial modeling are critical. Skilled financial modelers are highly adept at the use of shortcuts, and watching an expert modeler at work is impressive viewing. From 2012 to 2019, the ModelOff Financial Modeling World Championships were held annually, and the winner crowned world financial modeling champion. Sponsored by Microsoft, the championships were held through live online rounds, and a handful of finalists were flown to New York or London to compete. Each modeler was given modeling problems to complete in front of a live audience, a surprisingly entertaining spectacle. ModelOff was retired in 2020 and became the Full Stack Modeller program.

Nowadays other championship modeling competitions such as the Financial Modeling World Cup (FMWC) have taken its place. In addition to monthly online contests, FMWC holds online "battles" from time to time between modelers; thousands of spectators tune in live on YouTube to watch the world's top modelers display their speed, accuracy, and problem-solving prowess. Although there's a lot more to being a champion financial modeler than Excel skills, much of the speed required to perform well in these competitions can be attributed to keyboard shortcut usage.

Some of the most commonly used shortcuts are located on the top row of the keyboard; F2 (edit formula) and F4 (referencing $ toggle) are among the most popular. Strategically located between the F2 key and the Esc key is the F1 key, which is rarely helpful but often pressed accidentally when trying to press Esc or F1! For championship modelers, speed is paramount, and accidentally pressing F1 is very frustrating because it causes the modeler to lose valuable seconds. Many competitors actually remove the F1 key from their keyboards to avoid accidentally hitting it. The ModelOff world champion was presented with "The Golden Keyboard" trophy, which had the F1 key removed.

Alternatively, you can accomplish the same task using shortcuts:

1. **Select the cell.**
2. **Press Ctrl+C.**
3. **Use the Shift and arrow keys to move to the destination cells.**
4. **Press Enter (which clears the Clipboard) or press Ctrl+V (which leaves what you have copied on the Clipboard).**

Open Excel and try this for yourself. The second method is a lot quicker, especially with a little practice.

Hundreds of shortcuts are available in Excel. Table 6-1 lists those that are covered in this book and that you should, at a minimum, know. As you continue your journey as a modeler, you'll no doubt add many more shortcuts to your repertoire.

TABLE 6-1   ## Excel Shortcuts

Shortcut	Action
Editing	
Ctrl+S	Save workbook
Ctrl+C	Copy
Ctrl+V	Paste
Ctrl+X	Cut
Ctrl+Z	Undo
Ctrl+Y	Redo
Ctrl+A	Select all
Ctrl+R	Copies the far left cell across the range (after you highlight the range)
Ctrl+D	Copies the top cell down the range (after you highlight the range)
Ctrl+B	Bold
Ctrl+1	Format box
Alt+Tab	Switch program

(continued)

TABLE 6-1 *(continued)*

Shortcut	Action
Alt+F4	Close program
Ctrl+N	New workbook
Shift+F11	New worksheet
Ctrl+W	Close worksheet
Alt+E+L	Delete a sheet
Ctrl+Tab	Switch workbooks
Navigating	
Shift+Spacebar	Highlight row
Ctrl+Spacebar	Highlight column
Ctrl+– (minus sign)	Delete selected cells (note that the Del key only clears cells, it does not delete them)
Arrow keys	Move to new cells
Ctrl+Pg Up/Pg Down	Switch worksheets
Ctrl+Arrow	Go to end of continuous range and select a cell
Shift+Arrow	Select range
Shift+Ctrl+Arrow	Select continuous range
Home	Move to beginning of line
Ctrl+Home	Move to cell A1
In Formulas	
F2	Edit formula, showing precedent cells
Alt+Enter	Start new line in same cell
Shift+Arrow	Highlight within cells
F4	Change absolute referencing ($)
Esc	Cancel a cell entry
Alt+=	Sum selected cells
F9	Recalculate all workbooks
Ctrl+[	Highlight precedent cells
Ctrl+]	Highlight dependent cells
F5+Enter	Go back to original cell

TIP

To find the shortcut for any function, press the Alt key, and the shortcut keys will show on the Ribbon, as shown in Figure 6-16. For example, Remove Duplicates can be performed by selecting the range, and then pressing Alt+A+M.

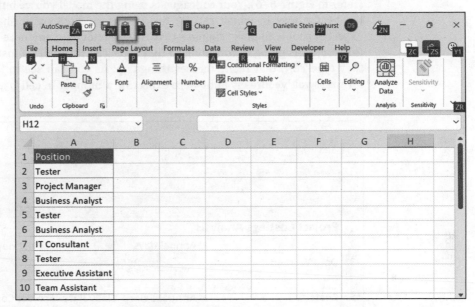

FIGURE 6-16: Shortcut keys are shown after pressing the Alt key.

In the upper-left corner, you can see the Quick Access Toolbar. You can change the shortcuts that appear here by clicking the tiny arrow to the right of the Quick Access Toolbar and selecting what you want to add from the drop-down box that appears. In Figure 6-16, Paste Special is in the first position, so Paste Special can be accessed with the shortcut Alt+1. Note that this only works when you've customized the Quick Access Toolbar; whatever you put in the first position will be accessed by the shortcut Alt+1.

Restricting and Validating Data

After you finish building a financial model, you may be tempted to keep it to yourself, because you don't want anyone to mess up your formulas or use the model inappropriately. Models should be collaborative, but you need to build your model in such a way that it's easy for others to use and difficult to mess up. One great way of making your model robust for others to use is to apply data validations and protections to the model. This way, the user can only enter the data they're supposed to.

Restricting user data entry

For a practical example of how to use data validation, let's take the Project Costings Analysis from the "Absolute cell referencing" section earlier in this chapter (refer to Figure 6-6). Your colleague is using the model you've built, and they can tell by the way in which cell D3 has been formatted (with shading) that you expected people to make changes to it. They're not sure anymore how many days this project is going to continue, so they type TBA into cell D3 instead. As soon as they type TBA, that really messes things up! As you can see in Figure 6-17, the formulas you've already built were expecting a number in cell D3, not text.

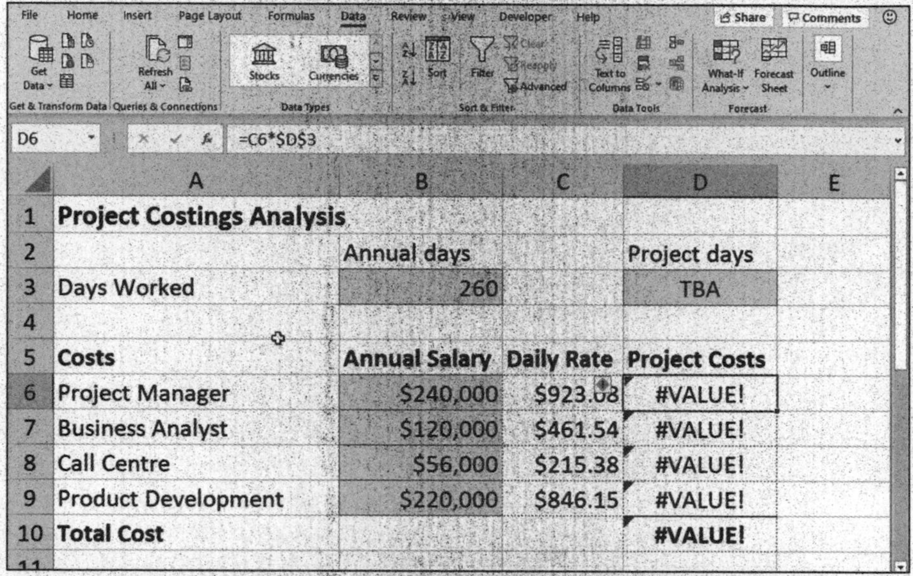

FIGURE 6-17: Text in an input causing errors.

Instead of allowing the user to put anything into any cell, you can change the properties of this cell to allow only numbers to be entered. You can also change it to allow only whole numbers or numbers in a given range.

Follow these steps:

1. Download File 0601.xlsx from www.dummies.com/go/financial modelinginexcelfd2e and select the tab labeled 6-17.

2. Select cell D3.

3. Go to the Data tab on the Ribbon and press the Data Validation icon in the Data Tools section (see Figure 6-18).

The Data Validation dialog box appears (refer to Figure 6-18).

4. On the Settings tab, in the Allow drop-down list, select Whole Number; in the Data drop-down list, select Greater Than; and in the Minimum field, enter 0.

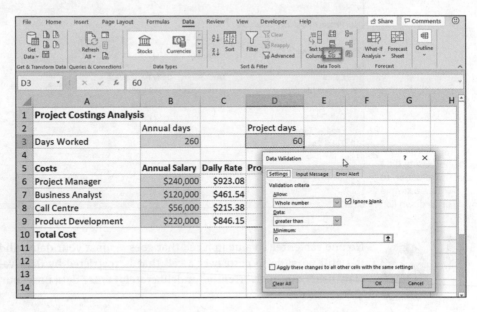

FIGURE 6-18: Using data validation to restrict entry into cells.

Now only allow whole numbers greater than zero to be entered into cell D3. Try entering text such as TBA. Try entering a negative value. Excel won't allow it, and an error alert will appear.

TIP

If you want, you can enter a warning message on the Input Message tab of the Data Validation dialog box. For example, you might want the following message to appear: "Warning! Only enter numerical values." On the Error Alert tab, you can enter another message that appears if someone ignores the warning and tries to enter invalid text. I'm usually tempted to type something mischievous, such as: "Invalid entry. Your hard drive will now be completely erased."

Creating drop-down boxes with data validations

Not only does the data validation tool stop users from entering incorrect data into your model, but you can also use it to create drop-down boxes. In the Data Validation dialog box, from the Allow drop-down list, select List, as shown in Figure 6-19. In the Source field, enter the values you'd like to appear in the list with a comma between them such as Yes, No. A simple drop-down list is created in cell B12 with only two options: Yes and No. The user can't enter anything else.

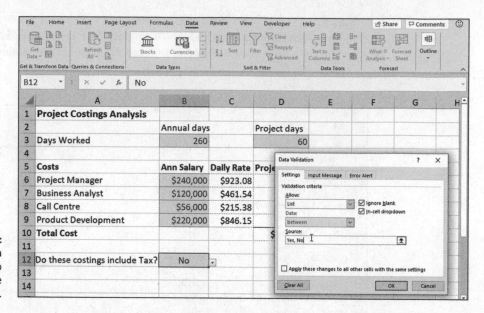

FIGURE 6-19: Using data validation to create a simple drop-down list.

WARNING

No one can enter a value in a cell that goes against your data validation rules, but it's still possible to *paste over* a cell that is restricted by data validation. In this way, users can inadvertently (or deliberately) enter data into your model that you did not intend.

You can also create a drop-down list that links to existing cells within the model. For example, in Figure 6-20, I don't want the users to include a region that is not included in the list shown in column F. So I've used a data validation list, but instead of typing in the values (which would be very time-consuming), I can link to the range already containing the regions — $F$2:$F$5 — which is a much quicker way of inserting a drop-down list.

TIP

Because I've linked the drop-down list, this drop-down is now dynamic. If someone edits any of the cells in the range F2:F5, the options in the drop-down list will automatically change.

Protecting and locking cells

You can also add protection to your model by going to the Review tab on the Ribbon and clicking the Protect Sheet button in the Changes section. Enter a password if you want one, and click OK. This will protect every single cell in the entire worksheet, so no one will be able to make any changes at all! If you want users to be able to edit certain cells, you'll need to turn off the protection, highlight those cells (and *only* those cells you want to change), go to the Home tab on the Ribbon, and click the Format button in the Cells section. Deselect the Lock Cell option that appears in the drop-down list. Turn the protection back on again, and only the cells that have been selected will be unlocked.

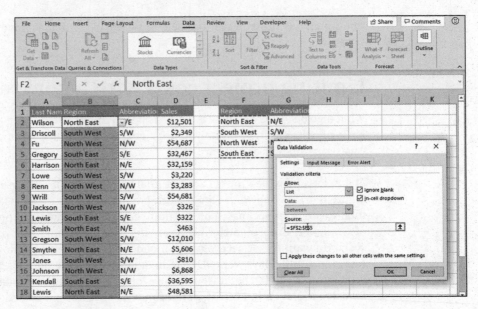

FIGURE 6-20:
Using data validation to create a linked, dynamic drop-down list.

WARNING

Keep in mind that it's reasonably easy to crack an Excel password (search the Internet for *Excel password cracker*), so if someone wants to get in and make changes to your protected model, they can. I recommend that you treat Excel passwords as a deterrent, not a definitive security solution.

Goal Seeking

Another tool that's very useful for financial modeling is goal seek. If you know the answer you want, but you want to know what input you need to achieve it, you can work backward using a goal seek.

In order to run a goal seek, you must have

» A formula

» A hard-coded input cell that drives this formula

It doesn't matter how complicated the model is. As long as there is a direct link between the formula and the input cell, the goal seek will calculate the result correctly.

REMEMBER

The input cell must be hard-coded. It won't work if the input cell contains a formula.

Limiting project costs with a goal seek

What a goal seek is and how it works is best demonstrated using a simple model. For a practical example of how to use a goal seek to limit project costings, follow this series of steps as shown.

Again, let's take the Project Costings Analysis from earlier in the chapter (refer to Figure 6-6). As shown in Figure 6-21, I've used simple formulas to calculate the total cost of a project based on the number of days worked, giving a total costing of $146,769. Unfortunately, however, I've only budgeted for $130,000 in staff costs. If I want the project to come in under budget, I need to know by how much I need to cut the days worked. I can manually tweak the number of days that has been input in cell D3, but it would take a long time to get the number exactly right. By using a goal seek, I can do it in seconds:

1. **On the Data tab of the Ribbon, in the Forecast section, select What-If Analysis and then select Goal Seek.**

   The Goal Seek dialog box (shown in Figure 6-21) appears.

2. **In the Set Cell field, make sure the cell contains the outcome you want, the total cost in cell D10.**

3. **In the To Value field, enter the number you want D10 to be,** $130,000.

4. **In the By Changing Cell field, enter the cell you want to change, the project days in cell $D$3.**

5. **Press OK.**

   The number of project days in cell D3 automatically changes to 53.1446540880503, which is a lot more information than you probably need! Round it down manually, by typing 53 into cell D3, which will change the total costings so that they come just under the $130,000 target you needed.

TECHNICAL STUFF

If you tried manually to enter a number with decimal places into cell D3, the data validation you created earlier in this chapter in Figure 6-6 would not allow it. Because a goal seek is essentially pasting the number into the cell, it circumvents the data validation rule, as though you had copied and pasted the value.

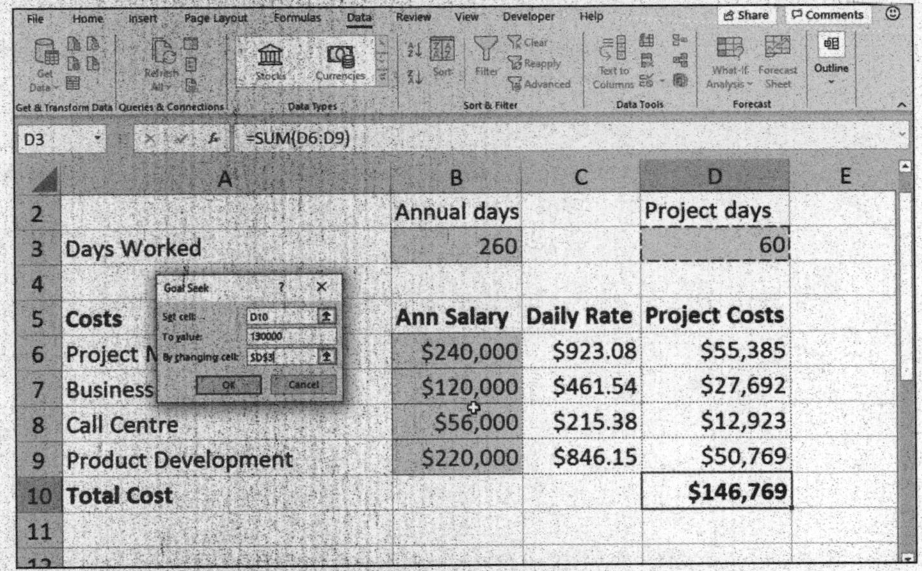

FIGURE 6-21: Using a goal seek to limit project costings.

Calculating a break-even point with a goal seek

Using goal seek is also very helpful for break-even analysis. In this section, you perform a simple break-even calculation using a goal seek. (For more detail on break-even analysis, see Chapter 6.)

For a practical example of how to use a goal seek to calculate a break-even point, let's work with the model you built earlier in this chapter. You've linked it through in such a way that if the number of units sold changes, the revenue changes, and so does the variable costs. You'd like to know the minimum number of units you need to sell in order to cover costs (the break-even point). Follow these steps:

1. **Go to** www.dummies.com/go/financialmodelinginexcelfd2e **and download and open** File 0603.xlsx.

2. **Go to the Assumptions worksheet, and try changing the number of units sold from 8,940 to 8,000.**

3. **Go back to the IS worksheet, and you'll see that the profitability has dropped from 20% to 14%.**

   You can continue to do this manually until you reach zero, but a goal seek will be much quicker and more accurate.

4. **On the Data tab on the Ribbon, in the Forecast section, select What-If Analysis and then select Goal Seek.**

   The Goal Seek dialog box appears (see Figure 6-22).

5. **In the Set Cell field, enter the cell that contains the outcome you want (the profit),** C24.

6. **In the To Value field, enter the number you want C24 to be,** 0.

7. **In the By Changing Cell field, enter the cell you want to change (the number of units on the Assumptions page),** $A$3.

8. **Press OK.**

   The number of units in cell A3 on the Assumptions page automatically changes to 6,424, which is the break-even point.

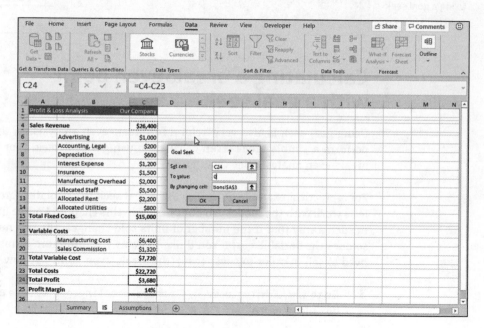

FIGURE 6-22:
Using a goal seek to calculate a break-even point.

IN THIS CHAPTER

» Understanding the difference
between functions and formulas

» Tracking down the right function for
the job

» Identifying the functions you need
for financial modeling

» Considering more advanced
functions

Chapter 7

Using Functions in Excel

The power of Microsoft Excel lies in its ability to do math for you. (Shh! Don't
tell your high school algebra teacher!) Of course, in order for Excel to work
its magic, you need to be able to tell it what you need. And you do that by
using formulas and functions. So, actually, you're not totally off the hook when it
comes to knowing math — you have to understand math in order to know which
formula or function to use.

In this chapter, I start by telling you the difference between a formula and a function. Then I explain how to find the function you need, when you're not quite sure
what it's called. Finally, as a financial modeler, you'll be expected to have a firm
grasp on the most commonly-used functions in Excel, at the very least; this chapter covers the functions that are absolutely critical for you to know.

Identifying the Difference between a Formula and a Function

In Excel, functions and formulas both help you calculate an answer. You may hear
the two words used interchangeably, but they're not technically the same. So,
what's the difference? A *formula* is an expression that uses cell references or hard-
coded numbers to calculate the value of a cell. For example, =A1+A2 and =923*12

are formulas. Sometimes a simple formula is all you need to get the right answer, but you can do so much more using functions. A *function* is a predefined formula already available in Excel. Functions streamline the process of creating a calculation. To date, Excel has more than 500 functions, and on Microsoft 365, more functions are added all the time, such as XLOOKUP, IFS, LET, and LAMBDA to name a few.

Functions can do complicated calculations that would be time-consuming to build manually. For example, if you wanted to add up a range of cells without using a function, you'd need to write something like =A1+A2+A3+A4+A5 instead of =SUM(A1:A5). Now, for five cells, writing it manually isn't such a big deal. But what if you're adding a range of hundreds of cells? Or thousands? Functions make calculations a lot easier.

So in summary, a formula is any calculation in Excel, but a function is a predefined calculation. For example:

=A1/A2 is just a formula.

=MAX(A1:B20) is a formula containing a function.

REMEMBER

There's a lot more to being a good financial modeler than simply knowing lots and lots of Excel functions. But the more functions you know, the more likely you are to choose the one that's most appropriate for the job at hand. As with many things in life, there are usually several ways to achieve the same result, but the best option is the one that's the clearest and easiest for others to understand, as well as the simplest to audit (see Chapter 5 for more on formula auditing).

Finding the Function You Need

If you're trying to perform a calculation in Excel and you aren't sure what the function you want is called, don't worry! Just follow these steps:

1. **Click the Formulas tab.**

2. **Click the Insert Function button.**

    The Insert Function dialog box, shown in Figure 7-1, appears.

TIP

You can also access the Insert Function dialog box by clicking the *fx* button to the left of the Formula Bar or by using the shortcut Shift+F3.

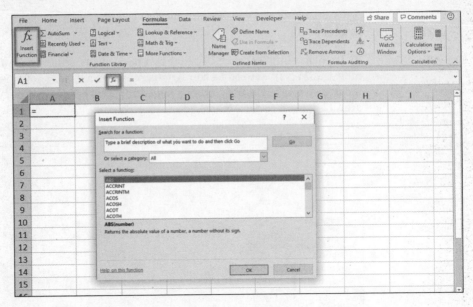

FIGURE 7-1:
The Insert
Function
dialog box.

3. **In the Search for a Function text box, type a brief description of what you want to do, and then click Go.**

A list of functions appears in the Select a Function box.

4. **If you're still not finding the function you're looking for, select a category of functions from the Select a Category drop-down list to narrow the list.**

5. **When you've found the function you think might be right, select it from the Select a Function box and click OK.**

TIP

The Insert Function dialog box appears. Click the Help on This Function link to get even more help on the function you've selected.

Getting Familiar with the Most Important Functions

You've arrived at the meaty part of the chapter. This is where things get interesting! In this section, I fill you in on all the functions you'll rely on most often and give you some examples of how and why to use them.

SUM

As its name implies, the SUM function is used to add a series of numbers. Normally, SUM is used to add a contiguous range of cells, as shown in Figure 7-2, but it can also be used to add cells in a noncontiguous range (in other words, cells that aren't adjacent to each other).

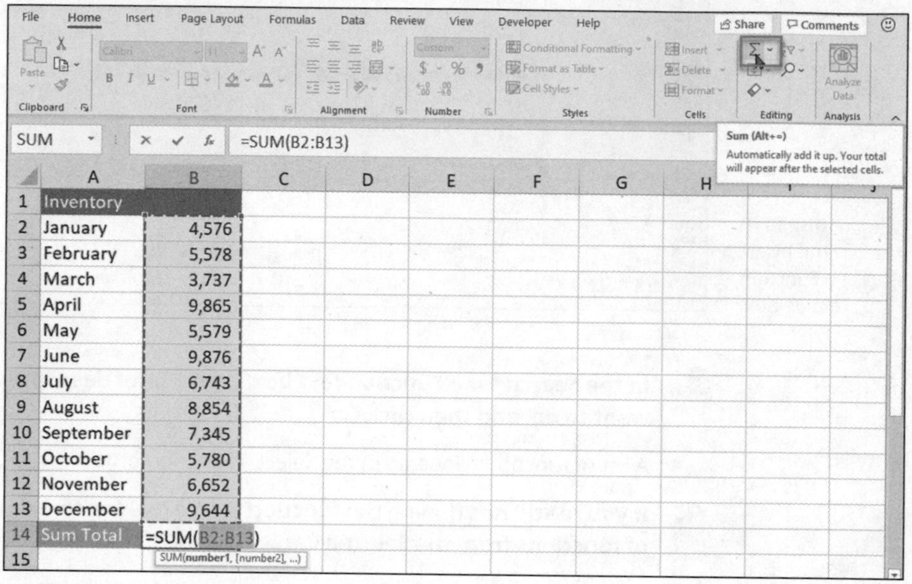

FIGURE 7-2:
Using the SUM
function to add
up a column.

Figure 7-2 shows an example of adding a column of numbers. To try this out for yourself, select a cell either at the bottom or the far right of a range of cells, and click the Σ AutoSum button on the Home tab or Formulas tab.

When you click the Σ AutoSum button, the SUM function tries to automatically determine the figures that you want to add up — and it usually gets it right. If it hasn't selected quite the right range you need to sum, you can fix it by doing any of the following:

>> Manually edit the range by retyping the references in the Formula Bar.

>> Select the correct range of cells with the mouse.

>> Drag the plus sign (+) in the corner of the summed range cell to add to the range of cells selected. To do this in the example in Figure 7-2, you would hover the mouse above the upper-right corner of cell B2.

Figure 7-3 shows an example of summing up a specific set of cells in a noncontiguous range. Because rows 8 and 15 already contain subtotals, you can't simply add up the entire column for the full-year total — it would include the subtotals as well at the values, so you'd end up with double the number. In the Formula Bar, enter the cell address of each cell that you want added together, so the formula in cell B16 is =SUM(B8,B15). Note that you need to enter a comma to separate each cell (or range of cells) from the others.

B16	=SUM(B8,B15)							
	A	B	C	D	E	F	G	H
1	Inventory Levels	2022	2023	2024				
2	January	10,400	11,315	10,378				
3	February	8,774	13,993	13,523				
4	March	12,504	10,837	11,513				
5	April	12,386	12,694	13,466				
6	May	9,301	9,325	12,349				
7	June	10,689	12,516	8,479				
8	Half-Year 1	64,054	70,680	69,708				
9	July	8,388	9,366	10,705				
10	August	13,393	8,157	10,730				
11	September	8,453	9,295	9,278				
12	October	10,204	12,228	8,217				
13	November	11,013	10,050	13,419				
14	December	10,987	9,386	8,897				
15	Half-Year 2	62,438	58,482	61,246				
16	Full Year	126,492	129,162	130,954				
17								

FIGURE 7-3: Using the SUM function to add noncontiguous cells.

TIP

Instead of pressing Σ AutoSum, you can use the shortcut Alt+=. Try selecting a cell either at the bottom or the far right of a range of cells, and press Alt+=. The SUM function is inserted, exactly as though you had pressed the Σ AutoSum button. Learning and using shortcuts like this one can save a lot of time when you're building financial models. See Chapter 6 for more on using shortcuts.

MAX and MIN

The MAX function helps identify the maximum value. The syntax for this function is the same as for the SUM function — you can enter a range of cells, individual cells separated by commas, or a combination of both. The MAX function returns an error if the cells you need to analyze have some text that can't be converted to numerical values.

For example, if you wanted to determine the maximum sales dollars for a year, you could use the MAX function to do so. In the example shown in Figure 7-4, the MAX function has been used to calculate the highest inventory level for the entire year with the function =MAX(B2:B13). Select cell B14 and you can complete this function in several different ways:

>> Type **=MAX(** and select the range with the mouse or the arrow keys.

>> Access the Insert Function dialog box (see "Finding the Function You Need," earlier in this chapter), and search for MAX.

>> Find the Σ AutoSum button on the Home tab or the Formulas tab (refer to Figure 7-2) and instead of clicking it, select MAX from the drop-down box next to the button.

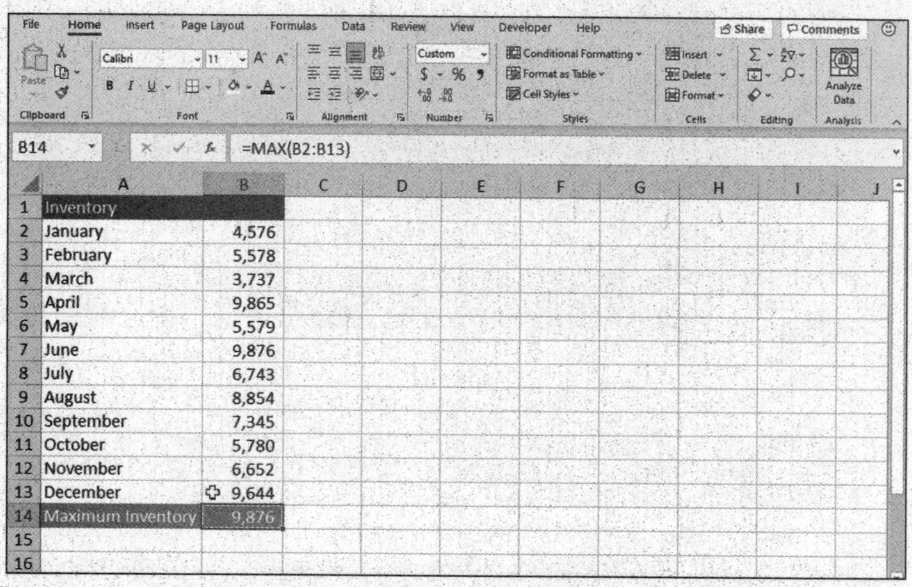

FIGURE 7-4:
Using the MAX function to calculate the maximum value.

The MIN function is the opposite of the MAX function: It calculates the *lowest* value in the column. The MIN function can also use any combination of ranged series and individual cells. The restrictions on what you enter and the results you get are similar to the MAX function. For example, if you wanted to determine the minimum inventory level for a year, you could use the MIN function, as shown in Figure 7-5 with the function =MIN(B2:B13).

FIGURE 7-5:
Using the MIN function to calculate the minimum value.

	A	B	C	D	E	F	G	H	I	J
1	Inventory									
2	January	4,576								
3	February	5,578								
4	March	3,737								
5	April	9,865								
6	May	5,579								
7	June	9,876								
8	July	6,743								
9	August	8,854								
10	September	7,345								
11	October	5,780								
12	November	6,652								
13	December	9,644								
14	Minimum Inventory	3,737								
15										
16										

B14 = =MIN(B2:B13)

Now that you've determined both the minimum and maximum values, you can use these formulas to calculate the spread, or *variance*, of the inventory levels between minimum and maximum values. Maybe your investors want to know how volatile your stock levels are. This calculation will give you some idea of the volatility of inventory.

For a practical example of how to use the MAX and MIN functions together, follow these steps:

1. Download File 0701.xlsx **at** www.dummies.com/go/financial modelinginexcelfd2e, **open it, and select the tab labeled 7-6, or open a new Excel file and enter and format the data as shown in Figure 7-6.**

2. In cell B16, enter the function =MAX(B2:B13) **to calculate the maximum inventory level for the first year.**

3. Copy that function across the row — in cells C16 and D16 — so that it calculates for all three years.

Because you *want* the cell referencing to change as you copy it across, no anchoring or dollar signs are required on the cell references.

TIP

4. In cell B17, enter the function =MIN(B2:B13) **to calculate the minimum inventory level for the first year.**

5. Copy that function across the row — in cells C17 and D17 — so that it calculates for all three years.

6. In cell B18, enter the formula =B16-B17 **to calculate the spread by deducting the minimum value from the maximum value.**

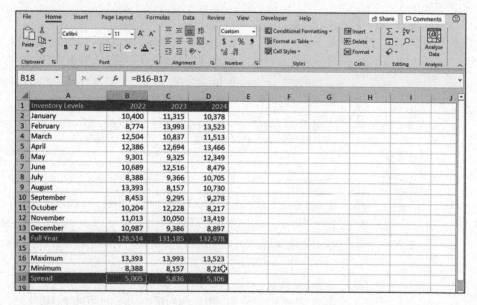

FIGURE 7-6:
Three years of
inventory levels.

	A	B	C	D	E	F	G	H
1	Inventory Levels	2022	2023	2024				
2	January	10,400	11,315	10,378				
3	February	8,774	13,993	13,523				
4	March	12,504	10,837	11,513				
5	April	12,386	12,694	13,466				
6	May	9,301	9,325	12,349				
7	June	10,689	12,516	8,479				
8	July	8,388	9,366	10,705				
9	August	13,393	8,157	10,730				
10	September	8,453	9,295	9,278				
11	October	10,204	12,228	8,217				
12	November	11,013	10,050	13,419				
13	December	10,987	9,386	8,897				
14	Full Year	128,514	131,185	132,978				
15								
16								

7. **Enter the titles** Maximum, Minimum, **and** Spread **in cells A16, A17, and A18, respectively, as shown in Figure 7-7.**

8. **Copy that formula across the row — in cells C18 and D18 — so that it calculates for all three years.**

The completed model is shown in Figure 7-7. Note that the second year has the widest range, with a spread of 5,836.

FIGURE 7-7:
Inventory Spread
over three years.

	A	B	C	D
1	Inventory Levels	2022	2023	2024
2	January	10,400	11,315	10,378
3	February	8,774	13,993	13,523
4	March	12,504	10,837	11,513
5	April	12,386	12,694	13,466
6	May	9,301	9,325	12,349
7	June	10,689	12,516	8,479
8	July	8,388	9,366	10,705
9	August	13,393	8,157	10,730
10	September	8,453	9,295	9,278
11	October	10,204	12,228	8,217
12	November	11,013	10,050	13,419
13	December	10,987	9,386	8,897
14	Full Year	128,514	131,185	132,978
15				
16	Maximum	13,393	13,993	13,523
17	Minimum	8,388	8,157	8,217
18	Spread	5,005	5,836	5,306
19				

TIP

This calculation could also have been done in a single row, using the formula =MAX(B2:B13)−MIN(B2:B13), but using this approach to build simple formulas first in separate cells makes your model easy to follow and it's sometimes necessary before attempting to build complex formulas. You can always put them together later, after you figure out what intermediary calculations you need.

AVERAGE

What if you have several hundred cells in a single spreadsheet column, each with a numerical value, and you want to find the average, or *mean*, value? Using ordinary formulas, you would have to sum up all the numbers, count the number of rows, and then divide the sum by the number of rows. Fortunately, Excel has an AVERAGE function, which makes this calculation a *lot* easier.

In the example shown in Figure 7-8, I quickly and easily calculated the average value of 7,019 with the AVERAGE function.

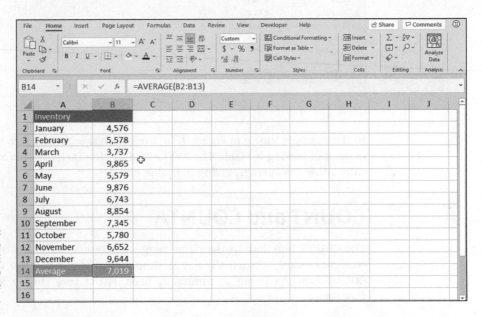

FIGURE 7-8:
Using the AVERAGE function to calculate the average value.

WARNING

The AVERAGE function only uses the cells with *values*. Make sure that this is what you intend with your calculation. In most situations, there isn't a lot of difference between a blank cell and a cell containing a zero value — and most functions treat a blank cell as though it contains a zero. When using the AVERAGE function, however, this is *not* the case. The AVERAGE function counts the cells with value zero, but it ignores empty cells and doesn't include them in the calculation. If you want those cells to be counted, you need to enter a value of zero in the cells.

In the example shown in Figure 7-9, I don't have any data yet for December, so cell B13 has been deliberately left blank. Although cell B13 has been included in the AVERAGE function's range, the function ignores it, and calculates the correct average for January to November as 6,780.

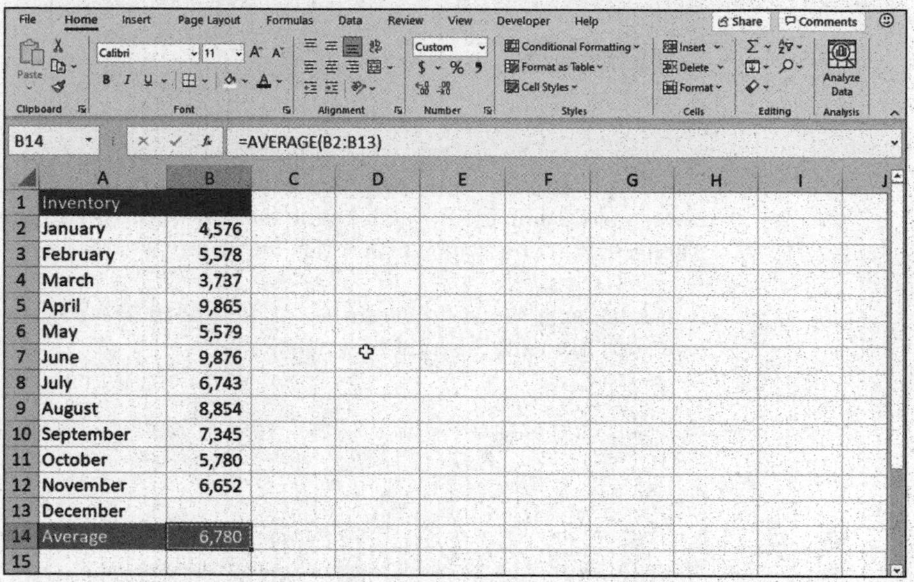

FIGURE 7-9:
The AVERAGE function ignores blank cells.

In the example shown in Figure 7-10, the user has entered a zero value in cell B13 instead of leaving it blank. The AVERAGE function includes this zero value when calculating the average, giving the value of 6,215.

COUNT and COUNTA

The COUNT function, as the name suggests, counts. Although this sounds very straightforward, it's actually not as simple as it seems and, for this reason, the COUNT function is not as commonly used as the very closely related COUNTA function.

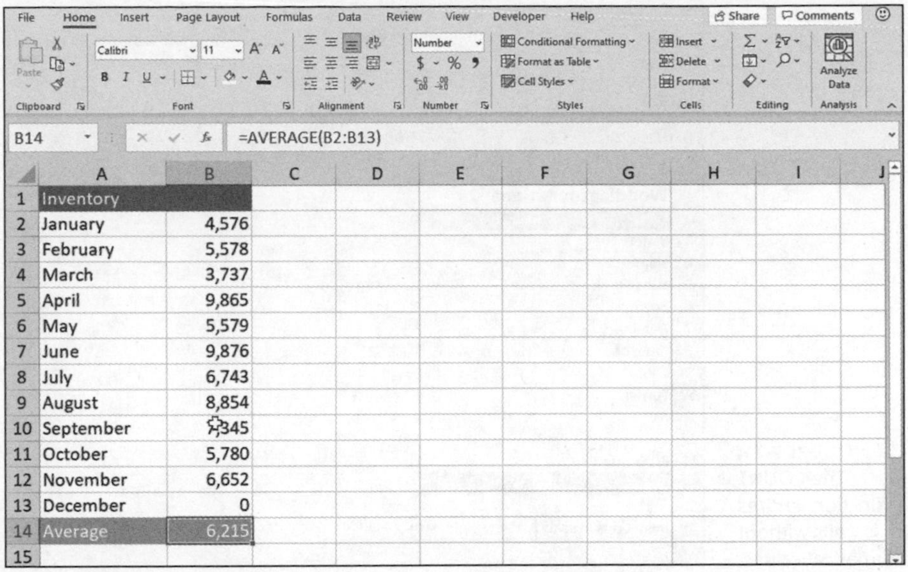

The spreadsheet shows:

	A	B
1	Inventory	
2	January	4,576
3	February	5,578
4	March	3,737
5	April	9,865
6	May	5,579
7	June	9,876
8	July	6,743
9	August	8,854
10	September	345
11	October	5,780
12	November	6,652
13	December	0
14	Average	6,215
15		

Formula bar: B14 =AVERAGE(B2:B13)

WARNING

The COUNT function only counts the number of cells that contain numerical values in a range. It will completely ignore blank cells and any cells within the range that don't contain numerical values, such as text. For this reason, the COUNT function is used only if you *specifically* want to count the numbers only.

In the example shown in Figure 7-11, I'm in the preliminary stages of planning for a wedding, and I need to calculate a couple different numbers from the data. I need to know the number of guests to be invited in order to figure out the maximum capacity for the venue. I also need to know the number of invitations to send, so I can order them from the printers. I'm not sure yet how many people are in the Fleming family, so I've inserted a question mark for now. The number of guests can be easily calculated using the SUM function; if I update the numbers in the future, the sum will automatically change without a problem. I can use the COUNT function to calculate the number of invitations, with the function =COUNT(B3:B13), but it will entirely ignore the cell containing the question mark and lead me to only order 10 invitations instead of 11.

The COUNTA function would be a much better solution to the problem shown in Figure 7-11. In fact, COUNTA is often used instead of COUNT. This is because the COUNTA function will count *all* cells containing data, not just numerical values, including error values and empty text (""), but it will still ignore cells that are completely empty.

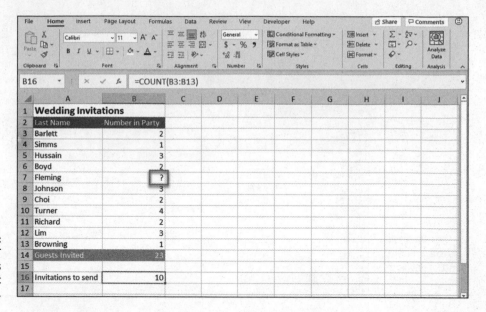

In the wedding-planning example, I could use the function =COUNTA(B3:B13) instead, and this will give the correct result. *Remember:* The COUNTA function ignores blank cells, so if you were to remove the question mark from cell B7 and leave it blank, the answer would be incorrect again. A better solution would be to count the number of names in column A, using the function =COUNTA(A3:A13), as shown in Figure 7-12.

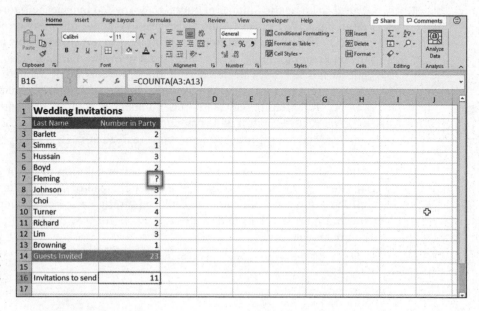

Calculating a full-year projection using COUNT functions

Let's try calculating a full-year projection using the COUNT and COUNTA functions. For example, say you have only ten months of data, and you want to do a full-year projection for your monthly budget meeting. As shown in Figure 7-13, you can calculate how many months' worth of data you have by using the function =COUNT(B2:B13), which will give you the correct number of elapsed months (10).

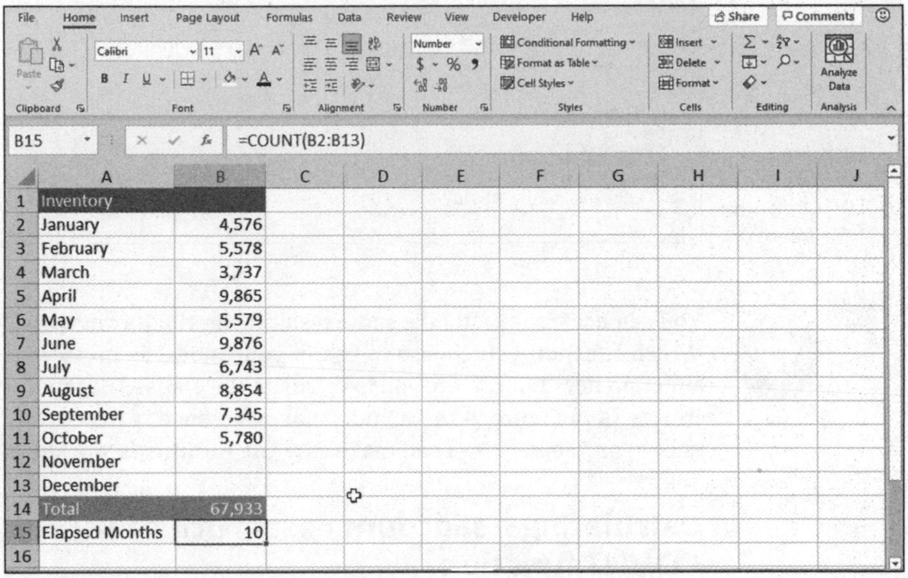

FIGURE 7-13: Using the COUNT function to count the number of values in a range.

	A	B	C	D	E	F	G	H	I	J
1	Inventory									
2	January	4,576								
3	February	5,578								
4	March	3,737								
5	April	9,865								
6	May	5,579								
7	June	9,876								
8	July	6,743								
9	August	8,854								
10	September	7,345								
11	October	5,780								
12	November									
13	December									
14	Total	67,933								
15	Elapsed Months	10								
16										

B15 — =COUNT(B2:B13)

TIP

To insert the function, you can either type out the formula in cell B15 (as shown in Figure 7-13), or select Count Numbers from the drop-down list next to the Σ Auto-Sum button on the Home tab or the Formulas tab.

Note that the COUNTA function would work just as well in this case, but you *particularly* want to count only numbers, so you should stick with the COUNT function this time.

Try adding in a number for November, and notice that the elapsed months changes to 11. This is exactly what you want to happen because it will automatically update whenever you add new data.

In cell B16, calculate the average monthly amount of inventory for the months that have already elapsed. You can do this using the formula =B14/B15. Then you can convert this number to an annual amount by multiplying it by 12. So, the entire formula is =B14/B15*12, which yields the result of 81,520, as shown in Figure 7-14.

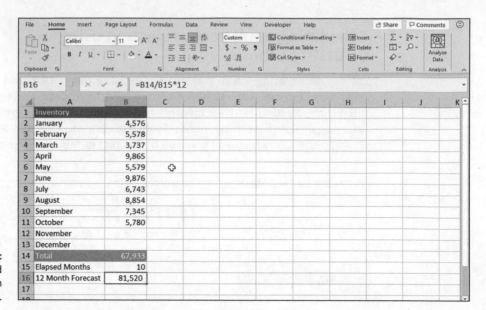

FIGURE 7-14:
A completed
12-month
forecast.

TIP

You can achieve exactly the same result using the formula =AVERAGE(B2:B13)*12. Which function you choose to use in your model is up to you, but the AVERAGE function does not require you to calculate the elapsed number of months as shown in row 15 in Figure 7-14. My personal preference is to see the number of months shown on the page so I can make sure the formula is working correctly.

Calculating headcount costs with the COUNT function

Let's take a look at another example where the COUNT function can be useful. I often use the COUNT function to calculate headcount in a budget as it's entered. For a practical example of how to use the COUNT function as part of a financial model, follow these steps:

1. Download File 0701.xlsx **from** www.dummies.com/go/financial modelinginexcelfd2e, **open it, and select the tab labeled 7-15 or enter and format the data as shown in Figure 7-15.**

2. In cell B17, enter the formula =COUNT(B3:B14) **to count the number of staff in the budget.**

You get the result of 9.

REMEMBER

Again, the COUNTA function would've worked in this situation, but I specifically wanted to add up only the number of staff for which I have a budget.

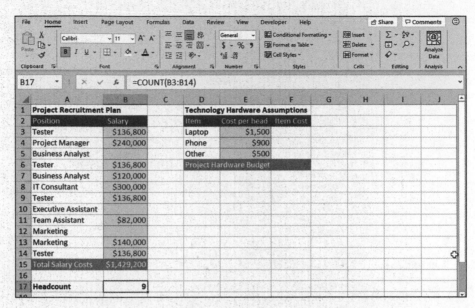

FIGURE 7-15:
Using a COUNT function to calculate headcount.

Try entering **TBD** in one of the blank cells in the range. What happens? The COUNT function doesn't change its value because it only counts cells with *numerical values.* Try using the COUNTA function instead (with TBD still in place in one of the formerly blank cells). The result changes from 9 to 10, which may or may not be what you want to happen.

After you've calculated the headcount, you can incorporate this information into your technology budget. Each of the costs in the budget is a variable cost driven by headcount. Follow these steps:

1. In cell F3, enter the formula =E3*B17.

This formula automatically calculates the total cost of all laptops based on the headcount numbers.

Because you want to copy this formula down, you need to anchor the cell reference to the headcount.

2. Change the formula to =E3*$B$17 by using the F4 shortcut key or typing in the dollar signs manually.

3. Copy the formula down the range, and add a total at the bottom, as shown in Figure 7-16.

When you've finished, test the model by adding a salary amount for Business Analyst in cell B5 (any number will do). You'll see that the headcount number automatically updates, as does the Project Hardware Budget in cell F6.

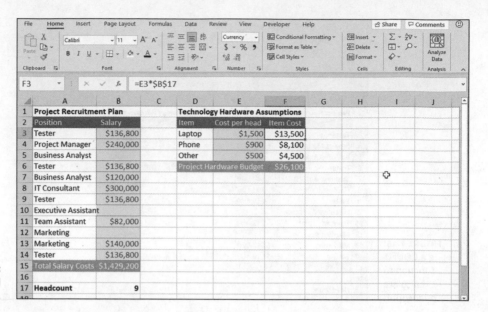

FIGURE 7-16:
The completed budget.

TIP

When you've finished a calculation in a model like this, it's always wise to run a quick test to make sure it's working the way you expect it to.

ROUND, ROUNDUP, and ROUNDDOWN

Several Excel functions round off numbers. The ones that are the most useful for financial modelers are ROUND, ROUNDUP, and ROUNDDOWN. The ROUND function rounds to the nearest specified value — whether it's up or down. The ROUNDUP function rounds up to the nearest specified value. And — you guessed it — the ROUNDDOWN function rounds down to the nearest specified value.

To understand how this particular function works, try it out for yourself by following these steps:

1. **Open a new file in Excel.**

2. **In cell A1, enter the number** 45215754.575.

3. **On the Home tab, in the Numbers section, click the comma button once to format the cell.**

   The formatting changes so the number now looks like this: 45,215,754.58. Note that the number remains the same; the third decimal place is still there but it's just not showing due to the way the cell is formatted.

4. **Select the blank cell A2, and enter the formula** =ROUND(A1,1).

The 1 in the last part of the formula means that you only want one decimal place. The decimal places are reduced to only one so that cell A2 contains the value 45,215,754.60. Note that the number really does only contain one decimal place; the extra decimal places are not being suppressed by formatting as they are in cell A1.

5. **Now select the blank cell A3, and enter the formula** =ROUND(A1,0) **to remove all decimal places completely.**

The result is 45,215,755.00. Now the cell value contains no decimal places at all.

6. **In the blank cell A4, enter the formula** =ROUND(A1,-1) **to round the number to the nearest ten.**

The result is 45,215,750.00.

7. **In cell A5, enter the formula** =ROUND(A1,-3) **to round the number to the nearest thousand.**

The result is 45,216,000.00.

8. **In cell A6, enter the formula** =ROUND(A1,-6) **to round to the nearest million.**

The result is 45,000,000.00, as shown in Figure 7-17.

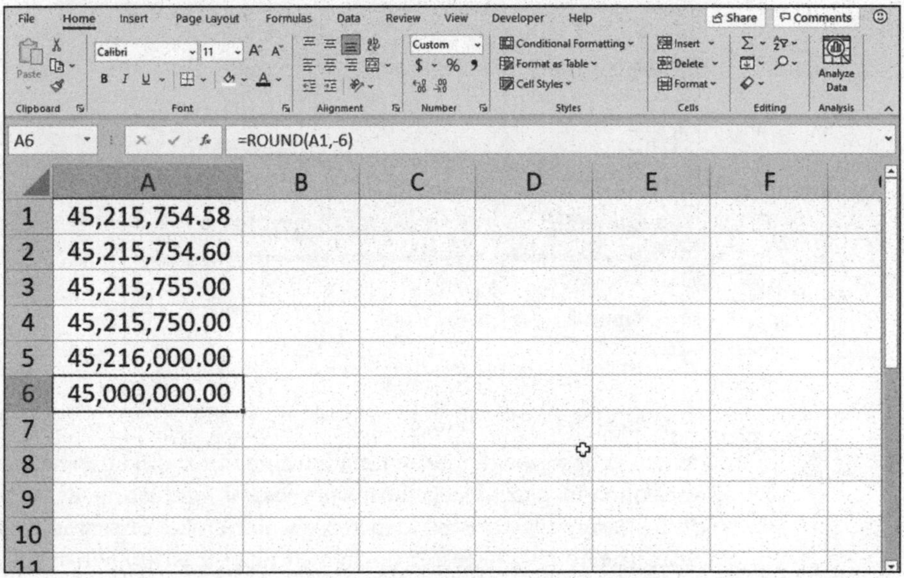

FIGURE 7-17:
Using the ROUND function.

For a practical example of how the ROUNDUP and ROUNDDOWN functions are used in a corkscrew cash flow in a financial model, see the Cash flow statement case study in Chapter 10.

Now let's look at an example of how to use the ROUNDUP function as part of a financial model. Let's say you're building a five-year plan for a call center. Each call operator can handle 40 customers. In the first year, you have 500 customers, and you expect that to increase by 20 percent per year. You have fixed costs of $250,000. The variable overheads are $100 per customer. Each call operator costs $65,000 per year. And all costs increase by inflation of 3 percent. How many call operators will you need each year? (*Hint:* Don't forget to round up!)

TECHNICAL
STUFF

This exercise demonstrates the difference between fixed, variable, and stepped costs, which are important concepts in management accounting and budget modeling. As shown in Figure 7-18, fixed costs do not change as the number of units produced increases. Variable costs change directly in line with the number of units produced, and are also very simple to model. Stepped costs, however, do not increase in a linear fashion; instead, they increase in increments or "steps," and these can be modeled using the ROUNDUP function.

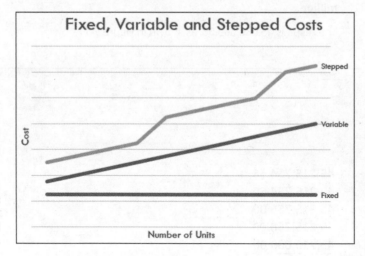

FIGURE 7-18:
Fixed, variable, and stepped costs.

This exercise also demonstrates a common escalation technique for increasing amounts by a growth rate, or inflation amount. You'll often need to be able to include escalation in your models for the purpose of forecasting, as you do in this exercise. In this exercise, you need to increase your number of customers by 20 percent each year. The number of customers in the first year is 500. When you add the 20 percent growth to this number, it becomes 600. Then you calculate the customer number in the third year based on this number (600) not the first year (500). This effect, whereby the growth increases exponentially, is called *compounding*.

TIP

To calculate growth, use the following formula:

Base Amount × (1 + Growth)

You're adding 1 (effectively 100 percent) to the growth rate (which is 20 percent) because you want the capital sum returned along with the accrued interest. Multiplying an amount by (1 + Growth) is a very common calculation in financial modeling.

Okay, finally, to answer the question posed earlier — "How many call operators will you need each year?" — follow these steps:

1. Download `File 0701.xlsx` **from** www.dummies.com/go/financial modelinginexcelfd2e, **open it, and select the tab labeled 7-19 or enter and format the data as shown in Figure 7-19.**

2. In cell C12, enter the formula =B12*(1+$B$4) **to calculate the number of customers expected in Year 2.**

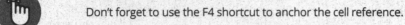

REMEMBER

Don't forget to use the F4 shortcut to anchor the cell reference.

3. Copy this formula all the way across the row.

The calculated result in Year 5 is 1,037.

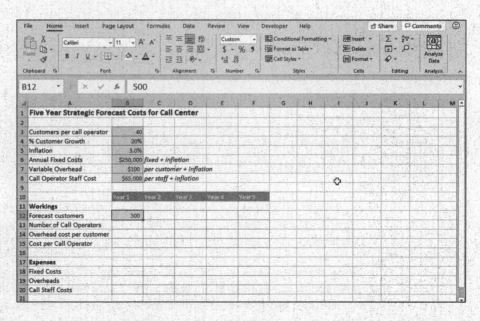

FIGURE 7-19:
Calculating number of call operators required with ROUNDUP.

4. **In cell B13, you need to work out how many call operators you need each year, so divide the number of customers by the customers per operator with the formula** =B12/$B$3.

Don't forget to use the F4 shortcut to anchor the cell reference.

The calculated result is 12.50.

Huh? That doesn't make sense. You can't employ a fraction of a person! You need to round up to the nearest whole person with the formula by wrapping a ROUNDUP function around the existing formula.

5. **In cell B13, change the formula to** =ROUNDUP(B12/$B$3,0).

6. **Copy that formula all the way across the row.**

The calculated result in Year 5 is 26. Compare your results to Figure 7-20.

B13	▾	:	× ✓ fx	=ROUNDUP(B12/$B$3,0)				

	A	B	C	D	E	F	G	H
1	Five Year Strategic Forecast Costs for Call Center							
2								
3	Customers per call operator	40						
4	% Customer Growth	20%						
5	Inflation	3.0%						
6	Annual Fixed Costs	$250,000	fixed + inflation					
7	Variable Overhead	$100	per customer + inflation					
8	Call Operator Staff Cost	$65,000	per staff + inflation					
9								
10		Year 1	Year 2	Year 3	Year 4	Year 5		
11	Workings							
12	Forecast customers	500	600	720	864	1,037		
13	Number of Call Operators	13.00	15.00	18.00	22.00	26.00		
14	Overhead cost per customer							
15	Cost per Call Operator							

FIGURE 7-20: Calculating number of call operators required with ROUNDUP.

You've now calculated the number of staff required. You can use this information later on in row 20 to work out their costs. For now, let's continue working down the page.

In row 14, you need to calculate the overhead amounts for each year. There are two parts to this calculation: First, you need to apply inflation, and second, you need to multiply it by the number of customers. You could do the entire calculation in a single row, but the formula would be difficult to follow.

When it comes to formula layout in a financial model, simple is best! It's far better to lay out the calculation step by step instead of trying to do the whole thing in one row.

Follow these steps to work out how much the staff will cost each year:

1. **In cell B14, enter** =B7 **to link this to the overhead assumption.**

2. **In cell C14, enter the formula** =B14*(1+$B$5) **to add inflation.**

   This technique is exactly the same as the one you used when increasing the number of customers, but you're picking up the inflation assumption instead of the growth assumption.

   Don't forget to use the F4 shortcut to anchor the cell reference.

REMEMBER

3. **Copy the formula all the way across the row.**

   The calculated result in Year 5 is 113.

Note that you have different formulas in cells B14 and C14. Ordinarily, you should try to have consistent formulas wherever possible, to reduce the number of formulas in the model, but in this case, it's just not practical.

In row 15, you need to calculate the staff costs per operator for each year. This works in exactly the same way as the overhead costs. You'll increase the per-operator costs by inflation each year and multiply it by the number of operators later on. Follow these steps:

1. **In cell B15, enter** =B8 **to link this cell to the cost per operator.**

2. **In cell C15, enter** =B15*(1+$B$5) **to add inflation to this number.**

   Don't forget to use the F4 shortcut to anchor the cell reference.

REMEMBER

3. **Copy the formula all the way across the row.**

   The calculated result in Year 5 is $73,158.

   You've finished the workings block, so you can start to calculate the costs below in row 18.

4. **In cell B18, enter** =B6 **to link this cell to the fixed cost assumption with the formula.**

5. **In cell C18, enter the formula** =B18*(1+$B$5) **to add inflation to this number.**

6. **Copy the formula all the way across the row.**

   The calculated result in Year 5 is $281,377.

7. In cell B19, enter the formula =B14*B12 to calculate the total overhead costs by multiplying the overhead cost per customer per year by the number of customers in that year.

No need to lock the cell referencing, because you *want* this to copy across the row.

8. Copy the formula all the way across the row.

The calculated result in Year 5 is $116,693.

9. In cell B20, enter the formula =B15*B13 to calculate the total call staff costs by multiplying the cost per operator by the number of operators.

10. Copy the formula all the way across the row.

The calculated result in Year 5 is $1,902,110.

11. In cell B21, enter the formula =SUM(B18:B20) to sum the total costs.

Another option is to select cell B21 and use the shortcut Alt+=.

12. Copy the formula all the way across the row.

The calculated result in Year 5 is $2,300,180. Compare your results to Figure 7-21.

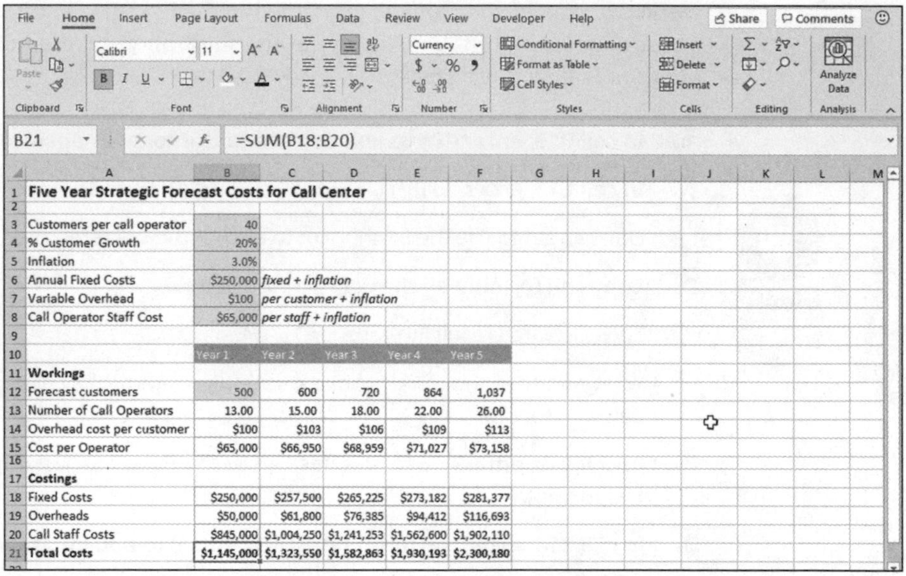

FIGURE 7-21:
The completed five-year strategic forecast.

	A	B	C	D	E	F
1	**Five Year Strategic Forecast Costs for Call Center**					
2						
3	Customers per call operator	40				
4	% Customer Growth	20%				
5	Inflation	3.0%				
6	Annual Fixed Costs	$250,000	*fixed + inflation*			
7	Variable Overhead	$100	*per customer + inflation*			
8	Call Operator Staff Cost	$65,000	*per staff + inflation*			
9						
10		Year 1	Year 2	Year 3	Year 4	Year 5
11	**Workings**					
12	Forecast customers	500	600	720	864	1,037
13	Number of Call Operators	13.00	15.00	18.00	22.00	26.00
14	Overhead cost per customer	$100	$103	$106	$109	$113
15	Cost per Operator	$65,000	$66,950	$68,959	$71,027	$73,158
16						
17	**Costings**					
18	Fixed Costs	$250,000	$257,500	$265,225	$273,182	$281,377
19	Overheads	$50,000	$61,800	$76,385	$94,412	$116,693
20	Call Staff Costs	$845,000	$1,004,250	$1,241,253	$1,562,600	$1,902,110
21	**Total Costs**	$1,145,000	$1,323,550	$1,582,863	$1,930,193	$2,300,180

IF

The IF function is very commonly used in financial models because it allows you to test certain conditions in your model and change outcomes or results depending on what the user inserts into the model. It's especially useful when building scenarios, because you can build the model so that the user can turn certain conditions on and off.

Type **=IF** and then use the Ctrl+A shortcut. The IF Function Arguments dialog box appears. There are three fields you need to fill in:

>> **The logical statement that is evaluated:** For example, is the weather sunny today? The answer to this will either be true or false.

>> **The result if the statement is true:** In this case, it might be "Go to the beach."

>> **The result if the statement is false:** In this case, it might be "Stay home."

The syntax looks like this:

```
=IF(statement being tested,value if true,value if false)
```

So, for this example, in plain language, the syntax looks like this:

```
=IF(the weather is sunny,go to the beach,stay home)
```

Written in an Excel formula, if the weather has been put into cell A1, the formula would look like this (see Figure 7-22):

```
=IF(A1="Sunny","go to the beach","stay home")
```

TIP

When using text within a formula, as you're doing in this example, you must put quotation marks (" ") around any text. However, if you use the IF Function Arguments dialog box, as shown in Figure 7-22, there is no need to put the quotation marks in manually — the dialog box will do it for you.

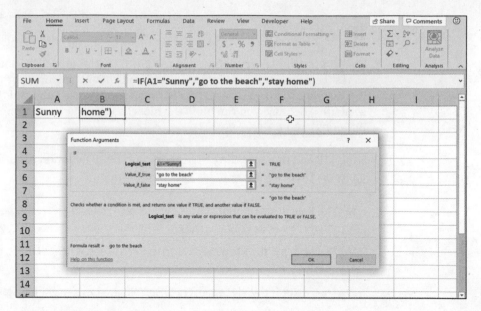

FIGURE 7-22:
Inserting an IF function using the Function Arguments dialog box.

The IF function can be used to automatically calculate whether a set of numbers meets certain conditions. For example, you can create a variance alert when comparing actual costs to budget — if the variance is greater than 10 percent, you want the formula to automatically alert us. For a practical example of how to use the IF function as part of a financial model, follow these steps:

1. **Download** File 0701.xlsx **from** www.dummies.com/go/financial modelinginexcelfd2e **and select the tab labeled 7-23-blank or enter and format the data in columns A through D, as shown in Figure 7-23.**

2. **In cell E3, enter the formula** =D3-C3 **to calculate the variance.**

   TIP

   When preparing an actual versus budget report, you should always show the variance as a positive if it's "better" than budget or a negative if it's "worse" than budget. This report shows expenses, so an actual amount higher than budget is a bad thing and should be shown as a negative value. For an expense report, the variance calculation is budget minus actual; for a revenue report, the variance calculation is actual minus budget.

   If you're showing an income or profit-and-loss statement with revenue at the top part of the report and expenses at the bottom, the formula can't be exactly the same all the way down the page. Although the consistency of formulas is an important part of financial modeling best practice, it's not always practical!

3. **Copy this formula down the column.**

   TIP

   When copying down a column, you can select the cell you want to copy, hover the mouse over the lower-left corner until the cross-hairs appear, and double-click. The formula is copied all the way down to the bottom.

4. **Select cell E13 and use the shortcut Alt+= and then press enter to sum the column.**

   The calculated value is $1,555.

5. **In cell F3, enter the formula** =E3/D3 **to calculate the variance percentage.**

6. **Copy this formula down the column.**

   You will notice an error value in row 11. This is because there was no budget for Other IT Costs and the formula can't divide by zero, so it shows an error value.

7. **Select cell F3 and suppress this error by editing the formula to** =IFERROR(E3/D3,0).

   Any formula errors will show a zero value instead of the error.

8. **Copy this formula down the column.**

REMEMBER

   Go back to the first cell (E3) to make the change and then copy it down, instead of making the change only where the error shows (E11). This way, if the numbers change in the future, the errors will always be suppressed.

9. **Ensure that the variance formula also copies all the way down to cell F13 and edit the formatting if necessary.**

   Now that you've set up the actual versus budget report, you can add an IF function to alert you when the variance is too high. First, you need to determine what you mean by "too high."

10. **In cell G1, enter the value** –10%.

    You'll link to this cell because this is the maximum variance to budget you can tolerate.

REMEMBER

    Don't forget to press F4 after referring to G1 to lock the cell reference so that you can copy it down.

11. **In cell G3, type** =IF(**and press Ctrl+A.**

    The Function Arguments dialog box appears.

12. **Enter the formula** =IF(F3<$G$1,"Over budget",0), **as shown in Figure 7-23.**

13. **Ensure that the variance formula also copies all the way down to cell G13 and edit the formatting if necessary.**

Your actual versus budget variance report is complete!

TIP

The zero values in the G column appear as a dash because of the way the cells have been formatted. This was done using the Comma Style in the Numbers section on the Home tab in the Ribbon. It looks much neater than showing a zero.

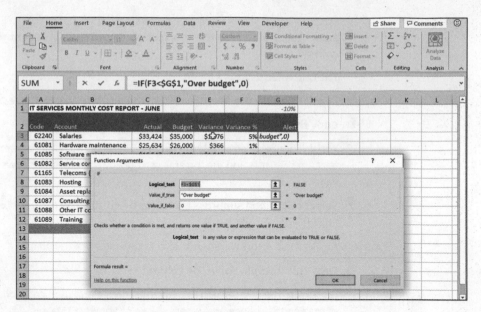

FIGURE 7-23:
Building a variance alert formula.

COUNTIF and SUMIF

COUNTIF and SUMIF are very handy functions to know for modeling. They add or count ranges of data, and are among some of my favorite, most frequently used functions.

Tallying sales with COUNTIF

COUNTIF is used to count the *number* of cells that match specified criteria. For example, you have a list of sales made by salesperson by region, as shown in Figure 7-24. You'd like to know how *many* sales were made in each region. To solve this problem, follow these steps:

1. **Download** File 0701.xlsx **from** www.dummies.com/go/financial modelinginexcelfd2e, **open it, and select the tab labeled 7-24.**

2. **Copy column B in its entirety to column E, as shown in Figure 7-24.**

3. **Leave column E selected, and on the Data tab, in the Data Tools section, click the Remove Duplicates button.**

4. **Click OK.**

   A message box displays how many duplicate values are to be removed.

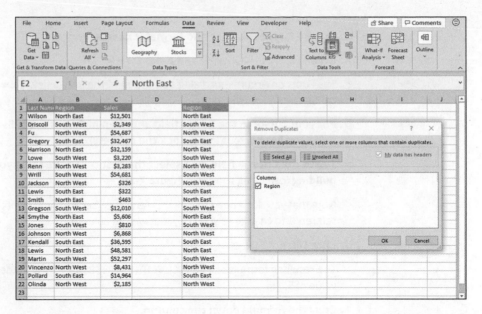

FIGURE 7-24:
The Remove
Duplicates
dialog box.

5. **Click OK.**

   The duplicate values are removed, leaving you with a unique list of regions, as shown in Figure 7-25.

   Alternatively, if you're using Excel on Microsoft 365 or later, you can use the UNIQUE function instead. The UNIQUE function is a type of dynamic array formula that's new to Microsoft 365. For more information on dynamic arrays, turn to Chapter 6.

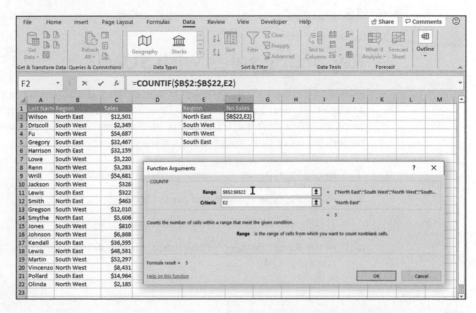

FIGURE 7-25:
The COUNTIF
Function
Arguments
dialog box.

6. In cell F1, type No. Sales **and format if necessary.**

7. In cell F2, type =COUNTIF(**and press Ctrl+A.**

The Function Arguments dialog box appears. The Range field shows the range containing the original data.

8. Put your cursor in the Range field and then highlight the cells B2:B22; press the F4 shortcut key to lock the cell references.

9. Tab to the Criteria field, and select the first cell in the table you're building (cell E2 as shown in Figure 7-25).

Note that you don't need to lock this reference because you *want* the cell reference to change as you copy it down the column.

10. Click OK.

The resulting formula will be =COUNTIF($B$2:$B$22,E2) with the calculated value of 5.

11. Copy the formula down the column.

12. Click cell F6, use the shortcut Alt+=, and press Enter to add the sum total.

The calculated value is 21.

13. Format as necessary.

14. In cell F7, enter the formula =COUNTA(B2:B22)-F6 **to make sure the totals are the same.**

15. Format the zero to a dash by clicking the comma button from the Number section of the Home tab.

16. Check your numbers against Figure 7-26.

Reporting sales with SUMIF

SUMIF is similar to COUNTIF, but it sums rather than counts the values of cells in a range that meet given criteria. Following on from the last example, let's say you want to know how *much* (in terms of dollar value) in sales were made in each region. To solve this problem, follow these steps:

1. In cell F1, type No. Sales **and format if necessary.**

2. In cell F2, type =SUMIF(**and press Ctrl+A.**

The Function Arguments dialog box appears.

3. In the Range field, enter the items you're adding together (B2:B22), and then press F4.

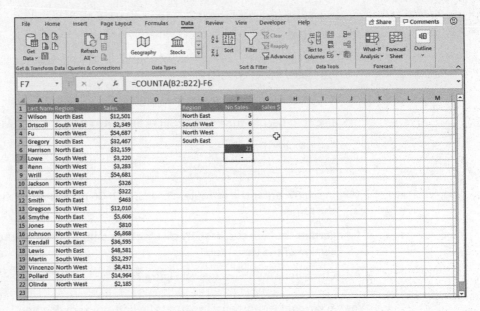

FIGURE 7-26:
The completed number of sales table with error check.

4. **In the Criteria field, enter the criteria you're looking for in that range** (E2).

    You don't press the F4 key here, because you *want* to copy it down the column.

5. **In the Sum_range field, enter the numbers you want to sum together** (C2:C22), **and then press F4.**

    Figure 7-27 shows what this should look like.

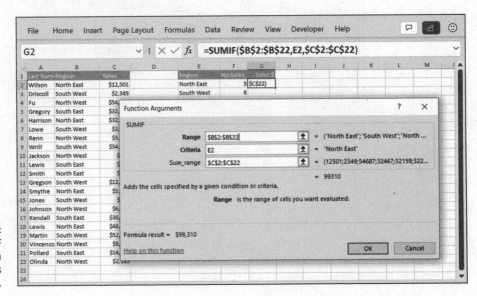

FIGURE 7-27:
The SUMIF Function Arguments dialog box.

6. Click OK.

The resulting formula will be =SUMIF($B$2:$B$22,E2,$C$2:$C$22) with the calculated value of $99,310.

7. Copy the formula down the column.

8. Click cell G6, use the shortcut Alt+= and press Enter to add the sum total.

The calculated value is $384,805.

9. Format as necessary.

10. In cell G7, enter the formula =SUM(C2:C22)-G6 to make sure the totals are the same.

11. Format the zero to a dash by clicking the comma button in the Number section of the Home tab.

12. Check your numbers against Figure 7-28.

You've now got a summary report at the bottom, showing you how much you've sold in terms of number and dollar value.

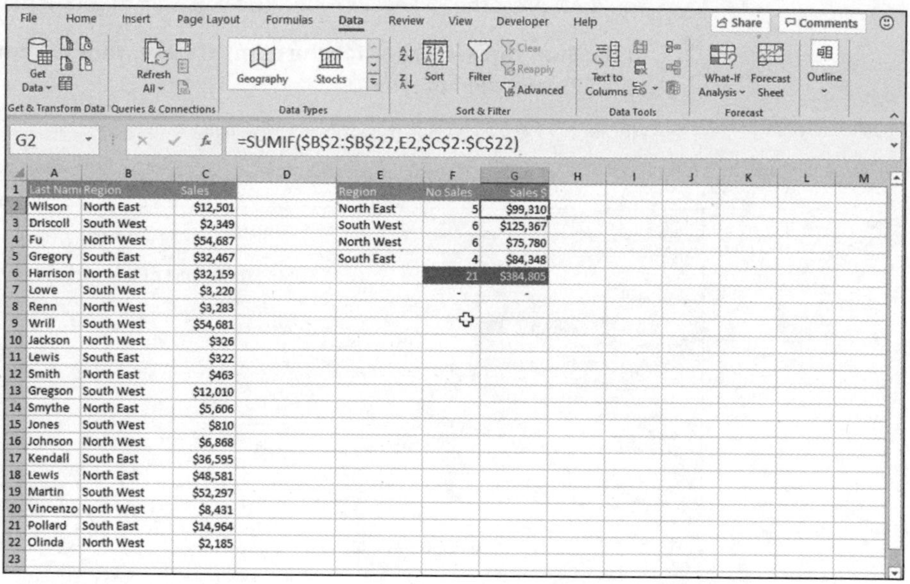

FIGURE 7-28:
The completed sales total table.

WHY ERROR CHECKS MATTER

If your Range and your Sum_range don't match up, your result will be wrong. For example, =SUMIF($B$2:$B$22,E2,$C$1:$C$22) — where one range includes the heading but the other does not — will give you an incorrect result without warning! This is a very easy mistake to make, and quite common in financial modeling. You can see in the following figure that the totals are not the same because the SUMIF function is picking up the incorrect range. Unfortunately, it does not return an error. Instead, it returns a number ($81,394) that *looks* as though it could be correct but is in fact entirely wrong! The same problem can occur for the COUNTIF function.

Building error checks into your model, as you've done in this example, can avoid error in formulas like this.

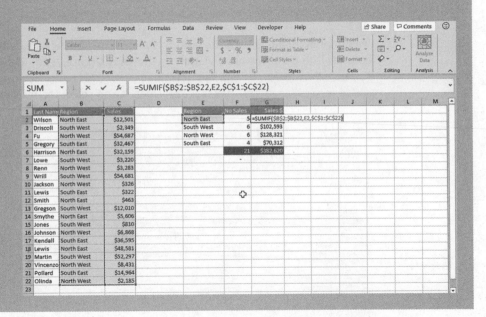

VLOOKUP, HLOOKUP, and XLOOKUP

The lookup functions — VLOOKUP, HLOOKUP, and XLOOKUP — are very often used in building financial models and are often the "go to" function for many modelers and analysts. Both the VLOOKUP and HLOOKUP functions have been superseded by the new XLOOKUP function available in Excel on Microsoft 365. Although XLOOKUP is superior to its predecessors, I'll still take you through how to use the VLOOKUP and HLOOKUP functions in case some people who need to use your model aren't on Microsoft 365.

Despite its popularity, the humble VLOOKUP is often misused and overused because many users — especially when they're just starting out — don't understand exactly how it works. VLOOKUP stands for *vertical lookup.* It can be used any time you have a list of data with a *unique* lookup field in the leftmost column. The VLOOKUP function searches through a data set and returns a corresponding match from a specified row and column.

HLOOKUP works in exactly the same way, except that the list of values is horizontally orientated instead of vertically oriented.

Mapping Data with VLOOKUP

Using the previous example from the last section, you have a list of sales and regions. Let's say you want to abbreviate the region names from "North West" to "N/W," because that's what your team is used to seeing.

If you followed along with the last example, simply insert an extra column before column D to enter the abbreviation as shown in Figure 7-29. Right-click column D, and select Insert. Or you can download File 0701.xlsx at www.dummies.com/go/financialmodelinginexcelfd2e. Open it and select the tab labeled 7-29.

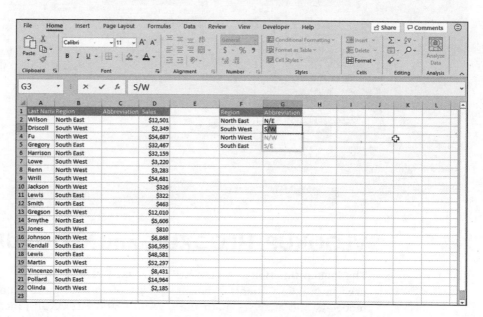

FIGURE 7-29:
Using Flash Fill.

To solve this problem, follow these steps:

1. In cell G2, start to enter the abbreviations for each region.

This is the mapping table you're using to map the regions to their abbreviated names. If you're using Excel 2013 or later, Flash Fill will begin to automatically populate the data for you as shown in Figure 7-29. Very cool.

2. Select cell C2 and then click the Insert Function command on the Formulas tab (or just press Shift+F3).

3. In the Select a Function box, scroll down until you see the VLOOKUP function; select VLOOKUP and click OK.

4. The first parameter is the criterion you're testing — in this case, the first region you need the abbreviation for, North East — so enter B2 in the Lookup_value field.

The next field is the table array, which contains the data you want to reference. This is where it gets tricky. The criteria you're looking for must *always* be in the far-left column of the data table you're referencing in the table array.

5. In the Table_array field, enter F2:G5, because in this case, the data you're referencing will be in that range.

REMEMBER

Press the F4 shortcut key to lock the cell reference.

In the Col_index_num field, you need to enter which column the value is found in. You need to tell the function which column in the table array you want it to return. In this case, you want it to tell you the abbreviation for the region. So, counting from the far-left side of the table array (starting in column F), you want it to return to the second column.

6. Enter a number 2 in the Col_index_num field, as shown in Figure 7-30.

The optional fourth field, Range_lookup, is where you specify whether a close match is okay.

7. If you want an exact match, enter zero in the Range_lookup field; otherwise, leave it blank.

You may also enter TRUE or FALSE, but typing a zero or leaving it blank is quicker.

WARNING

Make sure to enter a zero or FALSE in the last field. If you leave it blank, it will search for a "close" match and return an incorrect result. There are very few instances where you want a close match.

8. Click OK to complete the formula.

The completed formula will be =VLOOKUP(B2,$F$2:$G$5,2,0) with a returned result of "N/E."

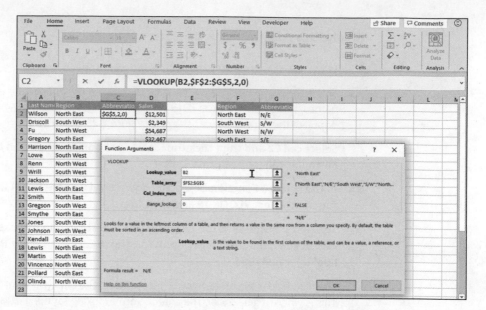

FIGURE 7-30:
The VLOOKUP
Function
Arguments
dialog box.

9. Copy cell C2 all the way down the column and compare your results to Figure 7-31.

10. Go to the mapping table and adjust the abbreviated names.

For example, change "N/E" to "NE," and you'll notice the abbreviations in column C also automatically change. In this way, you can save time in building your reports.

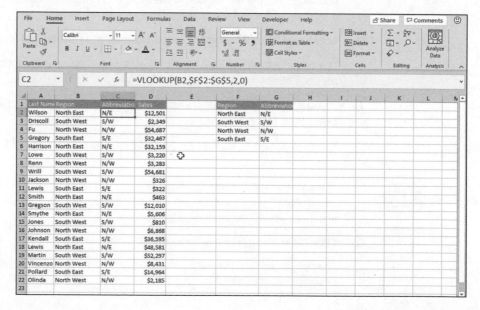

FIGURE 7-31:
The completed
report with
region
abbreviations.

Using the HLOOKUP function

The HLOOKUP function works in exactly the same way as the VLOOKUP function, except that the data values are arranged horizontally instead of vertically. HLOOKUP is subject to exactly the same issues as VLOOKUP, and it works in exactly the same way, except for the orientation. If your source data range is orientated vertically, use VLOOKUP, and if it's orientated horizontally, use HLOOKUP. For a practical example of using an HLOOKUP nested formula in a financial modeling context, turn to the section on building the scenario functionality in Chapter 10.

Breaking a VLOOKUP or HLOOKUP

If you've created a VLOOKUP function in a model such as the one in the preceding section, this should work well . . . until someone enters or deletes a column in your source data! A formula such as the following specifically asks for the second column, so it won't work if someone inserts a column range within the Regions range:

```
=VLOOKUP(B2,$F$2:$G$5,2,0)
```

It won't work because your required column becomes the third column, but the VLOOKUP function is still asking for the second. You'll get exactly the same problem with an HLOOKUP function, except when you add a row instead of a column.

WARNING

VLOOKUP and HLOOKUP are not very robust formulas — you can see how easy they are to break! Here's what you can do to avoid this problem and make your formula more robust:

>> Use an XLOOKUP instead (see the following section).

>> Protect the sheet to stop people from inserting or deleting rows or columns.

>> Use a "helper" row where the column number needs to be manually updated, or automatically calculated with a COLUMN or ROW function.

>> Insert an error to alert the user if this mistake has occurred.

>> Replace the hard-coded number 2 with a dynamic function such as a COLUMN or MATCH function that will automatically update.

Using the XLOOKUP function

REMEMBER

XLOOKUP is only available for Microsoft 365 users.

To use an XLOOKUP function to solve the problem shown earlier in the "Mapping Data with VLOOKUP" section, follow these steps instead:

1. **Select cell C2 and then click the Insert Function command on the Formulas tab (or just press Shift+F3).**

2. **In the Select a Function box, scroll down until you see the XLOOKUP function; select XLOOKUP and click OK.**

3. **The first parameter is the criterion you're testing — in this case, the first region you need the abbreviation for, North East — so enter** B2 **in the** Lookup_value **field.**

The next field is the table array, which contains the data you want to reference. Instead of selecting the entire array as you did before, this time only select the column that contains the data you want to look up.

4. **In the Table_array field, enter** F2:F5, **because in this case, the data you're referencing will be in that range.**

Press the F4 shortcut key to lock the cell reference.

5. **In the Return_array field, enter** G2:G5 **and then press F4 again to lock the reference range.**

6. **Leave the last two fields blank, unless you want to specify the value to show if the function can't find a value.**

If you don't want the error value #N/A to show if the function can't find a value, you can add a value such as **"n/a"** into the if_not_found field, as shown in Figure 7-32. This is entirely optional, and the formula will work fine if you leave this field blank.

7. **Click OK to complete the formula.**

The completed formula will be =XLOOKUP(B2,$F$2:$F$5,$G$2:$G$5,"n/a") with a returned result of N/E.

8. **Copy cell C2 all the way down the column, and compare your results to Figure 7-33.**

9. **Now, test the formula by inserting a column between F and G.**

Note that the formula doesn't break when a column is inserted between the two reference ranges, as shown in Figure 7-33.

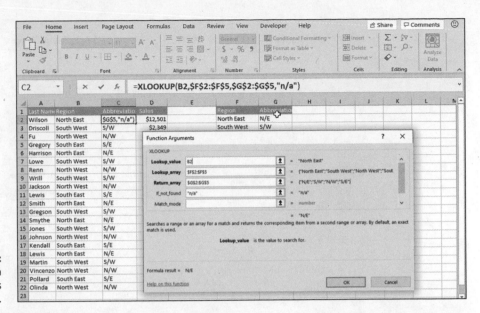

FIGURE 7-32:
The Function Arguments dialog box.

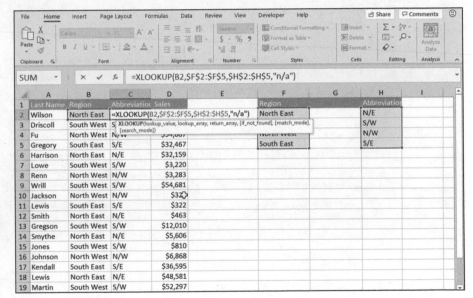

FIGURE 7-33:
The XLOOKUP references two separate columns and doesn't break when a column is inserted.

WORKING WITH NESTED FUNCTIONS

As you may have discovered by now, Excel allows you to include more than one function in a formula. For example, you can multiply a sum total by another number with the following formula:

    =SUM(B1:B20)*A3

But this does not make it a nested formula. A nested formula is a function that's included *inside* another function. This technique allows you to build more complex formulas. For example:

    =IF(SUM(D3:D23)<0,1,0)

This is a basic IF statement, but a SUM function has been included in one of the fields.

The IF statement is probably most commonly used as a nested function. You can actually nest up to 64 functions within a formula model, but this is not recommended, and it's certainly not good modeling practice!

With most functions covered in this chapter, I encourage you to make use of the Function Arguments dialog box. This dialog box doesn't work easily with nested formulas, but there is a bit of a trick to it.

Try typing in the nested formula:

    =(SUM(D1:D5)*AVERAGE(A1:A5))/12

Try to go into the Insert Function dialog box by pressing the *fx* button next to the Formula Bar. An unhelpful Function Arguments dialog box appears, as shown in the following figure.

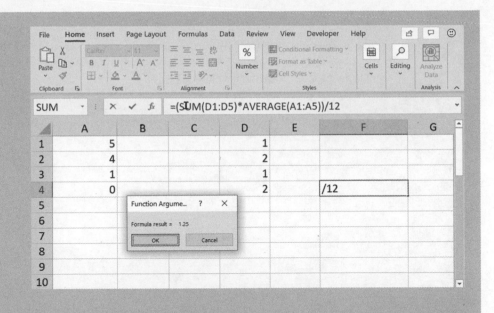

Now, try clicking within the formula or within the SUM part of the formula and press *fx*. The dialog box for the SUM part of the nested formula appears, as shown in the following figure.

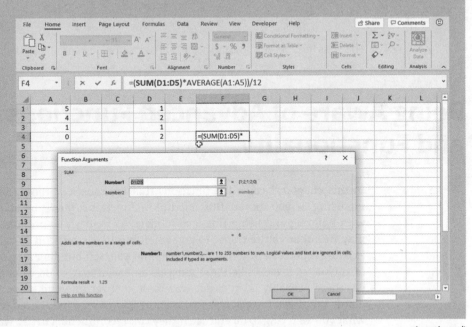

(continued)

(continued)

Now, do the same thing by clicking within the formula next to or within the AVERAGE part of the formula and press *fx*. The dialog box for the AVERAGE part of the nested formula appears, as shown in the following figure.

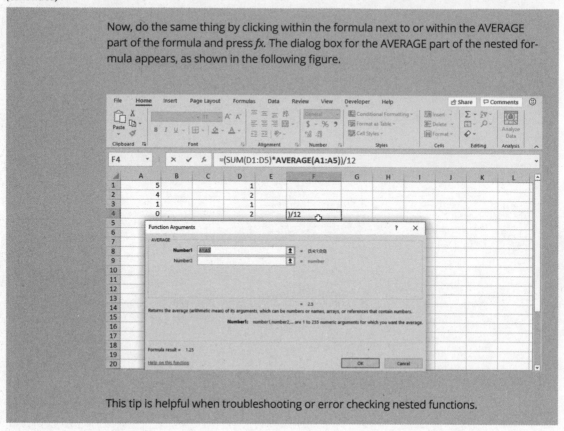

This tip is helpful when troubleshooting or error checking nested functions.

Being Aware of Advanced Functions and Functionality

In this chapter, I cover the functions that are most commonly used in financial modeling. If you master this handful of functions, you'll be able to get started with building and using financial models. As your skills progress, however, you may find that you're trying to do something that's difficult to achieve with your existing repertoire of functions. If you find yourself building long and complicated formulas, or it feels like there must be an easier way to do what you're trying to do, there probably is an easier way to do it. I recommend stopping what you're doing and if you have access to a mentor or a more experienced modeler, explain what you're trying to do and see if they can recommend a better way of approaching the problem. If you don't have access to someone you can ask, try to explain your problem in plain English to your favorite search engine and, chances are, you'll find what you need. If you don't have any success the first time, try explaining the problem a different way.

Say, for example, that you have a list of names, regions, products, and sales as shown in Figure 7-34. You'd like to summarize these numbers to show both regions and products on a dashboard. You think a SUMIF might do the trick, but you're limited to only one input range.

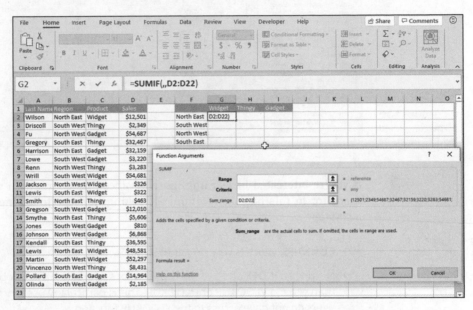

FIGURE 7-34:
Trying to use the SUMIF function to aggregate with multiple criteria.

So, you open your favorite search engine and search for "SUMIF with two ranges." You see a reference to the SUMIFS function. On further research, you discover some online tutorials that you work through carefully, and you discover that this might actually do the trick, as shown in Figure 7-35.

So now, the SUMIFS function is added to your repertoire of functions you can use if and when the situation requires. This is an example of how you can "learn on the job." By doing a little research, you can learn more advanced tools and functions.

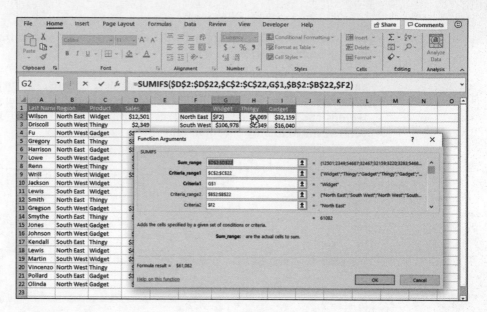

FIGURE 7-35:
The completed SUMIFS function.

If you're interested in learning more advanced functions than what I have the space for in this book, I recommend looking into the following functions as a next step:

» COUNTIFS, which is very similar to SUMIFS.

» Nesting an INDEX and two MATCH functions to create a more robust lookup than either a VLOOKUP or HLOOKUP. This is particularly useful if you or your users do not have access to the XLOOKUP function.

» Payment calculation functions, such as IPMT and PPMT (see Chapter 8 for more on PMT).

» Date functions such as EDATE and EOMONTH (see Chapter 9 for more on TODAY).

» The OFFSET function, which can be tricky to follow and audit but seems popular among some modelers.

» The INDIRECT function, which is similarly difficult to follow, but can be useful in certain situations.

Finally, to learn more advanced functions, check out *Using Excel for Business and Financial Modelling* by yours truly or *Excel All-in-One For Dummies* by Paul McFedries and Greg Harvey (both published by Wiley).

Chapter **8**

Applying Scenarios to Your Financial Model

One of the things that makes a financial model a financial model and not a spreadsheet is that it contains hypothetical outcomes or scenarios. When your model has been built properly, using links with data only entered once (see Chapter 4), adding scenarios to your model is a fairly straightforward process, and including scenarios doesn't require much work or redesign.

In this chapter, you take a couple of simple models that you've already built in previous chapters, and see how simple it is to add scenarios to improve the functionality. With a well-built model that has all inputs properly linked through to outputs, changing inputs and watching the outputs change is fairly easy. In fact, you could argue that this is pretty much the whole purpose of building a financial model in the first place!

Scenarios and sensitivity analysis are a great way to reduce risk by seeing all the possible outcomes of the project or venture you're modeling. What would be the absolute worst that could happen? If everything that can go wrong does go wrong, can you still afford to pay your staff? There are usually interdependent effects and interactions among multiple variables, which may change in the model. That's why it's so important to have links automatically calculating within a model. For example, if units sold increases, then revenue increases, so profitability increases, so cash flow increases, so borrowing decreases, so interest payable decreases, and so on. . . .

Scenarios can also help you make decisions. After you've built scenarios into the model, the hypothetical outcomes can be laid out so that the decision makers can see the expected impact of each course of action. How closely these outcomes reflect reality depends, of course, on the accuracy of the model as well as the assumptions that have been used — but you already knew that!

Identifying the Differences among Types of Analysis

Scenario analysis, sensitivity analysis, and what–if analysis are all very similar to each other. In fact, they're really only slight variations of the same thing. Here's a breakdown:

>> **What-if analysis:** What-if analysis is the process of testing to see "what would happen if" you change something in the model.

>> **Sensitivity analysis:** Sensitivity analysis is the process of tweaking one key input or driver in a financial model and seeing how sensitive the model is to the change in that variable.

For example, if you have an income statement with a profit of $1.2 million, you may want to know how that profit is affected by changes in price. If you reduce the per unit price of one of the products from $5.25 to $4.75, the profit may decrease to $975,000, so you can see that the business is quite sensitive to changes in the price for that product. This process of changing a single input in isolation is referred to as performing sensitivity analysis.

>> **Scenario analysis:** Scenario analysis is the process of tweaking a whole series of inputs or drivers in a financial model and seeing what happens with the model.

For example, a worst-case scenario could include not only the price decreasing but interest rates increasing, number of customers decreasing, and unfavorable exchange rates. Sometimes these inputs affect each other — for example, a reduction in sales affecting profitability may also cause sales commission or bonuses to go down, which would also affect profitability.

Building Drop-Down Scenarios

The most commonly-used method of building scenarios (and the one that I most often teach in my training courses) is to use a combination of formulas and drop-down boxes. In the model, you create a table of possible scenarios and their inputs and link the scenario names to an input cell drop-down box. The inputs of the model are linked to the scenario table. If the model has been built properly with all the inputs flowing through to the outputs, then the results of the model will change as the user selects different options from the drop-down box.

Data validation drop-down boxes are used for a number of different purposes in financial modeling, including scenario analysis. For an example of using data validations to reduce errors in a financial model, turn to Chapter 12.

Using data validations to model profitability scenarios

In Chapter 7, you create a simple one-page model to calculate the Five-Year Strategic Forecast Costs for Call Center based on particular inputs. I recommend that you build the model as described in Chapter 7 first so that you understand how this simple model works before adding the scenarios to it. Alternatively, you can find a copy of the completed model by downloading File 0801.xlsx from www.dummies.com/go/financialmodelinginexcelfd2e. Open it and select the tab labeled 8-1.

The way I've modeled this, the inputs are lined up in column B. You could perform sensitivity analysis simply by changing one of the inputs — for example, change the customers per call operator in cell B3 from 40 to 45, and you'll see all the dependent numbers change. This would be a sensitivity analysis, because you're changing only one variable. Instead, you're going to change multiple variables at once in this full scenario analysis exercise, so you'll need to do more than tweak a few numbers manually.

Note that the formulas still link to the inputs in column B, as you can see by selecting cell C12 and pressing the F2 shortcut key, as shown in Figure 8-1.

To perform a scenario analysis using data validation drop-down boxes, follow these steps:

1. **Take the existing model that you created in Chapter 7 (or downloaded), and cut and paste the descriptions from column C to column F.**

   You can do this by highlighting cells C6:C8, pressing Ctrl+X, selecting cell F6, and pressing Enter.

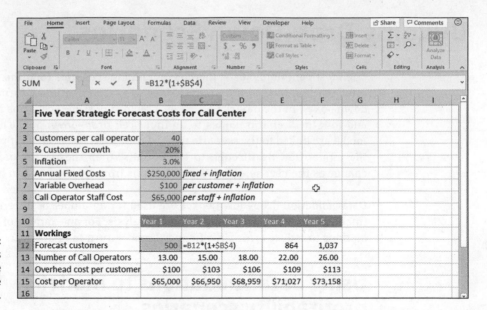

FIGURE 8-1:
Assumptions
drive the
formulas in the
model.

The inputs in cells B3 to B8 are the active range that drives the model and will remain so. However, they need to become formulas that change depending on the drop-down box that you'll create.

2. **Copy the range in column B across to columns C, D, and E.**

You can do this by highlighting B3:B8, pressing Ctrl+C, selecting cells C3:E3, and pressing Enter. These amounts will be the same for each scenario until we change them.

3. **In row 2 enter the titles Best Case, Base Case, and Worst Case, as shown in Figure 8-2.**

4. **Edit the inputs underneath each scenario.**

You can put whatever you think is likely, but in order to match the numbers to those in this example, enter the values as shown in Figure 8-2. Ignore column B for now.

Now you need to add the drop-down box at the top, which is going to drive your scenarios. It doesn't really matter where exactly you put the drop-down box, but it should be in a location that's easy to find, usually at the top of the page.

5. **In cell E1, enter the title** Scenario:.

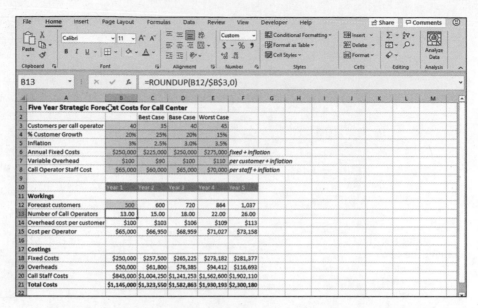

FIGURE 8-2: Setting up the inputs for scenario analysis.

B13 =ROUNDUP(B12/$B$3,0)

Five Year Strategic Forecast Costs for Call Center

	Best Case	Base Case	Worst Case	
Customers per call operator	40	35	40	45
% Customer Growth	20%	25%	20%	15%
Inflation	3%	2.5%	3.0%	3.5%
Annual Fixed Costs	$250,000	$225,000	$250,000	$275,000	fixed + inflation
Variable Overhead	$100	$90	$100	$110	per customer + inflation
Call Operator Staff Cost	$65,000	$60,000	$65,000	$70,000	per staff + inflation

	Year 1	Year 2	Year 3	Year 4	Year 5
Workings					
Forecast customers	500	600	720	864	1,037
Number of Call Operators	13.00	15.00	18.00	22.00	26.00
Overhead cost per customer	$100	$103	$106	$109	$113
Cost per Operator	$65,000	$66,950	$68,959	$71,027	$73,158
Costings					
Fixed Costs	$250,000	$257,500	$265,225	$273,182	$281,377
Overheads	$50,000	$61,800	$76,385	$94,412	$116,693
Call Staff Costs	$845,000	$1,004,250	$1,241,253	$1,562,600	$1,902,110
Total Costs	$1,145,000	$1,323,550	$1,582,863	$1,930,193	$2,300,180

6. **Select cell F1, and change the formatting to input so that the user can see that this cell is editable.**

The easiest way to do this is to follow these steps:

- Click one of the cells that is already formatted as an input, such as cell E3.

- Press the Format Painter icon in the Clipboard section on the left-hand side of the Home tab. Your cursor will change to a paintbrush.

- Select cell F1 to paste the formatting.

TIP

Format Painter is normally for single use. After you've selected the cell, the paintbrush will disappear from the cursor. If you want the Format Painter to become "sticky" and apply to multiple cells, double-click the icon when you select it from the Home tab.

7. **Now, in cell F1, select Data Validation from the Data Tools section of the Data tab.**

The Data Validation dialog box appears.

8. **On the Settings tab, change the Allow drop-down to List, use the mouse to select the range** =$C$2 : $E$2 **(see Figure 8-3), and click OK.**

9. **Click the drop-down box, which now appears next to cell F1, and select one of the scenarios (for example, Base Case).**

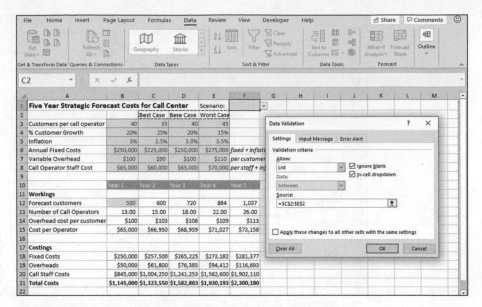

FIGURE 8-3:
Creating the data validation drop-down scenarios.

The spreadsheet shows:

	A	B	C	D	E	F
1	Five Year Strategic Forecast Costs for Call Center				Scenario:	
2			Best Case	Base Case	Worst Case	
3	Customers per call operator	40	35	40	45	
4	% Customer Growth	20%	25%	20%	15%	
5	Inflation	3%	2.5%	3.0%	3.5%	
6	Annual Fixed Costs	$250,000	$225,000	$250,000	$275,000	fixed + inflati
7	Variable Overhead	$100	$90	$100	$110	per customer
8	Call Operator Staff Cost	$65,000	$60,000	$65,000	$70,000	per staff + in
9						
10			Year 1	Year 2	Year 3	Year 4	Year 5
11	Workings					
12	Forecast customers	500	600	720	864	1,037
13	Number of Call Operators	13.00	15.00	18.00	22.00	26.00
14	Overhead cost per customer	$100	$103	$106	$109	$113
15	Cost per Operator	$65,000	$66,950	$68,959	$71,027	$73,158
16						
17	Costings					
18	Fixed Costs	$250,000	$257,500	$265,225	$273,182	$281,377
19	Overheads	$50,000	$61,800	$76,385	$94,412	$116,693
20	Call Staff Costs	$845,000	$1,004,250	$1,241,253	$1,562,600	$1,902,110
21	Total Costs	$1,145,000	$1,323,550	$1,582,863	$1,930,193	$2,300,180

Applying formulas to scenarios

The cells in column B are still driving the model, and these need to be replaced by formulas. Before you add the formulas, however, you should change the formatting of the cells in the range to show that they contain formulas, instead of hard-coded numbers. Follow these steps:

1. Select cells B3:B8, and select the Fill Color from the Font group on the Home tab.

2. Change the Fill Color to a white background.

REMEMBER

It's very important to distinguish between formulas and input cells in a model. You need to make it clear to any user opening the model that the cells in this range contain formulas and should not be overridden.

Now you need to replace the hard-coded values in column B with formulas that will change as the drop-down box changes. You can do this using a number of different functions; an HLOOKUP, a nested IF statement, an IFS, and a SUMIF will all do the trick. Add the formulas by following these steps:

1. Select cell B3, and add a formula that will change the value depending on what is in cell F1.

Here is what the formula will be under the different options:

- =SUMIF($C$2:$E$2,$F$1,C3:E3)

- =IF($F$1=$C$2,C3,IF($F$1=$D$2,D3,E3))

- `=IFS($F$1=$C$2,C3,$F$1=$D$2,D3,$F$1=$E$2,E3)` (Microsoft 365 only)

- `=XLOOKUP($F$1,$C$2:$E$2,C3:E3)` (Microsoft 365 only)

- `=HLOOKUP($F$1,$C$2:$E$8,2,0)`

Note that with this solution, you need to change the row index number from 2 to 3, and so on, as you copy the formula down. Instead, you could use a ROW function in the third field like this: `=HLOOKUP($F$1,$C$2:$E$8,ROW(A3)-1,0)`.

TIP

As always, there are several different options to choose from and the best solution is the one that is the simplest and easiest to understand. Any of these functions will produce exactly the same result, but in my opinion, having to change the row index number in the HLOOKUP is not robust, and adding the ROW may be confusing for a user. The nested IF statement is tricky to build and follow, and although the new IFS function is designed to make a nested IF function simpler, it's still rather unwieldy. I find the SUMIF quite simple to build and follow, and it's easy to expand if you need to add extra scenarios in the future.

WARNING

Note that IFS is a new function that is only available with Excel for Microsoft 365 and Excel 2016 or later installed. If you use this function and someone opens this model in a previous version of Excel, they can view the formula, but they won't be able to edit it.

2. **Copy the formula in cell B3 down the column.**

TIP

By using an ordinary copy and paste, you'll lose all your formatting. It's important to retain the formatting of the model so that you can see at a glance which inputs are in dollar values, percentages, or customer numbers. Use Paste Formulas to retain the formatting. You can access it by copying the cell onto the Clipboard, highlighting the destination range, right-clicking, and selecting the Paste Formulas icon to paste formulas only, and leave the formatting intact (see Figure 8-4).

Now for the fun part! It's time to test the scenario functionality in the model.

3. **Click cell F1, change the drop-down box, and watch the model outputs change as you toggle between the different scenarios, as shown in Figure 8-5.**

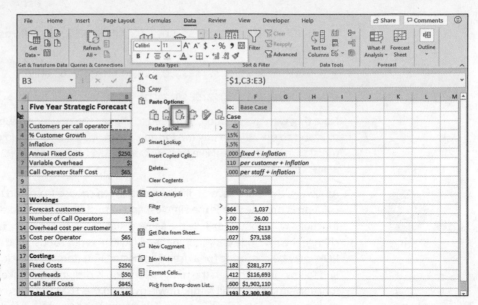

FIGURE 8-4:
Using Paste
Formulas to
retain formatting.

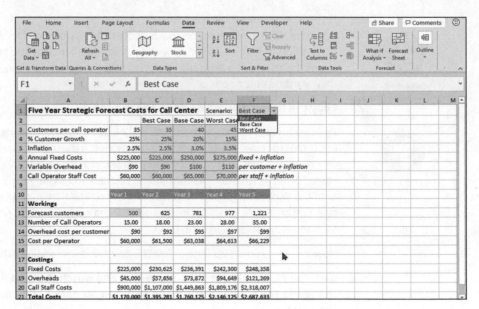

FIGURE 8-5:
The completed
scenario analysis.

Applying Sensitivity Analysis with Data Tables

Data tables are among the more advanced and complex financial modeling tools available. Data tables can be used for scenarios and sensitivity analysis, but they're less commonly used because they're more advanced. Data tables are unlike most other formulas in that you can't trace dependents, and they're very difficult to follow unless you're familiar with them. If anyone you work with doesn't know data tables, they won't be able to edit the table or make any changes.

Setting up the calculation

Let's go back to the profitability model you created in Chapter 6. I recommend that you work through the internal links exercise in Chapter 6, or download the completed version of this model, called File 0603.xlsx, from www.dummies.com/go/financialmodelinginexcelfd2e first so that you understand how this simple model works before adding sensitivities to it.

Because the model links directly to assumptions, you can use data tables to test the sensitivity of the profit margin to changes in assumptions such as the number of units sold and the cost per unit.

The existing model has a simple Income Statement linking to a number of input variables. You can test the sensitivity of one of the outputs, such as the profit margin, to variations in the input variables. Let's see how much the profit margin changes when the sales price and cost per unit inputs change. Of course, you could do this manually, but to see the various outputs in a single table, you need to use a data table.

Building a data table with one input

To create a data table in this model, follow these steps:

1. **Download** File 0802.xlsx **from** www.dummies.com/go/financial modelinginexcelfd2e, **open the file, and select the second tab.**

   You're testing how sensitive the profit margin is to changes in the sales price. The inputs for the sales price to be used in the data table have been entered in column A already. The next thing you need to do is to link the output cell to the data table. This needs to go at the top of the data table.

2. **Link cell B9 to the profit margin using the formula** =' Summary' !B9.

   Don't type this in — type **=** and then click the Summary tab, select cell B9, and press Enter.

3. **Highlight the entire data table in cells A9:B15, including the output cell, as shown in Figure 8-6.**

   Note that you must highlight all these cells in order for it to work.

4. **Select What-if Analysis from the Data tab and choose Data Table from the options (refer to Figure 8-6).**

   The Data Table dialog box appears.

   Because you're only doing a one-input data table, you only need to enter data for one variable, but which variable depends on how the data table is arranged and whether the input variable you're testing is in a row or a column. Because it's in a column, you should use the Column input cell field.

5. **Link the column input cell field to the input field for the sales price (cell A4) as shown in Figure 8-7.**

6. **Click OK.**

   Your data table populates with the completed sensitivity table, as shown in Figure 8-8.

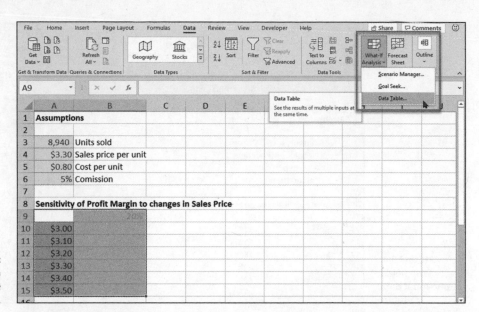

FIGURE 8-6:
Selecting the Data Table tool on the Ribbon.

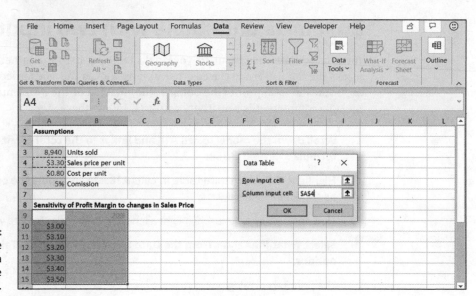

FIGURE 8-7:
Linking the one-input data table to the input cell.

Note that the formulas in the data table will have curly brackets around them like this =TABLE{,A4}. This is because it's an array formula. Array formulas work differently from ordinary formulas because array formulas treat the data like an array instead of a single data value. For this reason, you can't edit or delete a single cell within a data table in isolation. To make any changes, you need to use the Data Table tool or highlight all the formulas from cell B10 to B15, press Delete, and start again.

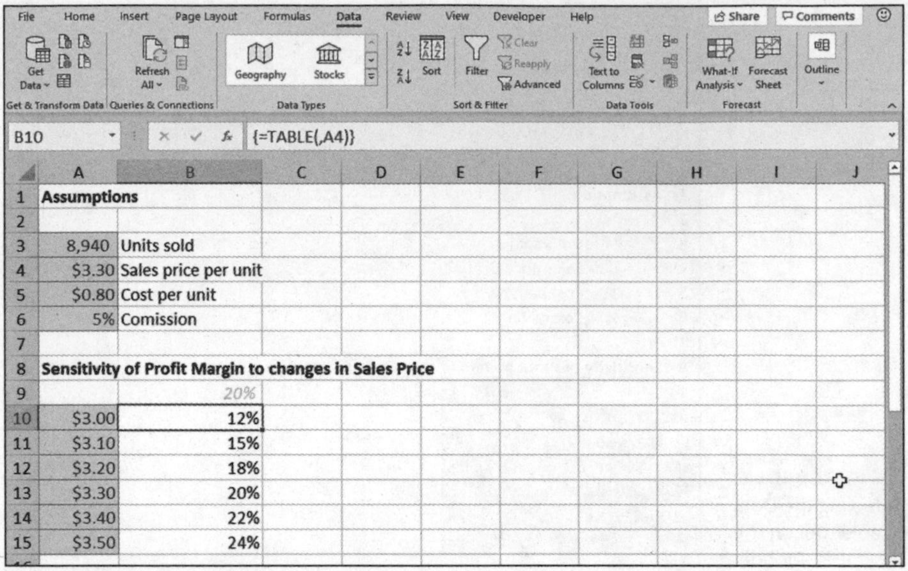

FIGURE 8-8:
Completed
one-input data
table.

Building a data table with two inputs

You can add another input to your data table by listing another input variable across the top. Let's add the cost per unit as well as the sales price, and this time, we'll test the total profit (the dollar value) instead of the profit margin (percentage). To complete this sensitivity analysis, follow these steps:

1. **Scroll down the model to cell A18 and link it to the total profit using the formula** =' Summary' ! B8.

2. **Highlight the entire data table in cells A18:E24, including the output cell, as shown in Figure 8-9.**

   Note that again, you must highlight all these cells in order for it to work.

3. **Select What-if Analysis from the Data tab and choose Data Table from the options.**

   The Data Table dialog box appears.

4. **Link the row input cell field to the input field for the cost per unit (A5) and the column field to the input field for the sales price (A4), as shown in Figure 8-9.**

5. **Click OK.**

   Your data table populates with the completed sensitivity table, as shown in Figure 8-10.

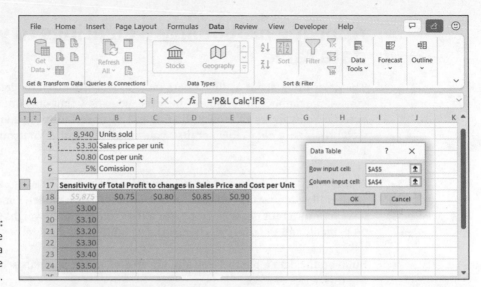

FIGURE 8-9:
Linking the two-input data table to the input cells.

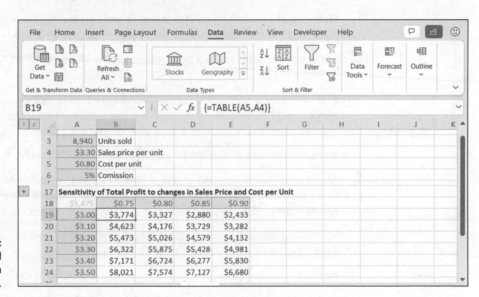

FIGURE 8-10:
Completed two-input data table.

TIP

Because data tables are an advanced feature of Excel, it may take you a few tries before you get the hang of them. Go through the practice examples a couple of times until you get it working, and then try it out on your own examples. The trickiest part is remembering which is the row input and which is the column input. Just remember that the dialog box is asking for the *original input* of the values that show in the column or in the row.

Applying probability weightings to your data table

The great thing about adding a data table to your financial model is that it gives you a large number of variables. However, you know that only one of these can be correct! You can try to reduce the amount of uncertainty by adding probability weightings to a data table because you know that not all outcomes are equally likely.

TIP

If you believe certain outcomes to be equally likely, then use the same weighting, while still retaining the probability functionality in the model. For example, if you have four different possible inputs for a data table, simply weight each of them at 25 percent, and the user can change the weighting inputs later.

Build on the data table that you already created in the previous section by following this series of steps:

1. **Download** File 0803.xlsx **from** www.dummies.com/go/financial modelinginexcelfd2e, **open the file, and select the first tab.**

2. **Enter the probability of each outcome in row 18 and column A, as shown in Figure 8-11.**

You may enter any weighting you like as long as the weightings add to 100 percent, but I recommend that you enter the same inputs as those shown in Figure 8-11 so that you can check that the output is accurate.

A check total has been added for you already in cells G18 and A26.

3. **Make sure that both column A and row 18 add to 100 percent, and add an error check that will alert the user if it does not because the model will be inaccurate if it does not tally.**

You can do this as follows: In cell G19, enter the formula **=1-G18**, as shown in Figure 8-11, and in cell B26 add the formula **=1-A26**.

Now add the data table just as you did in the last section.

4. **Link B19 to the output cell using the formula** = 'Summary' !B8.

5. **Highlight the entire range B19:F25.**

6. **Select the What-if Analysis from the Data tab and choose Data Table from the options.**

The Data Table dialog box appears.

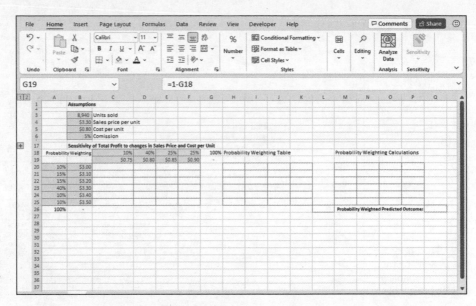

FIGURE 8-11:
Setting up the data table to add probability weightings.

7. **Link the row field to the input field for the cost per unit (B5) and the column field to the input field for the sales price (B4) and compare your results to those in Figure 8-12.**

   After you've finished the data table, you need to multiply out the probability weightings into the table so that you can work out how likely each outcome is.

8. **In cell H20, add the formula** =C$18*$A20.

   Don't forget your mixed cell referencing (see Chapter 6).

9. **Copy this formula across the block of data and then down to cell K25 and compare your results to those in Figure 8-12.**

   The total should add to 100 percent.

10. **Add an error check in cell L27 with the formula** =1-L26.

    When the data table and the probability weighting table have been built, you can use the results to calculate the probability-weighted outcomes.

11. **In cell M20, add the formula** =H20*C20.

    There is no need to add cell referencing for this calculation.

12. **Copy this formula across the block of data to cell P25 and compare your results to those in Figure 8-13.**

13. **In cell Q26, add the entire table together with the formula** =SUM(M20:P25)**, as shown in Figure 8-13.**

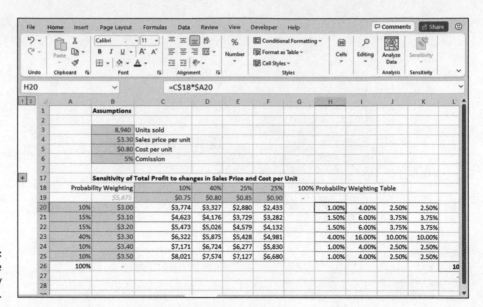

FIGURE 8-12:
Building the probability weighting table.

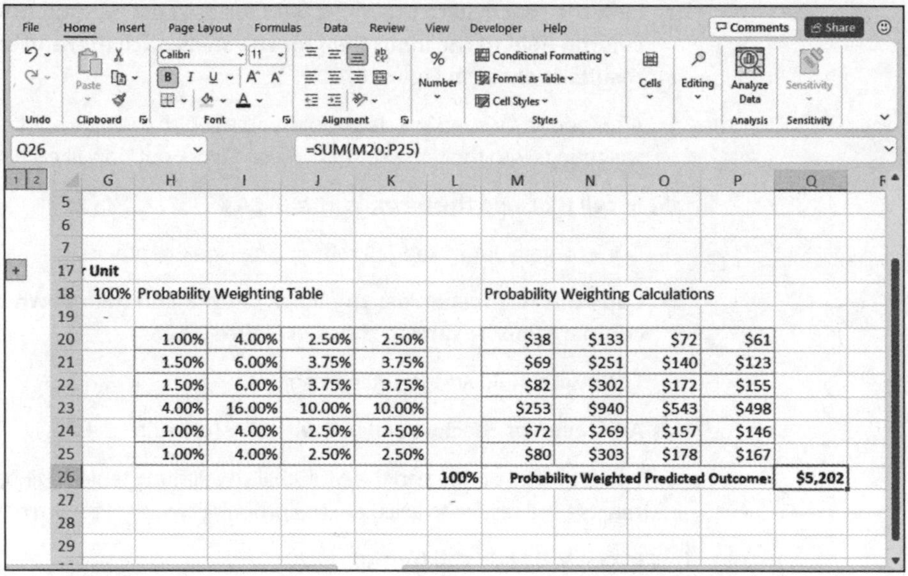

FIGURE 8-13:
Completed probability-weighted predicted outcome.

The calculated result is $5,202, which is the probability-weighted predicted outcome of this model. If you'd like to see a completed copy of this model, download File 0804.xlsx from www.dummies.com/go/financialmodelinginexcelfd2e.

THE LIMITATIONS OF DATA TABLES

You can see from the examples in this section that data tables are a great way to look at multiple scenarios or sensitivity analyses one at a time. Instead of manually changing the sales price or the cost per unit, you can display at a glance the impact of these changes.

However, data tables have a couple of limitations that make them inappropriate for some scenarios or sensitivity analysis situations:

- The inputs and outputs need to be on the same page.
- You can show only two inputs and one output at a time. This is not a restriction with other forms of scenario analysis.
- Formula auditing (trace precedents and trace dependents) doesn't work very well in data tables.

Data tables are extremely useful when you want to see the incremental change of one or two inputs on a single output. Data tables aren't appropriate if the output of your financial model is a full set of financial statements, for example. In this situation, a drop-down scenario would be best.

Using Scenario Manager to Model Loan Calculations

Scenario Manager is grouped together with Goal Seek and Data Tables in the What-If Analysis section of the Data tab. Being grouped with other tools that are so useful would lead you to believe that Scenario Manager is also a critical tool to know. However, despite its useful-sounding name and the good company it keeps, Scenario Manager is quite limited in its functionality and isn't as helpful as the name suggests! It's therefore not frequently used by expert financial modelers; however, for the sake of completeness, I cover it here very briefly.

Setting up the model

To demonstrate how to use Scenario Manager, let's apply it to a simple loan calculation model. The theory behind loan calculations is quite complex, but fortunately, Excel handles loans quite easily.

In the example shown in Figure 8-14, I've created an interest rate calculator upon which you can test the sensitivity of monthly repayments to changes in interest rates and loan terms. Follow these steps:

1. **Download** File 0804.xlsx **at** www.dummies.com/go/financial modelinginexcelfd2e, **open it, and select the first tab, or simply set up the model with hard-coded input assumptions as shown in Figure 8-14.**

2. **In cell B11, type** =PMT(**and press Ctrl+A.**

The Function Arguments dialog box appears.

The PMT function requires the following inputs:

- **Rate:** The interest rate.

- **Nper:** The number of periods over the life of the loan.

- **Pv:** The present value of the loan (the amount borrowed).

- **Fv:** The amount left at the end of the loan period. (In most cases, you want to pay the entire amount back during the loan period, so you can leave this blank.)

- **Type:** Whether you want the payments to occur at the beginning or the end of the period. (You can leave this blank for the purposes of this exercise.)

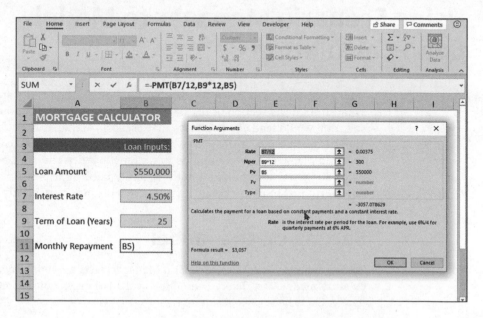

FIGURE 8-14:
Setting up the PMT function to calculate monthly loan repayments.

3. **Link the fields in the Function Arguments dialog box to the inputs in your model.**

TIP

The PMT function returns the *annual* repayment amount. Because you want to calculate the *monthly* repayment amount, you could simply divide the entire formula by 12, but because the interest is compounding, it's more accurate to divide each field by 12 within the formula. So, the rate in the first field is converted to a monthly rate, and the number of periods in the second field is also converted to a monthly rate.

4. **Click OK.**

The formula is =PMT(B7/12,B9*12,B5).

This function returns a negative value because this is an expense. For our purposes, change it to a positive value by preceding the function with the minus sign.

Applying Scenario Manager

Now you can use Scenario Manager to add some scenarios. You want to know the impact of changes in inputs on your monthly repayments. Follow these steps:

1. **On the Data tab, in the Forecast section of the Ribbon, click the What-if Analysis icon, and select Scenario Manager from the drop-down list.**

The Scenario Manager dialog box appears.

2. **Click the Add button to create a new scenario.**

The Add Scenario dialog box, shown in Figure 8-15, appears.

3. **Enter a name for the first scenario in the Scenario Name box (for example, Scenario One).**

4. **Enter the cell references for the variable cells in the Changing Cells box, as shown in Figure 8-15.**

Separate each reference with a comma (if there is more than one), but don't use spaces. You can also hold down the Ctrl key and click each cell in the spreadsheet to insert the references into the box.

5. **Click OK.**

The Scenario Values dialog box appears with the existing values (0.045 for the interest rate and 25 for the years).

6. **Click OK to accept these values as Scenario One.**

7. **Click Add to add another scenario.**

The Add Scenario dialog box appears again.

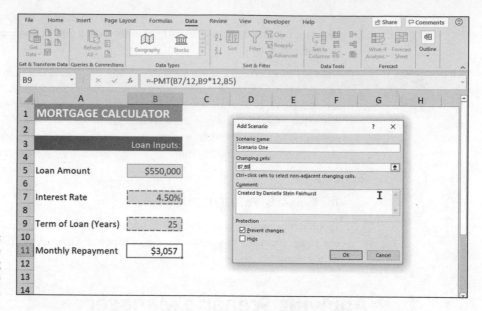

FIGURE 8-15:
Building the scenario using Scenario Manager.

8. **Enter a name for the second scenario in the Scenario Name box (for example, Scenario Two).**

9. **Click OK.**

   The Scenario Values dialog box appears again.

10. **Enter the variables' values for this scenario (for example, 0.05 for the interest rate and 20 for the years, as shown in Figure 8-16).**

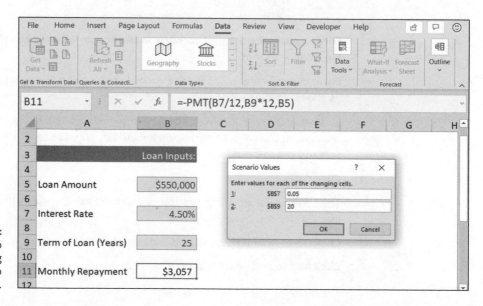

FIGURE 8-16:
Entering scenario values using Scenario Manager.

11. Click OK.

You're returned to the Scenario Manager dialog box.

12. Follow Steps 7 through 9 again to create additional scenarios.

13. After you've created all the scenarios, you can use the Scenario Manager to view each scenario, as shown in Figure 8-17, by clicking the Show button at the bottom.

The inputs are automatically changed to show the scenarios.

REMEMBER

Scenarios are sheet–specific, meaning they only exist in the sheet where you created them. So when you're looking for the scenarios you've created, you have to select the correct sheet in the model.

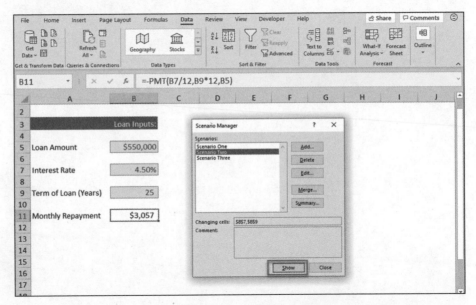

FIGURE 8-17:
The completed Scenario Manager.

THE LIMITATIONS OF SCENARIO MANAGER

Scenario Manager is fairly easy to build and use, but it's a rudimentary tool that simply changes hard-coded numbers. It isn't very easy to see, display, or print the different options unless you go into the Scenario Manager tool. Using the Summary tool creates a summary report of the scenarios created, but they aren't dynamic or interactive, so they're of little use as a modeling tool. The biggest downfall of Scenario Manager is that the user can't see the results on the sheet unless they actually go in to view the scenarios.

Chapter **9**

Charting and Presenting Model Output

The final stage of the model-building process is to present the outcome of the model. You've spent a lot of time on the calculations, making sure that the inputs and assumptions are correct and that all your scenarios are lined up ready for the decision makers to use. If you don't present the outputs of the model clearly, however, the users won't be able to understand what the model is showing, so they might not use it or, even worse, they might use it and misinterpret what the model is saying.

A well-designed report or presentation is the best way to display the model results clearly and concisely and get its message across. The output and presentation of the results are just as important as the rest of the model-building process. There's no point in having a beautifully designed, fantastically built model that none of the decision makers know (or care) about!

In this chapter, I walk you through conveying your model's output to an audience to ensure all your modeling efforts are put to good use.

Deciding Which Data to Display

The output of your financial model may be very detailed and contain a myriad of numbers, colors, and confusing calculations. A common mistake is to try to put as much information as possible into one chart in an attempt to make it look impressive. In reality, the chart just looks cluttered and fails to get the message across.

REMEMBER

Charts are built for the purpose of presenting information that is easier to digest visually than the raw data. Sometimes two charts may be easier for your audience to digest than one chart. For some tips on designing the output layout and using colors, see Chapter 3.

TIP

If you're not sure what data will look like visually, you can highlight it and press F11 to display an "instant chart" on a new tab.

Creating a summary sheet with visuals will help the viewer make sense of the financial model, but deciding which data to display is difficult. Your decision of what to show will depend on a couple of factors:

>> **What is your key message?** Sometimes the reason that you built the financial model in the first place is to convey a particular message to the audience — for example, "Supply costs are escalating. We need to increase pricing or risk eroding profits." In this example, you would show the supply cost per unit over time, versus the price over time, highlighting the key message for the decision maker.

>> **What is your audience interested in?** Sometimes you've built a model for a particular purpose, but you know that the audience is particularly interested in a certain cost or ratio, so this is what you need to highlight in your output report.

Let's look at the example shown in Chapter 8, where you create a five-year strategy for a call center with three scenarios. You can download File 0901.xlsx at www.dummies.com/go/financialmodelinginexcelfd2e and select the tab labeled 9-1 to see the model shown in Figure 9-1.

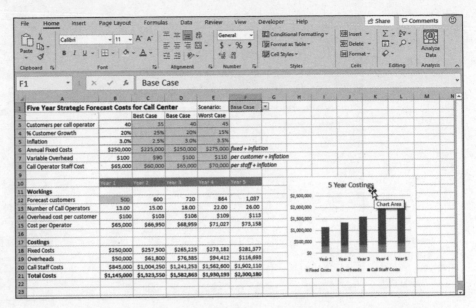

FIGURE 9-1:
Completed five-year model with costings chart.

The model calculates the costings for the next five years under different drop-down scenarios. To create a summary of the model's output, you have to decide which data to display. If you know that the audience is only interested in the cost-ings section, you can create a chart based on the costings data at the bottom of the page, as shown in Figure 9-1. For instructions on how to build this chart, see the "Bar charts" section, later in this chapter.

This case study is based on a simplified version of a model I built for a real-life client of mine. I know that the client was actually interested in the cost to serve each customer — finding this out was one of the purposes of building this model in the first place. So, add the cost per customer in row 24 with the formula =B21/B12 and copy it across the row.

The chart shows the cost per customer, as well as the forecast number of custom-ers, so you can see that although the number of customers increases steadily, the cost per customer fluctuates over the five-year period, as shown in Figure 9-2. For instructions on how to build this chart, see the "Combo charts" section, later in this chapter.

You can see in this case study that deciding which data to display can depend on what the message of the model is, as well as what the audience is interested in.

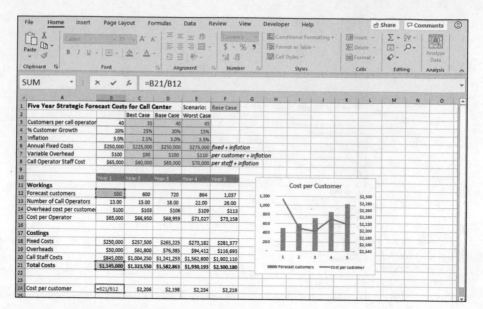

FIGURE 9-2:
Completed
five-year model
with cost per
customer chart.

Conveying Your Message by Charting Scenarios

As I mention in Chapter 8, the major limitation of drop-down scenarios such as the one built in the preceding section is that you can't see multiple scenarios side by side. The outputs of the five-year forecast model shown in Figure 9-2 only show the cost per customer under the base case scenario. To show the cost per customer under different scenarios, you need to change the scenario drop-down box in cell F1 — but you'll only be able to look at one scenario at a time.

To add a data table that will allow you to see the cost per customer of all three scenarios side by side, follow these steps:

1. Add the three scenario names — "Best Case," "Base Case," and "Worst Case" — below the Cost per Customer, as shown in Figure 9-3.

WARNING

Make sure that you spell the names correctly, and don't add trailing spaces or the data table won't work.

2. Select cells C2:E2 and press Ctrl+C.

3. Select cell A25, right-click, and select Paste Special ⇨ Transpose to paste the names in cells A25:A27 with exactly the same spelling.

4. Highlight cells A24:F27 (refer to Figure 9-3).

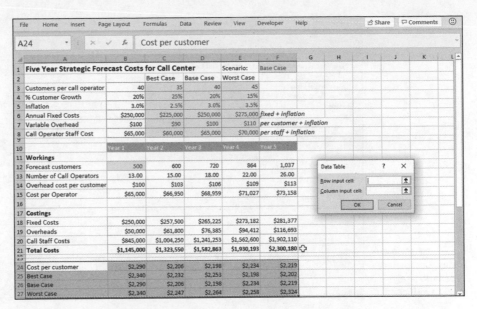

FIGURE 9-3:
Completing the
data table.

5. **On the Data tab of the Ribbon, in the Forecast group, select Data Table under the What-If Analysis button to display the Data Table dialog box (refer to Figure 9-3).**

   Because the variable you're changing is arranged in column A, you need to tell the Data Table dialog box where the *original* input is for the column, which is the Scenario cell in F1.

6. **Under the Column input cell field, select cell F1 (refer to Figure 9-3).**

REMEMBER

You can only show one output in a data table, so you chose to show the cost per customer only. If you want to show other values, you need to create additional data tables.

Now that you have the scenario results, they can be displayed in a line chart, as shown in Figure 9-4. For instructions on how to build this chart, see the "Line charts" section, later in this chapter.

The key message from this model can be seen in this chart. You can see that the cost per customer varies depending on the scenario, and the Best Case scenario doesn't necessarily mean that you'll experience a lower cost per customer.

TIP

Because the data table needs to be arranged in a single block, you can't insert a row above the scenario outputs to show that these are the results of the scenario analysis. You can change the formatting of row 24 and add the title "Scenario Analysis" in row 23 for clarity (refer to Figure 9-4).

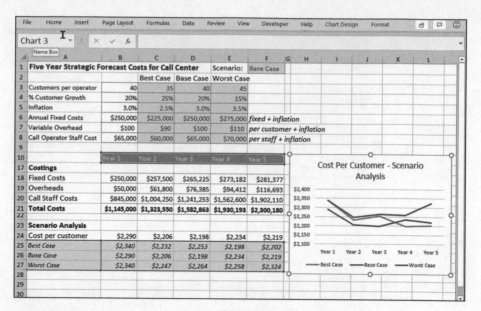

FIGURE 9-4:
Completed
scenario analysis
with chart.

Deciding Which Type of Chart to Use

When deciding how to display the output of your model, you have a lot of choices, especially in the later versions of Excel because they keep adding new charts to standard Excel. Looking back through the financial models I've created in the past couple of years, around 80 percent of them contain only one of the following charts:

» Line or area chart

» Bar or column chart

» Combo chart

» Pie or doughnut (less frequently used)

As with most elements of building a financial model, charting the output should be clear and straightforward, simple and easy to understand. If you can get your message across in a simple way, that's best. In some situations, though, you need to show more complex visualizations such as Waterfalls, Bubble charts, or Hierarchy charts, like a Treemap.

Of course, many more charts are available in Excel, but in this section, I stick to these because they're by far the most commonly used in financial modeling.

If you don't want to create a whole line chart, column chart, or bar chart to show your data, you can use a Sparkline instead. As I mention in Chapter 2, this is a new feature that was introduced back in Excel 2010. It shows the trend of the data in a tiny line or bar chart that fits into a single cell, as shown in Figure 9-5. Sparklines can be accessed via the Sparklines section of the Insert tab on the Ribbon.

	Year 1	Year 2	Year 3		Year 5	
10						
11 **Workings**						
12 Forecast customers	500	600		864	1,037	
13 Number of Call Operators	13.00	15.00	18.00	22.00	26.00	
14 Overhead cost per customer	$100	$103	$106	$109	$113	
15 Cost per Operator	$65,000	$66,950	$68,959	$71,027	$73,158	
16						
17 **Costings**						
18 Fixed Costs	$250,000	$257,500	$265,225	$273,182	$281,377	
19 Overheads	$50,000	$61,800	$76,385	$94,412	$116,693	
20 Call Staff Costs	$845,000	$1,004,250	$1,241,253	$1,562,600	$1,902,110	
21 **Total Costs**	**$1,145,000**	**$1,323,550**	**$1,582,863**	**$1,930,193**	**$2,300,180**	
22						
23 **Scenario Analysis**						
24 Cost per customer	$2,290	$2,206	$2,198	$2,234	$2,219	
25 *Best Case*	*$2,340*	*$2,232*	*$2,253*	*$2,198*	*$2,202*	
26 *Base Case*	*$2,290*	*$2,206*	*$2,198*	*$2,234*	*$2,219*	
27 *Worst Case*	*$2,340*	*$2,247*	*$2,264*	*$2,258*	*$2,324*	
28						
29						

FIGURE 9-5:
Sparklines.

Deciding which chart type to use is often just a matter of trial and error. Take a look at the data in a few different ways and see which chart makes the most impact and tells your model's story most effectively.

When deciding which chart to choose, highlight the data, and select Recommended Charts from the Charts section of the Insert tab on the Ribbon, as shown in Figure 9-6. This feature was introduced in Excel 2013, and it helps to visualize the data.

Line charts

Line charts are most appropriate for indicating trends. Like column charts, the simplicity of line charts makes them one of the favorites in displaying data. Column and line charts can be used interchangeably to display the same data, but line charts are normally used when there is a connection between the points on the x-axis, such as times or dates on a continuum. Line charts are best used for trending information such as time series, and columns are better for showing comparisons.

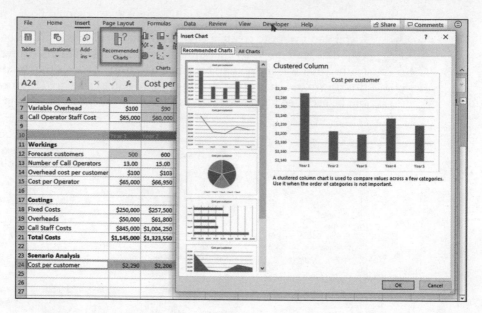

FIGURE 9-6:
Recommended
Charts.

In Excel, you also have stacked line and 100-percent stacked line chart options. Sometimes line charts convey information in a more meaningful manner when the data points are marked.

To build a line chart, such as the one shown in Figure 9-7, highlight the data, and simply select the first 2-D Line option from the Charts section of the Insert tab on the Ribbon, as shown in Figure 9-7.

TIP

The easiest way to add the labels on the x-axis in the chart in Figure 9-7 is to include the data in row 10 when creating the chart in the first place. To highlight data in nonconsecutive ranges, hold down the Ctrl key while highlighting with the mouse.

Move the chart across so that it isn't obscuring the data behind it, and add a label.

Take a closer look at the chart you just built. It looks attractive, but which scenario is shown by which line? Grasping the meaning is difficult, particularly if you're looking at the chart in black and white! Take a moment to put yourself in the viewer's shoes and see if your message is unambiguously clear. Not really, is it? By putting the legend at the bottom — even if the colors are showing — it's really difficult to figure out which line is which, so the viewer's eyes need to go backward and forward trying to understand the meaning.

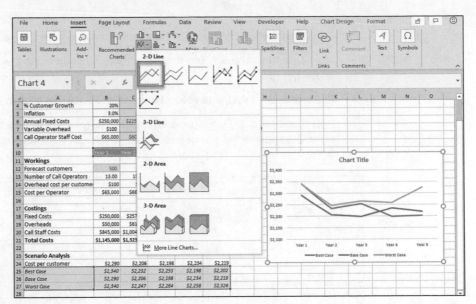

FIGURE 9-7:
Creating a line chart.

Instead of using a legend at the bottom, let's put the series names next to each line so that the chart will be easier to interpret. To do this, follow these steps:

1. Right-click one of the lines with the mouse.

2. Select Add Data Labels and then Add Data Labels again, as shown in Figure 9-8.

The data values appear. Don't worry — we're going to change that.

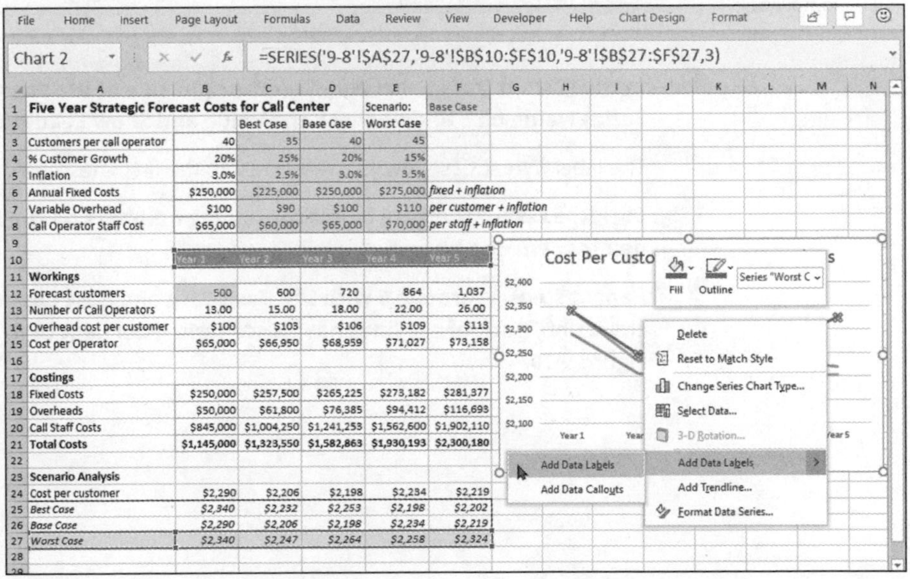

FIGURE 9-8:
Adding data labels to the line chart.

3. **Click the label on the far right-hand side (the one with the value $2,324).**

   Make sure that's the only one that's been selected; otherwise, it won't work properly.

4. **Right-click the label, and select Format Data Label, as shown in Figure 9-9.**

   Note that it must say Label (singular), not Labels (plural), because that would mean the entire series has been selected, which isn't what you want to do.

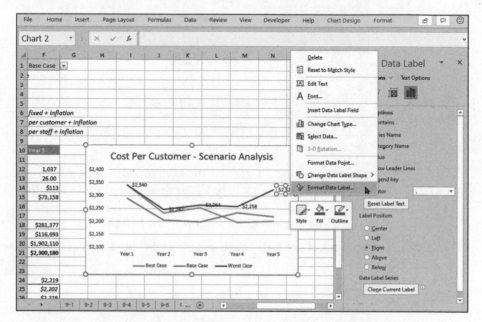

FIGURE 9-9:
Formatting the
data label.

5. **In the Format Data Label panel on the right side of the screen, check the Series Name box, and uncheck the Value and Show Leader Lines boxes.**

   The label "Worst Case" now appears next to the first line.

6. **Click the rest of the data labels containing numbers on the line, and delete them one by one.**

7. **Repeat steps 1 through 6 with the Base Case and Best Case lines on the chart until each of the lines has its scenario label next to it, as shown in Figure 9-10.**

8. Adjust the chart sizing as necessary, and move the labels so that each is next to the correct line.

Don't mix them up!

9. Remove the legend at the bottom of the chart and remove the gridlines if you wish by clicking them and pressing Delete.

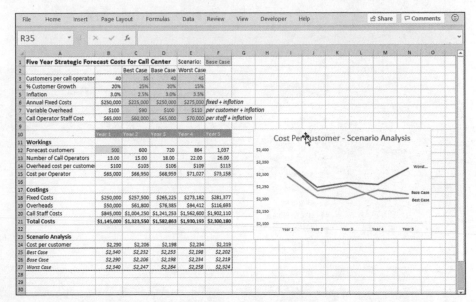

CHANGING A LINE CHART TO A STACKED AREA CHART

If the data you're displaying is continuous, such as in a time series, but it needs to be stacked, you can consider using a stacked line or stacked area chart. In the example where the three scenarios are shown as alternatives to each other, stacking them on top of one another doesn't make sense. If, however, you're looking at profitability from different products, for example, and you want to see how much each product contributes to a total, then stacking the chart would make sense.

To demonstrate the use of a stacked area chart, take a look at the case study from Chapter 3 where you looked at the contribution of different bus routes to the total for the purpose of evaluating the different scenarios. You can download the model in File 0302.xlsx at www.dummies.com/go/financialmodelinginexcelfd2e.

(continued)

(continued)

To change a line chart to a stacked area chart, right-click the chart and select Change Chart Type. Select the Stacked Area option, as shown in the figure.

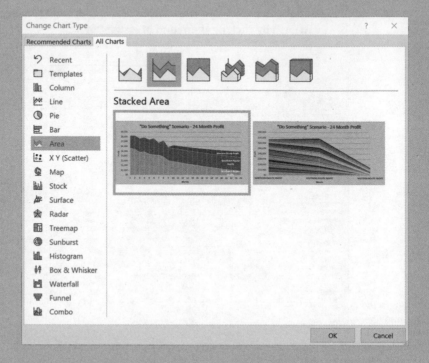

Note that in this area chart, I've also added the series name to label each route as described earlier, in the "Line charts" section.

TIP

Lining up the labels by hand is quite tricky. If you don't get them aligned properly, it can look messy. Try holding down the Alt key when you move the label — this will "snap to grid," which helps with alignment. Note that this method works with other objects such as whole charts, shapes, and images and in other programs, too.

Bar charts

Bar or column charts are one of the most commonly-used chart types available in Excel, second only to perhaps the line chart in their use in financial modeling. Bar charts are most useful for comparing unrelated data points graphically. They're very clear and easy to understand. When shown vertically, bar charts are sometimes called column charts. Horizontal bar charts represent exactly the same information as column charts from a different perspective. Most commonly, bar charts are used to represent time or future projections along the x-axis.

To build a simple bar chart with only one series, highlight the data, and simply select the first 2-D Column option from the Charts section of the Insert tab on the Ribbon.

To build a stacked bar chart, highlight all the data, including the series names and the years, as shown in Figure 9-11 (remember to hold down the Ctrl key to select nonconsecutive ranges), and select the stacked column (the second 2-D Column option) from the Charts section of the Insert tab on the Ribbon. Edit the title.

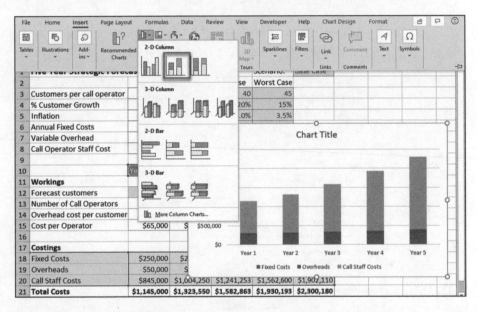

FIGURE 9-11: Building a stacked bar chart.

TIP

You may have noticed that there isn't a lot of difference in terms of the design between a stacked bar chart and a stacked area chart (see the "Changing a line chart to a stacked area chart" sidebar). Which option you choose is a matter of personal preference. Play around with your chart, trying a number of different chart types to see which shows the data best.

WARNING

Some data visualization specialists advise against the use of a stacked column chart because it makes the top columns difficult to compare because the bases don't start at the same value. I like to see the total amount as well as the breakdown, so although I appreciate that it can sometimes make comparison difficult, I still use stacked bar charts quite a lot when displaying the output of my financial models. You can try using a clustered column instead — that facilitates a better comparison. But with too many series, clustered columns can quickly become cluttered.

ADDING A DATA TABLE TO A BAR CHART

Data shown visually will always get the message across more clearly to the viewer, but as a financial modeler, I also like to see the numbers. In a stacked bar chart like the one shown in the figure, displaying the numbers in a table below will add more information, which is appreciated by numbers people like me.

Note: A data table added below a chart should not be confused with a data table performed for the purposes of sensitivity analysis, as described earlier in this chapter. Yes, Excel has two entirely different features with exactly the same name!

To add a data table to a chart, follow these steps:

1. **Click the chart, and press the Chart Elements button on the right, as shown in the figure.**

2. **Check the Data Table option.**

3. **The legend is now showing in the data table, so delete the one at the bottom, which is no longer required.**

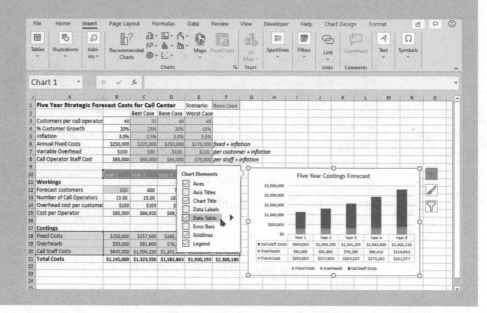

Combo charts

One of my favorite ways of showing different metrics in a single chart is to use a combination of bar and line chart types, which Excel calls a combo chart. I like combo charts because they can convey a lot of information without cluttering the chart. When you want to display as much information as possible in a small amount of space without making the graphic seem cluttered, combo charts are the answer.

You can also show correlations and make a point about cause and effect in your financial model simply and effectively with combo charts. For example, in the chart shown in Figure 9-12, the number of customers is increasing steadily, whereas the cost per customer changes erratically, making the point that just because demand increases, the cost per customer does not see any economies of scale as a result.

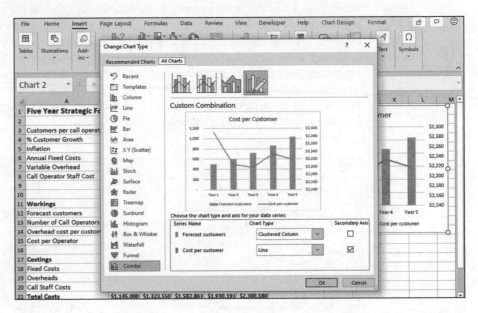

FIGURE 9-12: Building a combo chart.

The combo chart does not appear on the Ribbon, so to build a combo chart, follow these steps:

1. **Highlight the data, including the series titles (by holding down the Ctrl key to highlight nonconsecutive ranges) and select Recommended Chart from the Charts section of the Insert tab on the Ribbon.**

    The Insert Chart dialog box appears.

2. Click the All Charts tab.

3. Click the Combo icon at the bottom, and select the Clustered Column – Line on Secondary Axis option (refer to Figure 9-12).

4. Select the Cost per Customer Secondary Axis check box (refer to Figure 9-12).

Its data will now appear on the secondary axis on the right side of the chart.

5. Click OK.

6. Edit the colors and the chart title.

If you want to change the cost per customer to show on the primary axis (on the left instead of the right), select the Forecast Customers check box instead of the Cost per Customer check box in the dialog box shown in Figure 9-12.

WARNING

When you create the combo chart, the secondary y-axis (on the right-hand side) has automatically defaulted to starting at $2,140. This makes the difference between the years more noticeable, but it can be misleading, so you might decide to change the axis to start at zero instead. To do this, double-click the numbers in the secondary axis (or right-click and select Format Axis) and when the Format Axis panel appears, change the Minimum bounds from 2410 to 0, as shown in Figure 9-13. Compare this to Figure 9-12. You can see that the chart has less impact when the axis starts at zero.

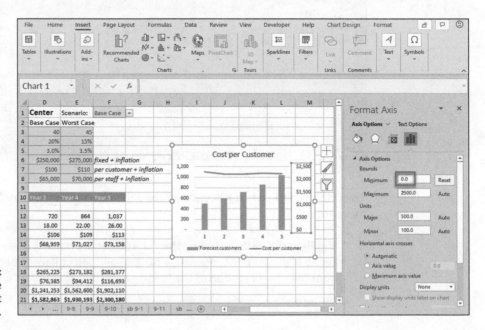

FIGURE 9-13:
Changing the
y-axis to start at
zero.

Try not to clutter the chart by adding too many series and, as always, look at the chart from your viewers' perspective and make sure your message is explicitly clear and understandable. In this example, it's fairly clear which axis contains which value because the secondary axis is formatted with dollars. But to make it even clearer, you might consider adding axis titles, which you can find under chart elements.

Pie charts

Pie charts have also been vilified in recent years because they make it even more difficult than stacked bar charts to compare data. Comparing the sizes of the different "slices" of the pie is extremely difficult. Pie charts aren't useful for comparison, or for time series. Particularly for dashboards where size is an issue, pie charts take up a lot of space without conveying much information. Pie charts *are* good, however, for displaying ratios or percentage information, such as market share or penetration. Pie charts are visually appealing, and I tend to use them when comparing only a few categories, such as male versus female.

To build a pie chart, highlight the data, including the series titles and simply select the first 2–D Pie option from the Charts section of the Insert tab on the Ribbon, as shown in Figure 9-14.

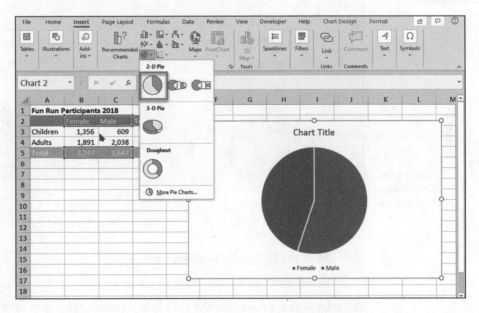

FIGURE 9-14:
Building a pie chart.

Edit the title, and you're done! Well, not quite. Take a closer look at the chart. Is it really clear which slice is male and which slice is female? Female is shown on the right, and male is on the left, but the data labels are the other way around. This happens sometimes in Excel, and it's not technically incorrect, but leaving the labels like this makes it much more difficult for someone to interpret the meaning of your data. Readers need to look very carefully to see which slice is which.

REMEMBER

Take time to check the outputs of the financial model, especially charts to make sure that the meaning and the message you want to get across can be easily inter-preted by others.

You can edit this chart so that it's easier to read and can be viewed properly in black and white by following these steps:

1. **Click the chart, and click the Chart Elements button on the right, as shown in Figure 9-15.**

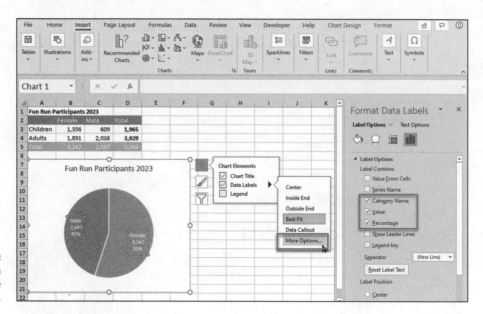

FIGURE 9-15:
Adding data labels to the pie chart.

2. **Check the Data Labels option.**

The value of each category appears on the pie chart.

3. **Hover the mouse over the Data Labels option again, and click the arrow that appears to the right.**

4. **Select More Options.**

The Format Data Labels panel appears at the right.

5. Check the Category Name, Value, and Percentage check boxes.

6. Change the Separator to "(New Line)."

Each of the labels is put on a separate line.

7. The legend is no longer required, so delete the one at the bottom, and add a chart title.

CHANGING A PIE CHART TO A DOUGHNUT CHART

Doughnut charts are another way of displaying exactly the same information as a pie chart. To change your pie chart to a doughnut chart, follow these steps:

1. Right-click the chart and select Change Chart Type.

2. Select the Doughnut Chart option, which is on the far right of the Pie section, and click OK.

The data labels don't look right, so play with some of the settings.

3. To change the size of the hole in the middle of the Doughnut, right-click the chart series and select Format Data Series, as shown in the figure.

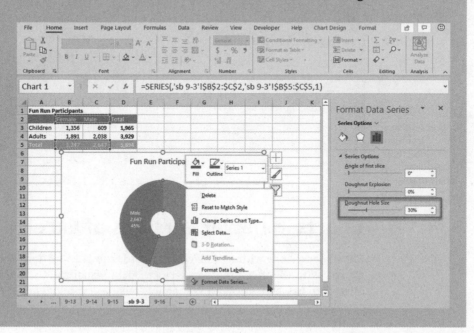

(continued)

(continued)

4. Reduce the hole size to around 30%.

The Doughnut hole size can be found in the Format Data Series panel on the right.

5. Reposition the data labels if necessary.

TECHNICAL STUFF

A doughnut chart is just a pie chart with a hole in the center. This difference may not seem significant at first, but this gap in the doughnut hole allows several series to be stacked in the same chart, which you couldn't do with a pie chart. Although this feature looks visually appealing, it's often misused and leads to confusing charts. To see this in action, add another series to the chart from earlier chart and overlay the male and female with the split between adult and children, as shown in Figure 9-16. This doesn't really tell you very much. A Sunburst chart, described later in this chapter, would be more useful in this situation.

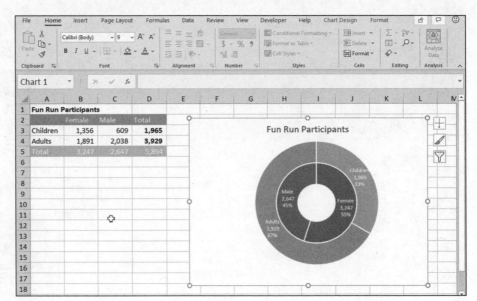

FIGURE 9-16:
A stacked doughnut chart (not recommended).

Charts in newer versions of Excel

The major change with later Excel versions is the introduction of a number of new charts. With the increased popularity of data visualization and graphic display, Microsoft has kept up with competing business intelligence and data analysis software by making it easier to create popular chart types in Excel. For more information about competing software and changes in Modern Excel, turn to Chapter 2.

As with most new features of Excel, the new charts aren't backward compatible. If, for example, you create a Sunburst in the current version, and someone tries to open it in a prior version, the chart will simply show as a blank area. So, make sure that your users have the same version of Excel as you do if you're planning to include newer Excel features such as these charts in your model.

Waterfall charts

Waterfall charts are very useful for displaying the output of financial models because they pull apart the pieces of a stacked chart and show their incremental effect side by side.

Take a look at the example shown in Figure 9-17. Showing an expense breakdown in a pie chart is not very helpful. Too many series are shown, and it's very difficult to compare each section without the help of the percentages shown in the data labels.

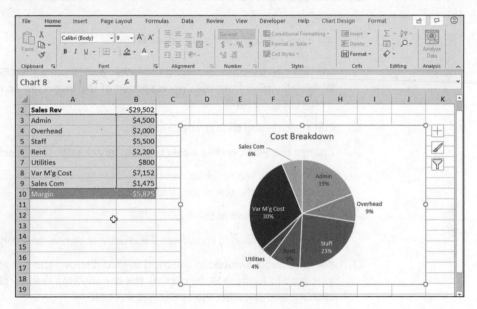

FIGURE 9-17:
A pie chart showing costs (not recommended).

This data is much better shown using a waterfall chart. Not only will you be able to see each of the cost categories side by side, but you'll be able to view the revenue amount and the margin as well for comparison. Download File 0901.xlsx from www.dummies.com/go/financialmodelinginexcelfd2e. Open it and select the tab labeled 9-18 or open a new workbook and enter the data as shown in Figure 9-18.

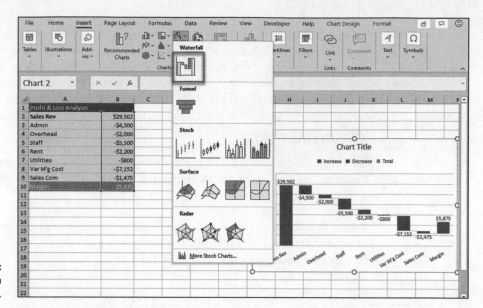

FIGURE 9-18:
Building a
waterfall chart.

To build a waterfall chart, follow these steps:

1. **Highlight all the data, including the labels and the margin, and select the Waterfall option from the Charts section of the Insert tab on the Ribbon (refer to Figure 9-18).**

2. **Edit the title and change the colors.**

3. **Change the labels on the *x*-axis so that they're orientated horizontally.**

   Showing labels at an angle makes the chart far more difficult to read. You may need to change the size of the chart to do this.

4. **Remove the legend at the top.**

   Everything you need to know from this chart is shown in the labels already.

5. **Set the margin amount as the total so that it shows the remainder only, as it does in Figure 9-19, by clicking the bar showing the margin, right-clicking, and selecting the option Set as Total.**

   This moves the margin column down so that it shows correctly against the *x*-axis, as shown in Figure 9-19.

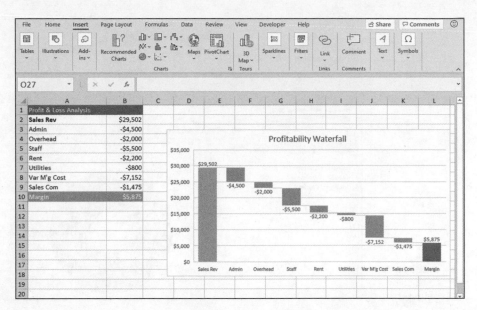

FIGURE 9-19:
A waterfall chart.

This waterfall chart won't appear if the file is opened in Excel 2013 or earlier. For instructions on how to build a waterfall chart using a "dummy stack" or up/down bars that can be opened and used in any version of Excel, go to www.plumsolutions. com.au/waterfalls.

REMEMBER

Sunburst charts

The stacked doughnut chart shown earlier in this chapter doesn't display gender and age data very well. If you have a hierarchical relationship within your data, you can use a hierarchical chart such as a Sunburst or Treemap.

To build a Sunburst chart, follow these steps:

1. **If necessary, reorganize your data so that it sits within hierarchical categories, as shown in Figure 9-20.**

2. **Highlight all the data, and select the Sunburst option from the Charts section of the Insert tab on the Ribbon.**

3. **Edit the title and change the colors.**

4. **Add the colors and edit the data labels, as shown in Figure 9-21.**

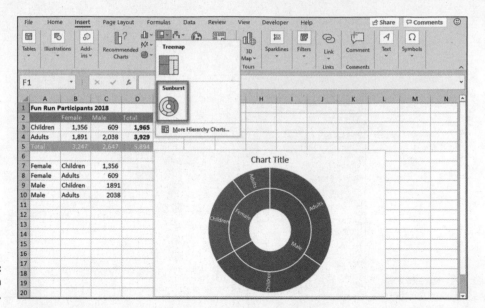

FIGURE 9-20:
Building a
Sunburst chart.

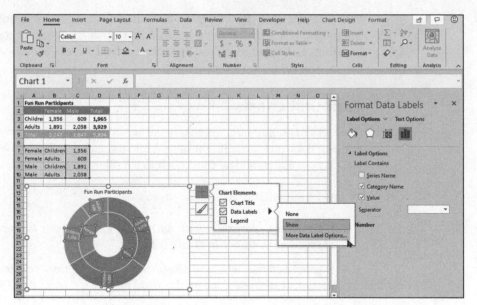

FIGURE 9-21:
A completed
Sunburst chart.

Treemap charts

A Treemap chart works in exactly the same way as the Sunburst, except that the segments are shown as squares instead of circles. The easiest way to change to a Treemap without having to change your settings again is to right-click the Sunburst, select Change Chart Type, and select the Treemap option, as shown in Figure 9-22.

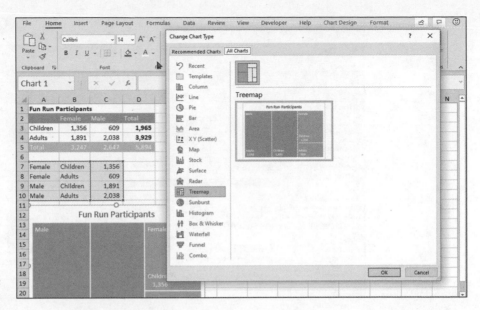

FIGURE 9-22:
A Treemap chart.

Although the Sunburst and Treemap charts show exactly the same data, be sure to try out both types to see which looks best with your data. In this example, the Sunburst looks better visually. If you had a larger number of series, however, the Treemap would probably be easier to understand.

TIP

Dynamic Charting

When you're creating charts in financial models or reports, you should still follow best practice and try to make your models as flexible and dynamic as you can. You should always link as much as possible in your models, and this goes for charts as well. It makes sense that when you change one of the inputs to your model, this should be reflected in the chart data, as well as the titles and labels.

Building the chart on formula-driven data

Take a look at the five-year strategic forecast model that you work on in the "Conveying Your Message by Charting Scenarios" section at the beginning of this chapter. Because the chart you built was based on formulas, the chart will automatically change when the drop-down box is changed. Download File 0901.xlsx from www.dummies.com/go/financialmodelinginexcelfd2e. Open it and select the tab labeled 9-23 to try it out for yourself, as shown in Figure 9-23.

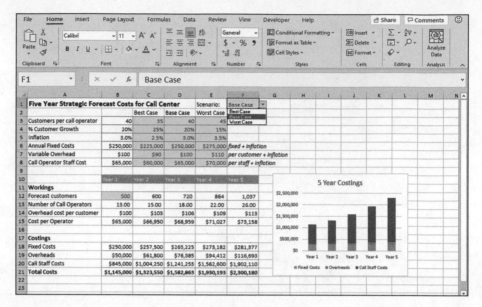

FIGURE 9-23:
Changing the
drop-down box.

WARNING

If you hide data in your source sheet, it won't show on the chart. Test this by hiding one of the columns on the Financials sheet and check that the month has disappeared on the chart. You can change the options under Select Data Source so that it displays hidden cells.

Linking the chart titles to formulas

Because all the data is linked to the drop-down box, you can easily create a dynamic title in the chart by creating a formula for the title and then linking that title to the chart. Follow these steps:

1. **In cell A1 of this model, change the title to the following:** =`"Five Year Strategic Forecast Costs for Call Center - "&F1.`

The ampersand (&) serves as a connector that will string text and values from formulas together.

TIP

Instead of the ampersand, you can also use the CONCATENATE function, which works very similarly by joining singular cells together, or the TEXTJOIN function is a new addition to Excel 2016, which will join together large quantities of data.

When you have the formula in cell A1 working, you need to link the title in the chart to cell A1.

2. **Click the title of the chart.**

This part can be tricky. Make sure you've only selected the chart title.

3. Click the formula bar.

4. Type = and then click cell A1, as shown in Figure 9-24.

5. Press Enter.

The chart title changes to show what is in cell A1.

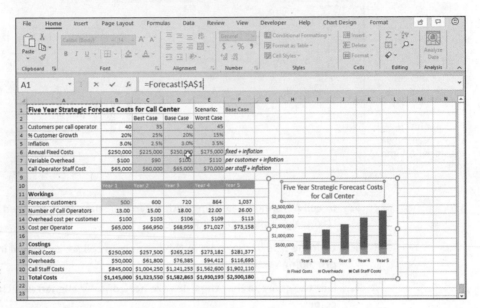

FIGURE 9-24:
Linking the chart
titles to formulas.

TIP

You can't insert any formulas into a chart. You can only link a single cell to it. All calculations need to be done in one cell and then linked to the title as shown.

Creating dynamic text

Take a look at the monthly budget report shown in Figure 9-25. We've already built formulas in columns F and G, which will automatically update as the data changes, and display how we're going compared to budget. (To see how to build this model, turn to Chapter 7.)

Now you'll create a chart based on this data, and every time the numbers change, you'll be able to see how many line items are over budget. Follow these steps:

1. Highlight the data showing the account, actual, and budget values in columns B, C, and D, respectively.

2. Select the first 2-D Column option from the Charts section of the Insert tab on the Ribbon to create a clustered column chart (refer to Figure 9-25).

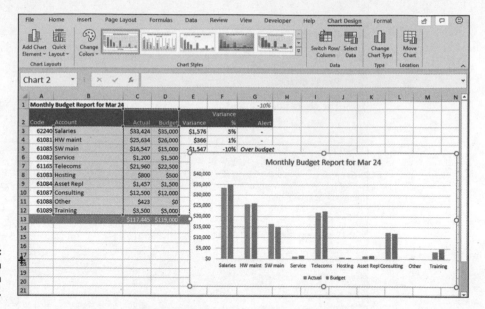

FIGURE 9-25:
Creating a clustered column chart.

3. **In cell A1, create a heading with a dynamic date (as described in the "Using dynamic dates" sidebar).**

4. **Link the title of the chart to the formula in cell A1, as shown in the preceding section.**

5. **Edit the chart so that the titles are horizontally aligned and change the colors.**

TIP

This chart will look much better if it's sorted so that the larger columns are on the left side.

6. **Highlight all the data including the headings, and click the Sort button (in the Sort & Filter section of the Data tab in the Ribbon).**

The Sort dialog box appears.

7. **Sort by Actual from largest to smallest, as shown in Figure 9-26.**

WARNING

It's very easy to mess up formulas when sorting, so be sure that you highlight all the columns from columns A to G before applying the sort.

Now, add some text commentary to the chart. You can do this by adding commentary in a single cell, which is dynamically linked to values in the model and link the cell to a text box to show the commentary on the chart.

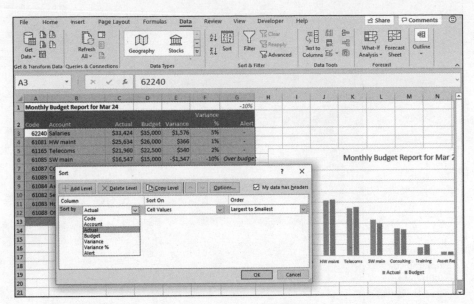

FIGURE 9-26:
Sorting the
chart data.

8. **In cell A15, create a formula that will automatically calculate how many line items are over budget.**

    You can do this with the formula =COUNTA(G3:G12)–COUNT(G3:G12), which calculates how many non-blank cells are in column G. (For more information on how the COUNTA and COUNT functions work, see Chapter 7.)

9. **You can see that two line items are over budget, so convert this to dynamic text with the formula** =COUNTA(G3:G12)–COUNT(G3:G12)&" Items over Budget" **(see Figure 9-27).**

10. **Insert a text box into the chart by pressing the Text Box button in the Text group on the Insert tab in the Ribbon.**

11. **Click the chart once.**

    The text box appears.

12. **Carefully select the outside of the text box with the mouse, just as you did in the last section when linking the chart titles.**

13. **Now go to the formula bar and type** =.

14. **Click cell A15 and click Enter.**

15. **Resize and reposition the text box as necessary.**

16. **Test the model by changing the numbers so that more items are over budget, and make sure that the commentary in the text box changes.**

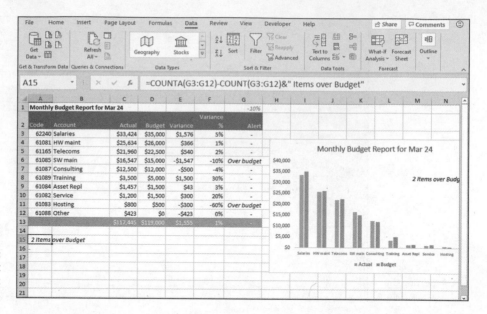

FIGURE 9-27:
Completed chart
with dynamic
text box.

Charting is an important part of the final stage of the model-building process. Make sure that the key messages from the model's output are accurately presented by using clear, attractive, and unambiguous charts and tables.

Data visualization is a discipline that is increasingly growing in popularity, and not one that comes naturally to many with an analytical background — like me! Although I readily admit that it doesn't come naturally to me, I've spent a lot of time learning about these principles to improve the models and dashboards that I build for clients. If you can educate yourself on even the most basic principles of visual design and apply them to your work, you and your financial models will have greater credibility and recognition in your organization and amongst your peers.

USING DYNAMIC DATES

Text containing a date can also be created in a single cell, and then linked to a title or text box in a chart. If you'd like the current date to always show on the chart, use the TODAY function in your formula, and format it using the TEXT function so that it shows the date in your preferred format.

Use the formula =`"Monthly Budget Report for "&TEXT(TODAY(),"mmm yy")`. Each time you open the file it will give you a title that includes the current month, such as "Monthly Budget Report for Nov 18," assuming the current month is November 2018.

Preparing a Presentation

You know your financial model best. No one is more qualified than you are to talk about your model, so you may be asked to communicate the results of the financial model as a formal presentation to the board or senior management. You need to decide how to communicate your findings in a clear and concise way. Understandably, many detail-oriented modelers find that distilling their 20MB financial models that have taken weeks to build into a ten-minute presentation is difficult!

WARNING

If you simply copy and paste a chart directly into Word or PowerPoint, the links to the underlying data in Excel will be maintained. This is fine if you're planning to make changes, but it can make the file size very large, and could also lead to your accidentally sending confidential information unintentionally embedded into another document. To avoid this, you need to paste the chart as a picture. Copy the chart and then use Paste Special in the destination document to paste the chart as a picture or JPG.

In this kind of environment where you need to convey lots of information, having the summary tables or charts on a PowerPoint slide behind you while you're speaking will be helpful. It can also help to take the focus off you if you're a little bit nervous.

Your audience is probably not interested in seeing the workings of the model (and I don't recommend showing those inner workings unless they've specifically requested it), but they might like to see live and changing scenarios. If the model is built correctly, you'll be able to make a single change to the input assumptions, and the audience will be able to see the effects of these changing scenarios in real time.

WARNING

Make sure that you test all possible inputs in advance. Having a #REF! error during a live sensitivity analysis is a real confidence and credibility killer.

Whether you're presenting in Excel or using PowerPoint slides, be sure to follow these basic rules of making financial presentations:

TIP

>> **Only display one key message at a time.** Don't crowd the screen with too much detail or try to convey too much at once.

>> **Use white space instead of gridlines.** Gridlines create clutter and the less like a boring Excel spreadsheet your presentation looks, the better. You might love Excel, but many people in the audience will switch off when they see the gridlines, so make it look more like a presentation and less like Excel.

>> **Give them a more detailed report to look through *after* the presentation.** Show only a high-level summary on the screen.

>> **Make sure the font is big enough and clear on the projector.** Test it in advance if you can. Sometimes colors look washed out, making text difficult to read when projected.

>> **If you're showing the model itself on the screen, increase the zoom in Excel so that your audience can see the numbers.** Test this in advance, and remember that you'll only be able to show a small portion of the screen in this way.

>> **Don't jump around in Excel.** Your audience isn't as familiar with the model as you are. They'll need some time to digest what they're seeing.

>> **Use charts and graphics to display your message instead of text and numbers.**

REMEMBER

Be prepared for questions regarding the output, inputs, assumptions, or workings of the model. Make sure that you can defend the assumptions you've used or the way you've calculated something. The model output is only as good as the assumptions that have gone into it, so you need to make sure that the audience accepts the key assumptions in order for them to accept the model results.

3

Building Your Financial Model

Identify and build the components of an integrated financial statement, an income statement, a cash flow statement, and a balance sheet in a working financial model.

Understand the theory of discounted cash flow and apply the concepts to a valuation model.

Transform a list of budgeted assets into a reusable budget model that calculates the cash flow and depreciation.

IN THIS CHAPTER

» Learning about financial statements

» Entering assumptions

» Calculating revenue and expenses

» Building the financial statements

» Adding scenarios

Chapter **10**

Building an Integrated Financial Statements Model

F inancial statements are the mainstay of many financial models. The financial statements consist of three reports:

>> Income statement

>> Cash flow statement

>> Balance sheet

TECHNICAL STUFF

Some financial models might include only an income statement (sometimes called a *profit-and-loss statement* or *P&L statement*), some might include simply a cash flow statement, but many include all three. If a financial model does contain all three, you might hear it referred as a *three-way financial model.*

What you really need to know about financial statements from a financial modeling perspective is that they should hang together and interrelate with each other with links. This is called an *integrated financial statement.*

Every output in a financial model is driven by inputs, and financial statements are no exception. So, it's very important that when you change one of the inputs or assumptions in your model, the outputs change, too. For example, if you've finished building a financial model and your balance sheet balances, if you change one of the inputs (sales price, for example) the balance sheet should still balance. Of course, you'll know right away if it doesn't balance, because you've built in error checks (see Chapter 4).

I've seen many examples of financial statements that do not link to each other. This is simply poor modeling practice because if one of the inputs changes, all the financial statements will be out of sync with each other.

The best way for me to explain how financial statements link and fit together is to build one, of course, but before we do that, if you'd like a detailed description of each of the three statements and how each of them can help you to build, manage, and understand a business, turn to the sections later in this chapter: "Building the Income Statement," "Building the Cash Flow Statement," and "Building the Balance Sheet."

Getting to Know the Case Study

In this case study, you're opening a small but (what you hope to be) busy café and applying for a business loan. The bank has asked you to put together a three-way financial model forecasting the business's income, balance sheet, and cash flow. You'll use all the tools and techniques covered in this book to build this financial model.

The bank has provided you with a general model template, but you have to create the model and project how your business will do in its first year. If you follow the steps as shown in this chapter, you'll end up with a fully integrated financial model. You can download the blank model template called `File 1001.xlsx` at `www.dummies.com/go/financialmodelinginexcelfd2e`.

Start by opening the file and selecting the Balance Sheet tab.

In order to open and operate the café, you expect the business will need a $10,000 coffee machine, $35,000 in furniture and fixtures, $5,000 in miscellaneous inventory (such as cups and coffee), and $5,000 in cash. The total amount of $55,000 is how much money you need to open the business, also called your *uses of funds*.

Enter these numbers into your model, as shown in Figure 10-1.

	I	J	K	L	M
		Sources of Funds			
		Borrowed from the Bank	$30,000		
		Equity raised	$25,000		
		Total sources of funds	**$55,000**		
		Uses of Funds			
		Working Cash	$5,000		
		Working Inventory	$5,000		
		Coffee Machine	$10,000		
		Furniture & Fixtures	$35,000		
		Total uses of funds	**$55,000**		

FIGURE 10-1:
Sources and uses
of funds.

Now that you've determined how much money your business needs to start, you have to determine how you'll fund this amount. This is called your *sources of funds.* Basically, you need to explain what you're planning to do with the money, and where you're planning to get it. In order to raise the required $55,000, you invest $25,000 in the form of equity (thanks, Ma and Pa) and borrow $30,000 as a bank loan.

REMEMBER

Your total sources of funds and uses of funds must always be equal. In other words, you have to raise enough money to fund what you purchase for the business.

Entering Assumptions

Now that you've figured out how to fund your business, you need to make future assumptions and project how the business will perform. You need to build a separate Assumptions worksheet with your business projections that will drive the rest of the financial model.

The Assumptions worksheet already has places for your key business drivers — it's up to you to input accurate and reasonable assumptions for the business.

REMEMBER

In modeling, all input variables should be formatted consistently (usually with blue font or using Input Style, which can be found on the Home tab in the Styles section of the Ribbon). Then anyone using this model knows that they can make changes to any of the cells formatted in that way.

Revenue assumptions

Based on your study of other cafés in the area (you've been drinking a lot of coffee the past few weeks, haven't you?), you expect the following assumptions for your business's revenue:

>> You'll sell an average of 120 cups of coffee per day throughout the year.

>> Forty percent of coffees sold will be in large cups; 60 percent will be in small cups.

>> You'll charge $4 for a large cup of coffee and $3.50 for a small cup of coffee.

These are your expectations for the business's sales; they represent your base case revenue assumptions. You aren't really sure whether you have the daily number of sales right — you're just estimating — so you'll adjust this number when you run the scenarios. You'll address the best- and worst-case assumptions later on, after the base case is complete, so you can leave the cells in rows 3 and 4 blank for now.

Go to the Assumptions page, and enter the business sales, as shown in Figure 10-2.

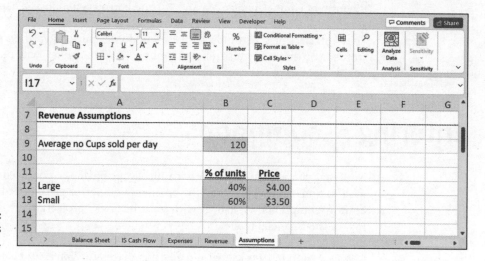

FIGURE 10-2: Sales assumptions.

WARNING

The model has already been formatted for you, but when you make your own models, be careful to format correctly, expressing percentage values as percentages and using dollar signs to show dollar values. One of the most common errors in financial modeling is confusing units, such as treating a number of units as a price. Proper formatting makes any report or model clearer and easier to read for the user. Pay particular attention to formatting when using percentages. If a cell is formatted as a percentage, any figure entered will automatically be converted to a fraction. For example, if you enter the number 5 in any normal cell, the value is 5. But if the cell is formatted as a percentage, the number 5 will automatically be converted to a value of 0.05 (or 5 percent). This could potentially lead to incorrect calculations.

Expense assumptions

In your analysis, you've also researched the operating costs of running a café, which are the following:

>> You think the rent expense will most likely be $1,200 per month. This is just an estimate, though — you'll enter some potential fluctuations into the scenario analysis later on.

>> Consumables — including coffee beans, cups, filters, and so on — will cost you $0.45 per cup. This amount has been averaged over both large and small cups, so you won't need to distinguish between size for the purpose of this model.

>> The barista's salary is $50,000 per year, plus 25% in other staff costs and benefits.

>> Monthly utilities, such as electricity, heat, and water, will cost $100 per month.

>> Interest rate on the loan is 7 percent.

>> The company income tax rate is 30 percent.

These are your expectations for the business's costs; they represent your base case expense assumptions.

Scroll down to the Expense Assumptions section on the Assumptions worksheet, and enter the assumptions as shown in Figure 10-3.

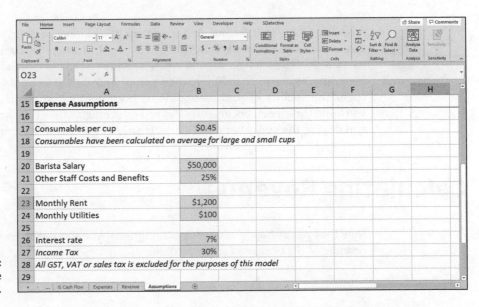

FIGURE 10-3: Expense assumptions.

Other assumptions

Finally, you also have some other assumptions regarding the number of business days you'll be open per month and how busy your café will be throughout the year, so you need to apply some seasonality because this will affect your cash flow. Follow these steps:

1. **Scroll down to the Other Assumptions section on the Assumptions worksheet, and based on next year's calendar, complete row 32 for the number of business days per month, as shown in Figure 10-4.**

2. **Based on historical seasonal and weather patterns, complete row 33 for the seasonality variance (refer to Figure 10-4).**

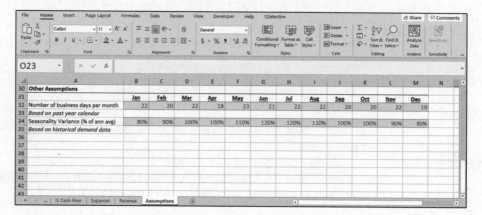

FIGURE 10-4:
Other assumptions.

REMEMBER

Models must be well documented and assumptions must be clearly stated. A properly documented model will not only help you and others follow it, but also help users if you're no longer around when a change needs to be made to the model. Including sources is handy for when you or someone else wants to go back and check the validity of your assumptions. Document assumptions and sources as you build the model. Documenting as you go is much easier than having to go back and do it at the end. After all, a model is only as good as its assumptions!

Calculating Revenue

Now that you're happy with your assumptions, you can use them to calculate the revenue of the business for the next year.

Projecting sales volume

You know that your base case assumption is that the café will sell 120 cups of coffee per day, so you need to multiply this assumption by the monthly seasonality to arrive at the number of cups sold per day in each month. Follow these steps:

1. **Go to the Revenue worksheet and select cell B5.**

In this cell, you're going to enter a formula to calculate the total number of cups of coffee.

2. **Type =.**

3. **Go to the Assumptions worksheet and select cell B9.**

4. **Press F4 to lock the reference.**

You need to anchor this reference because as you copy the formula across, you don't want B9 to change to another cell. For more information about cell referencing, see Chapter 6.

5. **Stay on the Assumptions worksheet and multiply this reference by the monthly seasonality assumption by typing * and selecting cell B34.**

There is no need to anchor the seasonality reference because you *want* the reference to change as you copy it along the row.

6. **Press Enter to finish the formula.**

Your formula will look like this: `=Assumptions!$B$9*Assumptions!B34`. The calculated result is 96.

7. **Copy this formula across the row by selecting cell B5, pressing Ctrl+C, selecting cells C5 through M5, and pressing Ctrl+V or Enter.**

You have the total number of cups sold per day. Now you need to project how many of these cups are large and how many are small based on your assumptions. You're going to use the calculated value of 96 and split it into large and small cups, based on your assumed split between large and small on the Assumptions worksheet. Follow these steps:

1. **On the Revenue worksheet, select cell B6 and type =.**

2. **Go to the Assumptions worksheet, select cell B12, and press F4 to lock the reference.**

3. **Multiply this value by typing *.**

4. **Go back to the Revenue worksheet and select cell B5.**

5. **Press Enter to finish the formula.**

Your formula will look like this: =Assumptions!$B$12*Revenue!B5. The calculated result is 38.

6. **Copy this formula across the row to calculate this for the entire year.**

You're going to repeat this process to find the number of small cups.

7. **On the Revenue worksheet, select cell B7 and type =.**

8. **Go to the Assumptions worksheet, select cell B13, and press F4 to lock the reference.**

9. **Multiply this value by typing *.**

10. **Go back to the Revenue worksheet and select cell B5.**

Your formula will look like this: =Assumptions!$B$13*Revenue!B5. The calculated result is 58.

11. **Copy this formula across the row to calculate this for the entire year.**

12. **On the Revenue worksheet, select cell B8 and enter the formula** =SUM(B6:B7).

If you prefer, you can use the AutoSum function or the shortcut Alt+=. The calculated result is 96.

13. **Copy this formula across the row to calculate this for the entire year.**

14. **Perform a sense-check by highlighting both cells B6 and B7.**

If you look at the status bar, the SUM will equal 96, the total number of cups sold per day.

Go one step further than sense-checking and add an error check in row 9.

15. **In cell B9, enter the formula** =B8-B5 **and copy it across the row.**

REMEMBER

Always sense-check your numbers as you build a model. Don't leave it to the end to check your numbers. Never take the number given for granted. Work it out in your head and use a calculator to make sure your numbers look right. This will help you make sure the numbers you've calculated are correct. When you're sure the numbers are right, add in an error check if you can just like you did in row 9. A good financial modeler is always looking for opportunities to put error checks into their models. For more information about error checks, see Chapters 4 and 13.

Projecting dollar sales

Now that you've projected how many cups and sizes you'll sell per day in each month, it's time to translate this into actual dollar sales figures. Follow these steps:

1. **On the Revenue worksheet, select cell B12 and multiply B6 (the number of large cups sold per day in January) by the price per large cup by typing the formula** =B6*Assumptions!$C$12**.**

   The calculated result is $154.

2. **Copy this formula across the row to calculate this for the entire year.**

3. **On the Revenue worksheet, select cell B13 and multiply B7 (the number of small cups sold per day in January) by the price per small cup by typing the formula** =B7*Assumptions!$C$13**.**

   The calculated result is $202.

4. **Copy this formula across the row to calculate this for the entire year.**

5. **Add the sum total in cell B14 by typing the formula** =SUM(B12:B13)**.**

   The calculated result is $355.

6. **Copy this formula across the row to calculate this for the entire year.**

   You now have sales per day figures for large cups, small cups, and total cups for each given month. In order to find each month's total sales, you must multiply daily sales by the number of business days per month.

7. **On the Revenue worksheet, select cell B15 and multiply the daily sales figure in cell B14 by the number of business days in January by typing the formula** =B14*Assumptions!B32**.**

   Note that you don't need to press F4 to add any cell referencing because you *want* the cell references to copy across. The calculated result is $7,814.

8. **Copy this formula across the row to calculate this for the entire year.**

   You've now projected your monthly sales for the year! Check your totals against Figure 10-5.

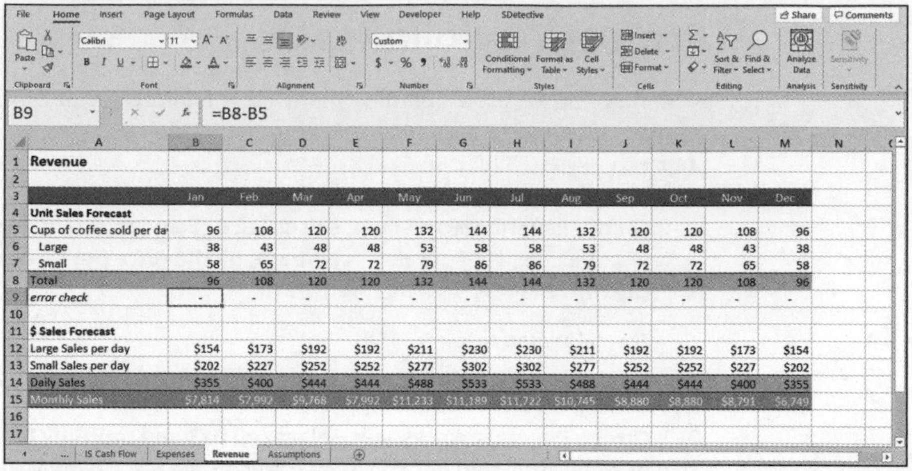

FIGURE 10-5:
Completed revenue calculations.

Calculating Expenses

Now that you've projected your revenue, it's time to project your expenses for the business.

Staff costs

Your assumption for the barista's annual salary is $50,000, so your annual projection should be divided by the 12 months of the year to arrive at the monthly amount. Follow these steps:

1. **Go to the Expenses worksheet and select cell D5.**

2. **Enter the formula** =Assumptions!$B$20 **and then press F4 to lock the reference.**

3. **Enter** /12 **in order to divide the annual salary by 12 months.**

4. **Press Enter to complete the formula.**

    The formula will be =Assumptions!$B$20/12. The calculated result is $4,167.

5. **Copy this formula across the row to calculate this for the entire year.**

    You've also assumed that it will cost an extra 25 percent of the barista's salary to cover other staff costs and benefits. Calculate this amount next.

6. **On the Expenses worksheet in cell D6 enter the formula**
=D5*Assumptions!$B$21.

The calculated result is $1,042.

7. **Copy this formula across the row to calculate this for the entire year.**

Make sure the formatting is correct. Often when you multiply a value by a percentage, Excel resets the formatting to show more decimals. If this happens, press Decrease Decimal in the Number section of the Home ribbon.

Your staff costs should total $5,208 every month of the year, shown in row 7.

Other costs

Now you need to calculate your other costs, like rent and utilities. Follow these steps, starting with rent, which has a base case assumption of $1,200 per month:

1. **On the Expenses worksheet, select cell D9, enter the formula**
=Assumptions!$B$23, **and press F4 to lock the reference.**

The calculated result for rent is $1,200.

2. **Copy this formula across the row to calculate this for the entire year.**

Your assumption for utilities is $100 per month.

3. **On the Expenses worksheet, select cell D10, enter the formula**
=Assumptions!$B$24, **and press F4 to lock the reference.**

The calculated result for utilities is $100.

4. **Copy this formula across the row to calculate this for the entire year.**

Your assumption for consumables expenses is an average of $0.45 per cup. You need to multiply this amount by the number of cups sold per month. You haven't calculated the number of cups sold per month, so you need to do this in the formula, too.

5. **On the Expenses worksheet, select cell D11 and enter** =Revenue!B8*Assumptions!B32*Assumptions!$B$17.

This formula multiplies

- The number of cups sold per day in January on the Revenue worksheet in cell B8

- The number of business days in January on the Assumptions worksheet in cell B32

- The cost of consumables per cup on the Assumptions worksheet in cell B17

The calculated result is $950.

Note that only the reference for the consumables per cup needs to be anchored as an absolute reference, because the other references need to change as you copy the formula across the row.

6. **Copy this formula across the row to calculate this for the entire year.**

7. **Add the subtotal of Other costs by selecting cell D11, entering the formula** =SUM(D8:D10), **and copying across the row.**

8. **Add the total of all costs by selecting cell D13, entering the formula** =D11+D6, **and copying across the row.**

Your costs should total $7,459 for January. You've just projected your cash expenses for the business! Check your totals against Figure 10-6.

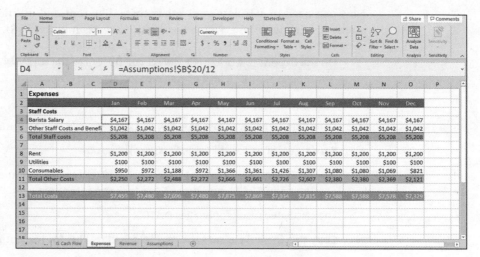

FIGURE 10-6: Completed expense calculations.

Depreciation and amortization

Depreciation and amortization (D&A) expenses are non-cash expenses used in accounting. They represent the cost of a long-term fixed asset, like property, plant, and equipment (PP&E), that is steadily allocated as an expense over the useful life of the asset. Because the business is generating revenue from this asset over an extended period of time, it makes sense to apportion the expense over the period of time for which it is going to be used.

So, for example, the coffee machine will cost you $10,000 and you expect it to last for three years. From an accounting perspective, it wouldn't be accurate to put the entire amount in the expenses on the income statement for the first month of operation because your income statement would show that you'd be making a huge loss in the first month and a huge profit thereafter. It makes more sense to spread the cost across the entire life of the assets because that will accurately reflect the costs of purchasing the coffee machine.

TECHNICAL STUFF

Amortization refers to the depreciation of intangible or nonphysical assets the company might hold on its balance sheet, such as goodwill, trademarks, or patents. For this example, your business only holds tangible assets so you only need to calculate the depreciation, not amortization.

When you decide that a large item of expenditure is an asset, rather than an operating expense, you need to put the cost of the asset onto the balance sheet and begin to depreciate it, which will be shown on the income statement. When you do this, the balance sheet changes as does the profitability shown on the income statement. The cash flow statement remains unchanged (because you need to pay for the item in any case). The process of taking a large item of expenditure and putting it onto the balance sheet rather than showing it on the income statement is called *capitalization.*

REMEMBER

When you capitalize an asset, the ongoing depreciation on the income statement affects the business's taxable income; there are all sorts of accounting rules and regulations that differ between regions about how large an asset needs to be before it can be capitalized and over how many years it should be depreciated.

The most common method of depreciation is the *straight-line method,* which means that the asset is depreciated equally over its useful life. For more information on other methods of depreciation and how to calculate them in Excel, see Chapter 9 of my book *Using Excel for Business and Financial Modelling,* Third Edition (Wiley).

You're going to make the assumption that your coffee machine ($10,000) will be depreciated over three years, and the furniture and fixtures ($35,000) will be depreciated over ten years. Using the straight-line method, you can calculate the depreciation simply by dividing the cost of the asset by the number of years. You need to enter this amount into the model to determine its depreciation.

You've already entered the capital costs on the Uses of Funds section on the balance sheet, so you can reference these numbers to build your depreciation schedule. Follow these steps:

1. **On the Expenses worksheet, enter the useful life of the coffee machine (3 years) in cell C20 and the useful life of the furniture and fixtures (10 years) in cell C21, as shown in Figure 10-7.**

2. **Select cell B20 and enter the formula =**'Balance sheet'!K11**.**

   This formula links this cell to the purchase price of the coffee machine on the Balance Sheet worksheet. The calculated result is $10,000.

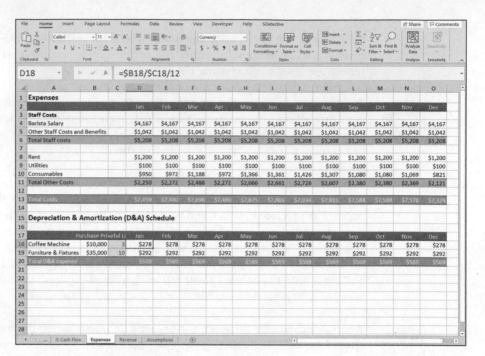

Cell reference: D18 | =$B18/$C18/12

	A	B	C	D	E	F	G	H	I	J	K	L	M	N	O
1	**Expenses**														
2				Jan	Feb	Mar	Apr	May	Jun	Jul	Aug	Sep	Oct	Nov	Dec
3	**Staff Costs**														
4	Barista Salary			$4,167	$4,167	$4,167	$4,167	$4,167	$4,167	$4,167	$4,167	$4,167	$4,167	$4,167	$4,167
5	Other Staff Costs and Benefits			$1,042	$1,042	$1,042	$1,042	$1,042	$1,042	$1,042	$1,042	$1,042	$1,042	$1,042	$1,042
6	Total Staff costs			$5,208	$5,208	$5,208	$5,208	$5,208	$5,208	$5,208	$5,208	$5,208	$5,208	$5,208	$5,208
7															
8	Rent			$1,200	$1,200	$1,200	$1,200	$1,200	$1,200	$1,200	$1,200	$1,200	$1,200	$1,200	$1,200
9	Utilities			$100	$100	$100	$100	$100	$100	$100	$100	$100	$100	$100	$100
10	Consumables			$950	$972	$1,188	$972	$1,366	$1,361	$1,426	$1,307	$1,080	$1,080	$1,069	$821
11	Total Other Costs			$2,250	$2,272	$2,488	$2,272	$2,666	$2,661	$2,726	$2,607	$2,380	$2,380	$2,369	$2,121
12															
13	Total Costs			$7,459	$7,480	$7,696	$7,480	$7,875	$7,869	$7,934	$7,815	$7,588	$7,588	$7,578	$7,329
14															
15	**Depreciation & Amortization (D&A) Schedule**														
16															
17		Purchase Pri	seful Li	Jan	Feb	Mar	Apr	May	Jun	Jul	Aug	Sep	Oct	Nov	Dec
18	Coffee Machine	$10,000	3	$278	$278	$278	$278	$278	$278	$278	$278	$278	$278	$278	$278
19	Furniture & Fixtures	$35,000	10	$292	$292	$292	$292	$292	$292	$292	$292	$292	$292	$292	$292
20	Total D&A expense			$569	$569	$569	$569	$569	$569	$569	$569	$569	$569	$569	$569

FIGURE 10-7:
Completed expenses including depreciation and amortization.

Worksheet tabs: IS Cash Flow | **Expenses** | Revenue | Assumptions

3. **Select cell B21 and enter the formula** ='Balance sheet'!K12.

This formula links this cell to the assumed furniture and fixtures amount on the Balance Sheet worksheet. The calculated result is $35,000.

Finally, you have to figure out the monthly depreciation and amortization expense using the straight-line method. This is done by dividing the cost of the long-term asset by its useful life to find the annual depreciation expense, and then dividing by 12 to find the monthly expense.

4. **In cell D20, enter** =B20/C20/12.

This formula divides the price of the coffee machine ($10,000) by the useful life (3 years) and then converts it to monthly by dividing it by 12. The calculated result is $278. Don't worry about the cell referencing just yet.

TIP

Although financial modeling best practice tells you to *never* hard-code a number into a formula, entering 12 for the number of months is okay because it's not a variable that is likely to change in the near future!

Because you can copy this formula down to the next row as well as across the page, you can save time by making use of mixed cell referencing.

5. **Go back into your formula in cell D20 and add a dollar sign before the column referencing.**

The formula should now be =$B20/$C20/12.

You can do this by manually typing it in, or click *within* each cell reference and press the F4 shortcut key three times. The calculated result is still $278.

6. **Copy this formula across the row as well as down to row 21 to calculate the depreciation for both assets for the entire year.**

7. **Add the sum total in row 22 by entering the formula =SUM(D20:D21); and copy it across the entire row.**

The calculated result for each month is $569.

You've just projected your depreciation costs for the business. Check your totals against Figure 10-7.

Building the Income Statement

The income statement, also called the profit-and-loss (P&L) statement, shows the underlying profitability of the company — in other words, exactly how much money the business is making. This information is useful for the purposes of calculating taxes; it also helps the owner or manager run the business. Of all the three statements that make up the financial statements, the income statement is the simplest to understand because it simply shows the revenue earned by the business and the operating costs associated with generating that revenue for the business.

The income statement is usually more detailed than the other statements, so when building a financial model from scratch, you'll normally tackle this one first.

TIP

One of the things that differentiates the income statement from the other financial statements is that each column refers to only one period. Most income statements are built on a monthly basis; some are also annual. With a cash flow or a balance sheet, you need to carry over the amount from the previous period, but with an income statement, each period starts fresh.

An income statement can also be used as a tool to compare current performance with past months or years, tracking the performance of the business, and providing a basis from which to create a forecast or budget. The model you're building is for the purpose of budgeting the projected income for the business over the next 12 months for the bank, and the income statement is a critical component.

All income statements follow a similar format:

	Revenue
−	Cost of Goods Sold
=	Gross Profit
−	Expenses
=	Operating Income or Earnings before Interest, Tax, Depreciation, and Amortization (EBITDA)
−	Depreciation and Amortization
=	Earnings before Interest and Tax (EBIT)
−	Interest
=	Earnings before Tax (EBT)
−	Tax
=	Net Income

WARNING

You don't need to be an accountant to build a financial model, but you do need to be familiar with basic accounting concepts, and the format of an income statement is about as fundamental as it comes. If you don't lay out an income statement in this order, your model will lose all credibility.

Most of these line items you'll find in the income statement for the financial model you're building in this chapter, but cost of goods sold is not relevant for a business like yours, so it isn't shown on your income statement. Some income statements may differ between companies and not show every single line item. For example, EBT is sometimes not shown, and the income statement jumps directly from EBIT to net income, without showing the earnings before tax has been applied.

Operating income or EBITDA is useful for knowing what the underlying profitability of the company is before you deduct tax, interest, depreciation, and amortization. EBITDA is sometimes used for company valuations because it gives managers, shareholders, and other interested parties a better indication of how the company is doing before other elements relating to the capital structure of the company come into play. Similarly, EBIT takes into account the depreciation and amortization but does not include interest and tax. Some managers' key performance indicators (KPIs) and other targets are set based on EBIT or EBITDA because these items cannot be controlled easily by management.

CALCULATING PROFIT MARGIN

We use the components of the income statement for ratio analysis, too. For example, one of the most useful ratios is profit margin (also called return on sales or gross profit ratio), which gives a very useful indication of how the company is doing. To calculate profit margin, use the following formula:

$$\text{Profit Margin} = \frac{\text{Profit before Tax}}{\text{Revenue}}$$

The profit margin is one of the many ratios that investors and creditors use to check the financial health of a company. Dividends and returns are paid from profit, so if an investor buys shares in the company, how likely is it that they will receive dividends? Banks or other creditors use the profit margin to see whether they're likely to get their money back.

See the exercise in Chapter 6 for a practical example of calculating the profit margin ratio.

Now that you know the basics of an income statement, you need to build one! For simplicity's sake, the income statement will go on the same worksheet as the cash flow: the IS Cash Flow worksheet.

If you've been following along with this chapter from the beginning, you've already projected most of the income statement line items. The first part of the income statement simply requires you to "pull through" the revenue and expense summary lines by linking them to the Revenue and Expenses worksheets. Follow these steps:

1. **Go to the IS Cash Flow worksheet, select cell C5, and enter the formula** =Revenue!B15.

This links cell C5 to cell B15 on the Revenue worksheet. The calculated result is $7,814.

2. **Copy this formula across the row to calculate this for the entire year.**

3. **Select cell C7 and enter the formula** =Expenses!D7.

This links cell C7 to cell D7 on the Expenses worksheet. The calculated result is $5,208.

4. **Copy this formula across the row to calculate this for the entire year.**

5. **Select cell C8 and enter the formula** =Expenses!D12.

This links it to cell D12 on the Expenses worksheet. The calculated result is $2,250.

6. Copy this formula across the row to calculate this for the entire year.

7. Calculate the sum total in cell C9 by entering the formula =SUM(C7:C8); copy it all the way across the row.

8. In cell C11, calculate the EBITDA by deducting the expenses from the revenue by entering the formula =C5-C9.

The calculated result is $356.

9. Copy this formula across the row to calculate this for the entire year.

10. Select cell C13 and enter the formula =Expenses!D22.

This links cell C13 to cell D22 on the Expenses worksheet where you calculated the depreciation earlier. The calculated result is $569.

11. Copy this formula across the row to calculate this for the entire year.

12. In cell C14, calculate the EBIT by deducting the depreciation and amortization from the EBITDA by entering the formula =C11-C13.

When the depreciation and amortization have been deducted, the café is making a loss for the first month. The calculated result is –$214.

13. Copy this formula across the row to calculate this for the entire year.

The bank loan you're applying for carries a 7 percent annual interest rate that you'll pay monthly. In order to calculate the interest payable, you need to pick up the loan amount from the Balance Sheet worksheet and the interest amount from the Assumptions worksheet.

14. Still on the IS Cash Flow worksheet, select cell C16 and link it to the Balance worksheet tab by typing =, selecting the amount of the loan in cell K3, and pressing F4 to lock the reference. Then multiply it by the interest rate in cell B26 on the Assumptions worksheet, and lock the reference by pressing F4.

The formula is = 'Balance Sheet'!$K$3*Assumptions!$B$26/12 and the calculated result is $175.

This formula multiplies the borrowed amount in cell K3 on the Balance Sheet worksheet by the annual interest amount in cell B26 on the Assumptions worksheet and divides it by 12 to convert it to a monthly amount.

The formula calculated result is $175.

15. Copy this formula across the row to calculate this for the entire year.

16. Select cell C17 and enter the formula =C14-C16 to calculate the Earnings before Tax (EBT).

The calculated result is –$389.

17. Copy this formula across the row to calculate this for the entire year.

To calculate your tax expense, you need to multiply your EBT by your tax rate of 30 percent.

18. Select cell C19 and link this to the EBT by entering the formula =C17*Assumptions!$B$27.

19. Press F4 to lock the reference.

The calculated result is –$117.

TIP

Notice that the tax is a negative value, which forms a tax credit. When a business reports a *negative net income,* also called a *net loss,* these losses are tax-deductible, and the business benefits from a tax credit when this happens. Although the business won't realize the credit right away because tax is not paid every month, you still need to show the calculated tax amount each month in order to derive an accurate profit amount.

20. Copy this formula across the row to calculate this for the entire year.

You may need to adjust the decimal formatting.

21. In row 20, enter the formula =C17-C19.

This formula calculates the net income by deducting the tax from the EBT. The calculated result is –$272.

WARNING

Be sure to get your plus and minus signs around the right way! Mixing up the positives and negatives is the most common error on a financial statement. Go over the logic of your income statement carefully, and make sure the tax is either positive or negative, depending on whether you've made a profit or a loss.

22. Select cell O5 and press Alt+=.

This automatically sums up the entire year with the formula =SUM(C5:N5). The calculated total is $111,755.

23. Copy this down the column to row 20 to add up the totals for each line.

TIP

By simply copying and pasting the formula down the column, it will copy the cell format as well as the formulas. Use Paste Formulas to copy only the formulas, and leave the formatting as it is.

To use Paste Formulas:

a. Copy cell O5 onto the Clipboard and press Ctrl+C.

b. Highlight cells O5:O20 with the mouse.

c. Right-click with the mouse, and select the Paste Formulas icon under Paste Options.

24. Look down the column and remove the unnecessary zero values in rows 6, 10, 12, 15, and 18. Select these cells and press Delete.

You've just completed the income statement — your first financial statement for the business! Check your totals against Figure 10-8.

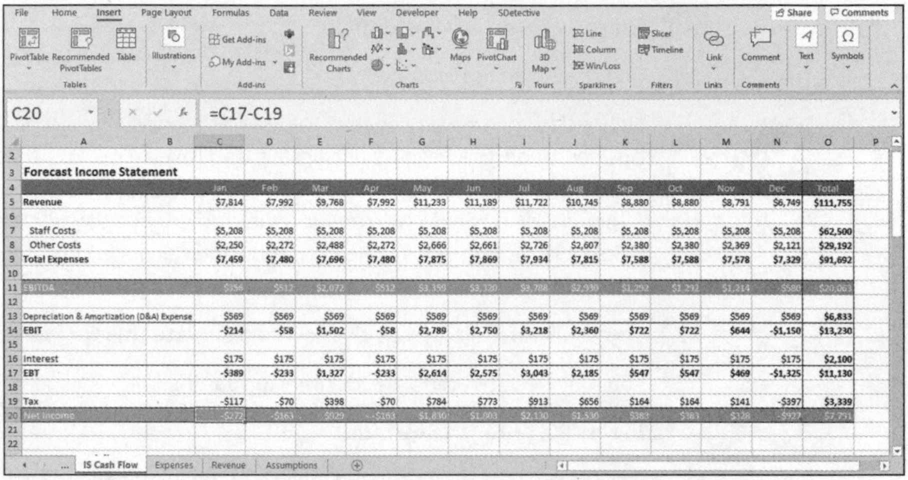

FIGURE 10-8:
The completed income statement.

The spreadsheet shows cell C20 with formula =C17-C19.

Forecast Income Statement

	Jan	Feb	Mar	Apr	May	Jun	Jul	Aug	Sep	Oct	Nov	Dec	Total
Revenue	$7,814	$7,992	$9,768	$7,992	$11,233	$11,189	$11,722	$10,745	$8,880	$8,880	$8,791	$6,749	$111,755
Staff Costs	$5,208	$5,208	$5,208	$5,208	$5,208	$5,208	$5,208	$5,208	$5,208	$5,208	$5,208	$5,208	$62,500
Other Costs	$2,250	$2,272	$2,488	$2,272	$2,666	$2,661	$2,726	$2,607	$2,380	$2,380	$2,369	$2,121	$29,192
Total Expenses	$7,458	$7,480	$7,696	$7,480	$7,875	$7,869	$7,934	$7,815	$7,588	$7,588	$7,578	$7,329	$91,692
EBITDA	$356	$512	$2,072	$512	$3,358	$3,320	$3,788	$2,930	$1,292	$1,292	$1,214	$580	$20,063
Depreciation & Amortization (D&A) Expense	$569	$569	$569	$569	$569	$569	$569	$569	$569	$569	$569	$569	$6,833
EBIT	$214	-$58	$1,502	-$58	$2,789	$2,750	$3,218	$2,360	$722	$722	$644	-$1,150	$13,230
Interest	$175	$175	$175	$175	$175	$175	$175	$175	$175	$175	$175	$175	$2,100
EBT	-$389	-$233	$1,327	-$233	$2,614	$2,575	$3,043	$2,185	$547	$547	$469	-$1,325	$11,130
Tax	-$117	-$70	$398	-$70	$784	$773	$913	$656	$164	$164	$141	-$397	$3,339
Net Income	-$272	-$163	$929	-$163	$1,830	$1,803	$2,130	$1,530	$383	$383	$328	-$927	$7,791

Building the Cash Flow Statement

Cash is king! When running a business like this — particularly a new business — you should never ever run out of cash. You may have a business that's highly profitable, but if you can't pay your staff next month, then you don't have a business. For this reason, cash flow is the most important out of all the financial statements.

A cash flow statement helps to plan your business's cash flow, which identifies and eliminates shortfalls or surpluses in cash projections. If you find your cash flow is projecting a shortfall, you need to alter the business's financial plans in order to provide more cash. You can arrange an overdraft from the bank, adjust inventory, or take other measures that will free up some more cash. If your cash flow forecast reveals surplus or excess cash, it might mean you're borrowing too much or that you have idle money that could be invested. The objective is to keep the business with a cash reserve that is large enough for unknown eventualities but small enough that it doesn't waste cash sitting in a low-interest account that could otherwise be put to better use. Keeping tabs on your cash flow with a well-built and regularly updated cash flow model is imperative for avoiding cash flow problems.

TIP

Profit and cash flow don't necessarily go hand in hand. *Cash flow* is actual cash coming in and out of your bank account; *profit* is the underlying profitability of the business. You can have a very profitable business, but if you don't have the cash to pay wages at the end of the month, the business won't last very long.

Often the discrepancies between cash flow and profit are due to timing differences. If you were to take a large number of orders for a new product for which the customer had not paid a deposit, you would need to purchase raw materials, hire staff, or outlay other expenditure in order to fulfill that order. If you've sent the customer the invoice, but the terms of credit to the customer were, say, 60 days, then that means you won't receive any payment for the goods until 60 days *after* the goods have been received by the customer. In the meantime, you've had to pay staff and possibly pay for raw materials, so cash flow is going to be a problem until that invoice is paid. Because you've already sent the customer the invoice, the funds will show on that month's income statement, but the cash won't turn up for another two months. Your income statement will look healthy, but you'll run into problems with cash flow unless you're able to arrange funding from elsewhere until the invoice is paid. A good financial model will help identify and mitigate these potential problems.

To model the cash flow, start with the opening cash balance, add income, and deduct outflows from payments. This will give you an idea of whether you have a surplus or a deficit for that period. If financing is needed, you'll add that as an amount coming into the bank account, and then calculate any repayments or interest payable going forward. The closing balance of one period becomes the opening balance of the next period, like a corkscrew, as shown in Figure 10-9.

	July	August	September	October	November
Opening Cash	$1,000	$2,000	$1,000	$1,990	$3,490
Add: Inflow from receipts	$10,000	$9,000	$11,000	$8,000	
Less: Outflow from payments	($9,000)	($12,000)	($8,000)	($6,500)	
Surplus / Deficit	$2,000	($1,000)	$4,000	$3,490	
Add: Financing or repayments		$2,000	($2,010)		
Cash at end	$2,000	$1,000	$1,990	$3,490	

FIGURE 10-9: Corkscrew cash flow modeling.

When calculating a cash flow forecast for the café model, you need to consider these differences between cash flow and profit. You've built an income statement already, so you can use this as a base, making a few key adjustments in order to calculate cash flow. To begin forecasting the cash flow for the new business, you need to outline the initial flows of cash when opening the business in the Pre-Open column.

Capital expenditures (CapEx) represent funds that are spent to acquire, upgrade, or replace physical assets such as property, plant, and equipment (PP&E). Capital expenditures are often used to invest in equipment for new projects or maintain old ones. The coffee machine and furniture and fixtures that the café needs to open are PP&E, so the purchases of these assets are classified as capital expenditures.

REMEMBER

Getting your starting position right is important, because it will affect the entire statement. Unlike the income statement, any changes in prior months will flow on and affect the balances in later periods because of the "corkscrew" nature of cash flow.

The starting point for the cash flow statement is the pre-open amounts in column B. The starting cash balance (the amount you have in the bank before opening the doors) is $5,000, and this is made up of the following:

» $5,000 in purchased inventory (consumables such as cups, coffee, milk, and so on that you need to purchase prior to opening the café). Note this is a purchase and will, therefore, be expressed on the cash flow statement as a negative value.

» $45,000 in CapEx for the coffee machine ($10,000) and furniture and fixtures ($35,000). This is also cash out, so it's shown as a negative value on the cash flow statement.

» $30,000 for the money you received from bank loan.

» $25,000 for the capital raised.

REMEMBER

You need to calculate the pre-open by entering the amounts as just described. Although you may be tempted to type these numbers in, it's very important that you follow financial modeling best practice by *only entering data once.* All these numbers have already been entered into your model, so you must access them, or "pull them through," by linking from other parts of the model — in this case, the balance sheet. If you simply type the numbers in, this model will cease to be a fully integrated financial model, because any changes made won't be reflected in the calculations.

Follow these steps to pull the numbers through:

1. On the IS Cash Flow worksheet, in cell B30, enter the formula =-'Balance sheet'!K10.

This formula links cell B30 to the –$5,000 for inventory from the uses of funds on the Balance Sheet worksheet. No need to anchor the cell referencing this time because you aren't copying this formula across.

TIP

Accounts receivable and accounts payable are not material in this model, so you won't include the calculations, but you'll leave the lines there (rows 31 and 32) to show where they go if you want to come back later and add them in.

2. **In cell B35, enter the formula** =-'Balance sheet'!K11-'Balance sheet'!K12.

This formula links cell B35 to the $45,000 in CapEx to where you entered them on the uses of funds on the Balance Sheet worksheet. You need to add them up but because you need a negative value, you're prefacing the formula with a minus sign after the equal sign, and deducting it rather than adding it. The formula gives the total of –$45,000.

3. **In cell B38, enter the formula** ='Balance sheet'!K3.

This formula links cell B38 to the $30,000 amount you expect from the bank loan to where you entered it on the sources of funds section of the Balance Sheet worksheet.

4. **In cell B39, enter the formula** ='Balance sheet'!K4.

This formula links to the $25,000 amount you've raised from where you entered it on the sources of funds section of the Balance Sheet.

5. **Calculate the closing cash in cell B42 by entering the formula** =SUM(B26:B41).

The calculated value is $5,000, which is what we expect it to be. This represents the amount of working cash your business needs to operate.

6. **You need to calculate the closing cash for each month on this statement, so copy this formula all the way across the row to calculate this for the entire year.**

Even though the values are now zero, they'll update as you fill in the cash flow statement.

Closing cash will represent the opening cash for the next month, so you need to link your opening cash amount to the balance from the prior month.

7. **In cell C26, enter the formula** =B42.

8. **Copy this formula all the way across the row to calculate this for the entire year.**

The calculated value for each month is $5,000, which is not yet correct, but these cells will update as you fill in the cash flow statement.

Your net income from the income statement also represents cash inflows, but not all income statement items are cash expenses. Revenues, operating expenses, interest, and taxes are all cash expenses, but D&A expenses are accounting expenses that don't represent cash outflows. So, not only should you add your net income as a cash inflow, but you should also add back your D&A expense that you subtracted from net income earlier.

9. Link the net income in cell C28 to the net income calculated farther up the page by entering the formula =C20.

The calculated value is –$272.

10. Link the D&A (noncash) amount in cell C29 to the D&A expense calculated farther up the page by entering the formula =C13.

The calculated value is $569.

11. Copy the formulas in rows 28 and 29 across the rows to calculate for the entire year.

Because you've already entered the opening and closing balances into the cash flow statement, these will automatically update.

You have just completed the cash flow statement! Check your totals against Figure 10-10.

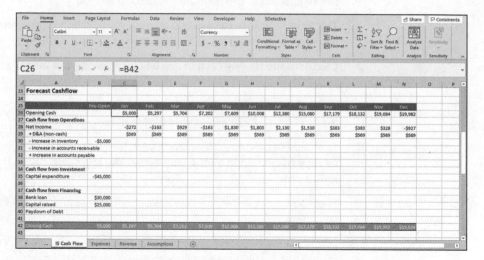

FIGURE 10-10:
The completed cash flow statement.

Building the Balance Sheet

The accounting equation as shown on the balance sheet is perhaps the single most important concept to understand in terms of financial statements modeling:

Assets = Liabilities + Shareholders' Equity

Let's take a look at each of these components:

>> **Assets:** All property owned by the company. This includes cash in the bank, factories, materials, and even money you're owed. You can think of assets as the resources that are used to generate revenue.

Assets are split into two categories:

- **Current assets:** Current assets can be easily converted into liquid assets or cash. This includes assets such as stocks and shares, account receivables (money that is owed to the company), and stock that will sell soon for cash.

- **Fixed assets:** Fixed assets are still property owned by the company, but they may take longer to convert into liquid assets. This includes large capital items such as factories or equipment, as well as nonphysical assets such as intellectual property or goodwill.

>> **Liabilities:** All debts owed. Similarly, current liabilities are short-term debt that needs to be paid back within a year, such as accounts payable (money you owe to suppliers), credit card debt, or overdrafts. Long-term liabilities are more formal borrowings such as bank loans.

>> **Shareholders' equity:** What the owner has after all the debt has been repaid. If the company were sold, theoretically, this is what the shareholders would have.

The balance sheet shows the financial position of a company at any given moment. Just as with the income statement, the elements of a balance sheet need to be arranged in a specific order:

ASSETS

Current Assets

Fixed Assets

LIABILITIES

Current Liabilities

Long-Term Liabilities

EQUITY

Common Stock

Additional Paid in Capital

Retained Earnings

TOTAL EQUITY

TOTAL LIABILITIES AND EQUITY

Now that you've projected your income and cash flow, you need to complete your balance sheet and connect all three financial statements.

Your café's beginning balance sheet at Year 0 will be tied to your sources and uses of funds. Your uses of funds will be your starting assets, and your sources of funds will represent your liabilities and equity. Breaking down the concepts, your uses of funds are assets that you're purchasing in order to operate the business. Your sources of funds are how you fund the purchases of said assets — money can be raised through liabilities that you owe, such as a bank loan, or it can be equity invested by an owner (in this case, you!).

Start with the current assets (which for your business consists of your cash) and inventory. Follow these steps:

1. **On the Balance Sheet worksheet, select cell B5 and link it to the cash amount by entering the formula** ='IS Cash Flow'!B42.

   This formula links cell B5 to the closing cash amount you calculated in the last section on the cash flow statement. This represents the starting cash of $5,000 your business has on hand.

2. **Select cell B6 and enter the formula** =K10.

   This formula links cell B6 to the working inventory on the uses of funds you entered earlier on the same worksheet. This represents your starting inventory amount of $5,000.

3. **Leave accounts receivable in cell B7 blank, and sum the current assets in cell B8 by entering the formula** =SUM(B5:B7); **copy the formula across to the second year.**

4. **Select cell B11 and add cells K11 and K12 on the same worksheet by entering the formula** =K11+K12.

   The calculated value is $45,000. This represents your starting PP&E.

5. **Leave depreciation in cell B12 blank for now and sum the fixed assets net of depreciation by entering the formula** =SUM(B11:B12); **copy it across to the second year.**

6. **Sum the current and fixed assets in cell B15 by entering the formula** =B13+B8; **copy it across to the second year.**

   This gives you the calculated total asset value of $55,000.

7. **Leave row 20 blank because you don't have any current liabilities at this point.**

8. **Select cell B23 and enter** =K3.

This formula links cell B23 to the bank loan amount of $30,000 you entered earlier into the sources of funds section on the same worksheet. This represents the amount you have borrowed from, and owe to, the bank.

9. **Sum total long-term liabilities in cell B24 by entering the formula** =SUM(B23) **and copy it across to the second year.**

It may seem strange to only sum one number, but it's important to do so for consistency. If at a later date you add other rows for long-term liabilities, they'll also be included in this total.

10. **Select cell B27 and enter the formula** =K4.

This formula links cell B27 to the $25,000 equity amount raised that you entered earlier in the sources of funds section on the same worksheet. This represents the amount you've invested and your equity in the business.

11. **Row 28 relates to retained earnings, which will come from the profit shown on the income statement.**

This is not relevant for Year 0 because you haven't yet begun operations.

12. **Select cell B29 and enter the formula** =SUM(B27:B28).

13. **Sum total the liabilities and equity in cell B31 by entering the formula** =B29+B24; **copy it across to the second year.**

You know that total assets *must* be equal to liabilities and equity in order for the balance sheet to balance, so this is a perfect opportunity to include an error check.

14. **Add an error check in cell B32 by entering the formula** =B31-B15 **and copy it across to the second year.**

Now that you've completed the balance sheet for the pre-open year, you need to link your balance sheet to the income and cash flow statements to determine what the balance sheet will look like after the first year of operations.

The café's cash at bank will change by the amount of cash flow from your cash flow statement. You've already calculated this on a monthly basis, and you have a closing cash figure at the end of December of Year 1.

15. **Go back to the top of your balance sheet, select cell C5, and link it to the closing cash balance of $19,624 on the IS Cash Flow worksheet by entering the formula** ='IS Cash Flow'!N42.

16. **In cell C6, enter the formula** =B6-SUM('IS Cash Flow'!C30:N30).

17. **In cell C11, enter the formula** =-SUM('IS Cash Flow'!C35:N35).

This formula calculates the total amount of fixed assets on the books at the end of the second year. If you've purchased additional assets during the year, it will show on the cash flow statement, so you need to link that through with the formula. Note that any CapEx purchases on the cash flow statement are shown as negative values so you need to add a minus sign to the beginning of the sum to show it as a positive value. The total will be zero at this point, but that may change in future iterations of these financial statements.

You also need to add the existing fixed asset amount of $45,000 carried over from the previous year.

18. **Add this amount to the beginning of the formula you already have in C11 so that it looks like this:** =B11-SUM('IS Cash Flow'!C35:N35).

TIP

Note that fixed assets need to be shown at their *original cost* (regardless of whether they've increased or decreased in value since purchase) and then the accumulated depreciation is shown on a separate line to give us the total written-down value of the asset at that point in time. A long-term asset like the ones shown here will be depreciated until it's worth nothing on the balance sheet at the end of its useful life.

Because the fixed assets' value is depreciated, you need to pick up the D&A amount already calculated on the income statement.

19. **Select cell C12 and enter the formula** =-'IS Cash Flow'!O13.

You need to enter the minus sign because D&A subtracts from gross PP&E.

20. **Check your totals.**

The total amount of D&A expensed throughout Year 1 is $6,833, total fixed assets is $38,167, and total assets is $62,791.

Moving on to liabilities, in cell C23 you need to take into consideration any paying down of debt that may have occurred during the year. If there is any, it would show up in the cash flow on row 40.

21. **Although there isn't any at the moment, you should still link this row through to the balance sheet by entering the formula** =SUM('IS Cash Flow'!C40:N40).

The calculated value is zero.

22. **You then need to add the bank loan carried over from the previous year, so adjust the formula in cell C23 to** =B23+SUM('IS Cash Flow'!C40:N40).

The calculated value is $30,000.

23. For owners' funds in cell C27, simply carry this over to the next year by entering the formula =B27.

Finally, your retained earnings represent the amount of economic profit, or net income, your business has earned that has been retained in the company. This can be kept in the company to reinvest in the business or pay down debt, or it can be paid out as dividends to shareholders.

24. Select cell C28 and link it to cell O20 on the IS Cash Flow worksheet by entering the formula ='IS Cash Flow'!O20.

The calculated value is $7,791 and represents the total net income earned throughout the year.

Congratulations! You've linked all three financial statements. Check your totals against Figure 10-11 and make sure that you perform a balance sheet error check to see if your total assets equal your total liabilities and equity, and thus balances.

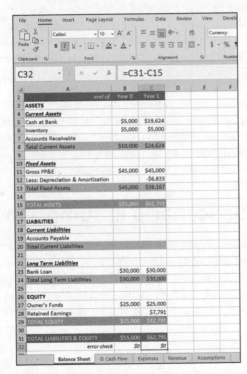

FIGURE 10-11:
The completed
balance sheet.

TIP

The balance sheet check is the most important one because it's the most common place where an error will surface due to the many moving pieces that all need to be correct in order for both sides of the balance sheet to balance. Many times, the error will be between the balance sheet and cash flow statement and may be because of an incorrect minus or positive value. When trying to reconcile a balance sheet that does not balance, I find it helpful to remember that the total assets must be equal to the total liabilities and equity, so if I add an item to the assets side of the equation, I need to add an amount of the same value to the other side of the equation.

Building Scenarios

Now that you've determined your base case assumptions that reflect how you believe the business will perform, you also want to run worst-case and best-case scenarios. Not only do you want to see how you believe the business will do, but you also want to see how the business will perform if it does worse than expectations or better than expectations.

Running multiple scenarios is a very important part of financial modeling — some would say it's the whole *point* of financial modeling — because it allows the user to gauge the different outcomes if certain assumptions end up being different. Because no one can see into the future and assumptions invariably end up being wrong, being able to see what happens to the outputs when the main assumption drivers are changed is important.

Because you've built this integrated financial model such that all the calculations are linked either to input assumption cells, or to other parts of the financial statements, any changes in assumptions should flow nicely throughout the model. The proof is in the pudding, however. In this section, you see what happens when you make major changes to this model with scenario analysis!

Entering your scenario assumptions

Going back now to the Assumptions worksheet, you believe that the main drivers of profitability for your café will be the average number of cups you sell per day and the rent you'll pay. You believe that reducing cups sold per day by 20 cups and increasing rent by 10 percent is a reasonable worst-case scenario, and increasing cups sold per day by 20 cups and reducing rent by 10 percent is a reasonable best-case scenario.

At the very top of the Assumptions worksheet, enter the scenario input assumptions as shown in Figure 10-12.

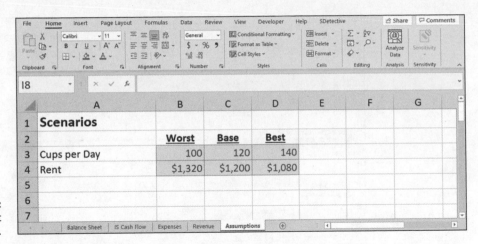

FIGURE 10-12:
Scenario input assumptions.

Building a drop-down box

You've decided on your scenario assumptions, so now you need to build a drop-down box, which is going to drive your scenario analysis. You have a full, working financial model, so you want the ability to switch between your scenarios to see how the outputs change in real time. You can put the scenario drop-down box on either of the financial statements, but for this example you'll put it at the top of the income statement.

Follow these steps:

1. **Go to the IS Cash Flow worksheet and select cell B1.**

2. **Select Data Validation in the Data Tools section of the Data Ribbon.**

The Data Validation dialog box appears.

3. **From the Allow drop-down list, select List.**

You could type the words Best, Base, and Worst directly into the field, but it's best to link it to the source in case you misspell a value. To review how to use a data validation drop-down box, turn to Chapter 6.

4. **In the Source field, type = and then click the Assumptions worksheet, and highlight the scenario names Worst, Base, Best.**

Your formula in the Source field should now be =Assumptions!$B$2:$D$2, as shown in Figure 10-13.

5. **Click OK.**

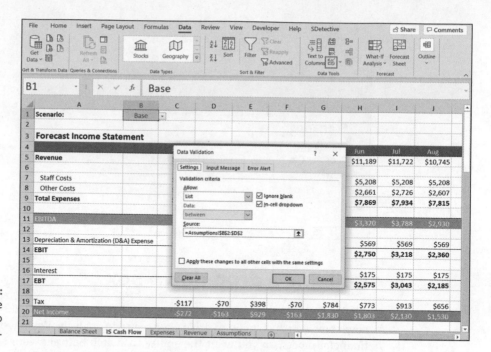

FIGURE 10-13:
Building the scenario drop-down box.

6. Go back to cell B1 on the IS Cash Flow worksheet, and test that the drop-down box is working as expected and gives the options Worst, Base, Best.

7. Set the drop-down box to Base for now.

Building the scenario functionality

You need to edit your input assumptions for number of cups sold per day and monthly rent so that as the drop-down box on the IS Cash Flow worksheet changes, the input assumptions change to the corresponding scenario. For example, when Best has been selected on the IS Cash Flow worksheet, the value in cell B9 on the Assumptions worksheet should be 140, and the value in cell B23 should be $1,080. This should be done using a formula.

TIP

Often, many different functions will achieve the same or similar results. Which function you use is up to you as the financial modeler, but the best solution will be the one that performs the required functionality in the cleanest and simplest way, so that others can understand what you've done and why.

In this case, there are several options you could use: a HLOOKUP, a SUMIF, or an IF statement. In my opinion, the IF statement, being a nested function, is the most difficult to build and is less scalable. If the number of scenario options increases, the IF statement option is more difficult to expand. In this instance, I have chosen to use the HLOOKUP with these steps.

Follow these steps (and see Chapter 7 for more information on HLOOKUP):

1. **Select cell B9 and press the Insert Function button on the Formulas tab or next to the formula bar.**

2. **Search for HLOOKUP, press Go, and click OK.**

   The HLOOKUP dialog box appears.

3. **Click the Lookup_value field, and select the drop-down box on the IS Cash Flow worksheet.**

   This is the criterion that drives the HLOOKUP.

4. **Press F4 to lock the cell reference.**

   In the Table_array field, you need to enter the array you're using for the HLOOKUP. Note that your criterion must appear at the top of the range.

5. **Select the range that is the scenario table at the top — in other words, B2:D4 — and then press F4 to lock the cell references.**

   The cell references will change to $B$2:$D$4.

6. **In the Row_index_num field, enter the row number, 2.**

7. **In the Range_lookup field, enter a zero or false, because you're looking for an *exact* match.**

8. **Check that your dialog box looks the same as Figure 10-14.**

9. **Click OK.**

   The formula in cell B9 is =HLOOKUP('IS Cash Flow'!B1,$B$2:$D$4,2,0) with the calculated result of 120.

10. **Perform the same action in cell B23 by entering the formula** =HLOOKUP('IS Cash Flow'!$B$1,$B$2:$D$4,3,0).

TIP

Instead of re-creating the entire formula again, simply copy the formula from cell B9 to cell B23 and change the row reference from 2 to 3. Copying the cell will change the formatting of the number, so you'll need to change the currency symbol back to $ again.

11. **Go back to the IS Cash Flow worksheet and change the drop-down to Best.**

   Check that your assumptions for average number of cups sold per day and monthly rent on the Assumptions worksheet have changed accordingly. Cups will have changed to 140 and rent to $1,080.

   Now, the important test is to see if the balance sheet still balances!

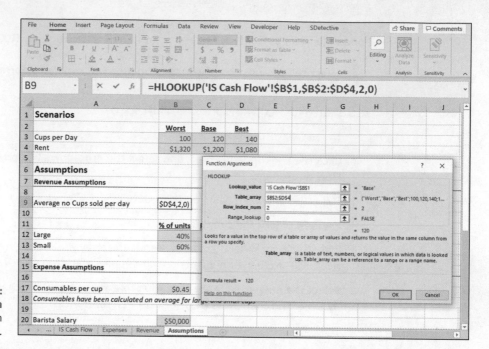

FIGURE 10-14:
Building a scenario with HLOOKUP.

12. **Go back to the Balance Sheet worksheet and make sure that your error check is still zero.**

13. **Test the drop-down again by changing it to Worst.**

Cups will have changed to 100 and rent will be $1,320. Check the error check on the Balance Sheet worksheet again.

Congratulations! Your entirely integrated financial model, together with scenario analysis, is now complete! You can download a copy of the completed model in File 1002.xlsx at www.dummies.com/go/financialmodelinginexcelfd2e.

IN THIS CHAPTER

» **Getting acquainted with discounted cash flow models**

» **Calculating free cash flow to firm**

» **Calculating weighted average cost of capital**

» **Finding terminal value**

» **Discounting cash flows and valuation**

Chapter **11**

Building a Discounted Cash Flow Valuation

The discounted cash flow (DCF) model is one of the most commonly-used methods of finding the value of a company or any other cash flowing asset. In fact, many other methods of valuation — such as cash flow multiples and the leveraged buyout model — are proxies or derivatives of the DCF model. Normally, modelers use the DCF method when trying to decide what the value of an asset is. For example, you may be considering purchasing a company or a large piece of equipment and want to know what the value of the asset is *for you*.

DCF calculations are normally an add-on to an existing, working financial model, but in order to use the DCF method to arrive at a value for the asset, you need to make sure that the model contains the following three pieces of information:

» Free cash flow to the firm, or the information necessary to calculate this

» Weighted average cost of capital

» Perpetuity growth rate (an assumption)

In this chapter, I explain how to pull out the pieces of information you need in order to calculate value using the DCF method. Of course, before you do so, you need to make sure that you have all the necessary inputs. If you didn't build the financial model that contains the information you'll be using, make sure that you understand the information you've been given and that the financial model is correct. For more information on working with an inherited model, see Chapter 5.

Understanding How the Discounted Cash Flow Valuation Works

The core concept of the DCF valuation is that of the basic finance concept of the *time value of money,* which states that money is worth more in the present than the same amount in the future. In other words, a dollar today is worth more than a dollar tomorrow.

The idea behind the time value of money is that if you have to wait to receive your funds, you're missing out on other potential investment opportunities, not to mention the risk of not receiving the money at all. If you have to wait to get your money, you'd expect some compensation — hence, the concept of interest. For example, if you invest $100 at a 10 percent annual interest rate today, it will be worth $110 in one year. Conversely, $110 in one year would only be worth $100 today. In this example, the 10 percent is referred to as the *discount rate.* As the name suggests, the discount rate is a key input you need to calculate the DCF.

A DCF valuation uses a modeler's projections of future cash flow for a business, project, or asset and discounts this cash flow by the discount rate to find what it's worth today. This amount is called the *present value* (PV). Excel has a built-in function that automatically calculates PV.

TECHNICAL STUFF

If you want to know the math behind the function, here's how to calculate PV, where *CF* is the cash flow for the projected year, *r* is the discount rate, and *n* is the number of years in the future:

$$PV = \frac{CF_1}{(1+r)^1} + \frac{CF_2}{(1+r)^2} + \frac{CF_3}{(1+r)^3} + \cdots \frac{CF_n}{(1+r)^n}$$

In the case of a project or asset with finite cash flows, the modeler would forecast all the cash flows and discount them to find the present value. For example, if you were purchasing an asset such as a large piece of machinery that has an expected life of ten years, you would model the entire ten years. When purchasing a business, however, which is expected to be a going concern and the cash flows are expected to continue into perpetuity, a DCF analysis must find a terminal value at the end of a certain forecast period instead of forecasting cash flows into eternity.

The *terminal value* represents the projected value of the company or asset at the end of the forecast period. Forecast periods are typically projected to the point at which cash flows are expected to grow at a stable and predictable rate. When the cash flows become stable, you can then reasonably estimate a fair value for the steady cash flows that are earned after that point in time.

There are variations of the DCF analysis in which the cash flows, discount rates, and terminal values can differ, but the most common method is to project free cash flow to firm, find a terminal value using the perpetuity growth method, and discount these values by the business's weighted average cost of capital.

For the case study in this chapter, assume that you've been provided with the projected financial model containing the financial statements for a company. It's your responsibility to perform a DCF analysis to arrive at a valuation for the business and ultimately a fair value for its equity shares.

Download the file File 1101.xlsx from www.dummies.com/go/financial modelinginexcelfd2e, open it, and spend a few minutes reviewing and familiarizing yourself with the financial statements. If you've completed the case study in Chapter 10, you'll recognize these financials. In Chapter 10, you build a financial model containing a full set of integrated financial statements, covering a 12-month period. To perform a DCF analysis, however, you need several years of financial statements, which are provided in this new model.

Step 1: Calculating Free Cash Flow to Firm

The DCF analysis will discount projected free cash flow that the business will earn, also called the *free cash flow to firm* (FCFF). A business's FCFF represents the cash flows the business will earn, disregarding cash flows associated with the capital structure, such as interest expense, debt paydown, dividends, or capital raises. The DCF analysis yields the value of the whole business.

The financial model provided in File 1101.xlsx has a projection period of seven years for the business and includes the Income Statement, Cash Flow Statement, and Balance Sheet for this period. Your job is to calculate the projected FCFF and then use this to calculate the DCF.

TIP

There are different variations of the DCF that may use a different FCFF to discount. For instance, a levered free cash flow DCF may project a future capital structure for the business and project a *free cash flow to equity* (FCFE), which accounts for costs of financing like debt interest and paydown. In this chapter, I explain the more common method of discounting FCFF.

Although there are different ways to arrive at FCFF, a common equation derived from net income is the following:

Free Cash Flow to Firm = Net Income + Depreciation and Amortization and Other Noncash Charges + Interest * (1 – tax rate) – Capital Expenditures + Change in Working Capital

To calculate FCFF, follow these steps:

1. **Add depreciation and amortization and other noncash charges to the net income.**

   These noncash expenses do not represent actual cash outflows from the business. Depreciation and amortization is the most common noncash expense to add back, but all other noncash expenses found in the income statement should be added back as well.

2. **Add the interest expense to the number you arrived at in Step 1.**

   You add back the interest because you have to disregard the charges associated with the capital structure and debt. Because interest expense is tax-deductible on the income statement, you need to add back interest adjusted for the taxes saved by its deduction.

3. **Subtract capital expenditures from the amount you arrived at in Step 2.**

   Capital expenditures and long-term investments are real cash outflows for the business that are required to keep the business going and properly invested in for the future.

4. **Add the working capital to the amount you arrived at in Step 3.**

   Working capital is calculated by subtracting current liabilities from current assets and includes line items like inventory, accounts receivable, and accounts payable. These items are continually required on the balance sheet for the business to operate. If more working capital is required due to an inventory increase, this represents a cash outflow because the business will need to spend cash to purchase said inventory. Conversely, if less working capital is required due to an increase in accounts payable (the ability to pay vendors later), this represents a cash inflow for the business.

Now that you know how to arrive at FCFF from net income, you need to link these projected line items from the included financial statements. On the DCF tab of the model you have open, you'll find these labels in cells A14:A19. Follow these steps:

1. **Select cell C14 and link it to the Year 1 Net Income in the Income and Cash Flow tab using the formula** =`'IS Cash Flow'!C27`**; copy this formula across the row.**

2. **Select cell C15 and link it to the Year 1 Depreciation & Amortization in the Income and Cash Flow tab using the formula** =`'IS Cash Flow'!C13`; **copy this formula across the row.**

3. **Select cell C16 and link it to the Year 1 Interest and multiply it by (1 – Year 1 Tax Rate) in the Income and Cash Flow tab using the formula** =`'IS Cash Flow'!C19*(1-'IS Cash Flow'!C25)`; **copy this formula across the row.**

REMEMBER

You're adding back interest and tax-adjusting it to account for the tax savings of the expense.

4. **Select cell C17 and link it to the Year 1 Capital Expenditures in the Income and Cash Flow tab using the formula** =`'IS Cash Flow'!C45`; **copy this formula across the row.**

5. **Select cell C18 and sum all Year 1 Working Capital cash flows in the Income and Cash Flow tab, including increases in inventory, accounts receivable, and accounts payable using the formula** =`SUM('IS Cash Flow'!C38:C40)`; **copy this formula across the row.**

6. **Select cell C19 and sum all these cash flow adjustments including Net Income, D&A, Interest, Capital Expenditures, and Changes in Working Capital to arrive at FCFF using the formula** =`SUM(C14:C18)`; **copy this formula across the row.**

You've just completed the FCFF calculation, your first step in the DCF analysis. Check your totals against Figure 11-1.

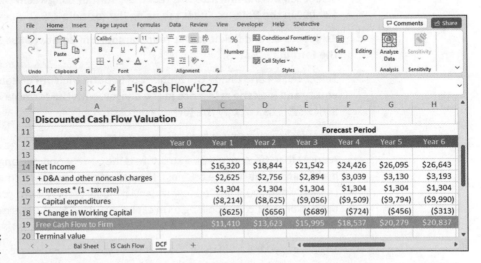

FIGURE 11-1:
Calculating FCFF.

Step 2: Calculating Weighted Average Cost of Capital

The most common discount rate used for a FCFF DCF analysis is the company's *weighted average cost of capital* (WACC), which is the company's cost of capital weighted by how much debt and equity it has:

WACC = (Proportion of Equity × Cost of Equity) + (Proportion of Debt × Cost of Debt, Less Tax)

The *cost of equity*, or the return required by the market in exchange for owning the company's equity, is multiplied by the percentage of the business's capital structure that is equity. The *cost of debt*, or the interest required by lenders in exchange for lending money to the company, is similarly multiplied by the percentage of the business's capital structure that is debt. The cost of debt is also multiplied by 1 minus the tax rate because interest is tax-deductible, which effectively lowers the cost of having debt by the amount of tax savings.

In this case study, you have a capital structure made up of 45 percent debt and 55 percent equity. You need to multiply each of these by the cost of equity and the market rate of the debt to come up with the WACC for the company. Follow these steps:

1. **Select cell B3 and link it to the Year 1 amount of Long-Term Debt of $30,000 in the Balance Sheet tab using the formula** =`'Bal Sheet'!$C$28`.

2. **Select cell C3 and link it to the Year 1 amount of Equity of $36,320 using the formula** =`'Bal Sheet'!$C$34`.

3. **Select cell B4 and divide the amount of debt by the sum of debt and equity and lock the reference in the divisor, with the formula** =`B3/SUM($B$3:$C$3)`; **copy the formula across to cell C4.**

   Now you have the percentage of the capital structure that is debt and equity.

   Assume that the Year 1 capital structure is the current optimal long-term mix of debt and equity for the business. Because capital structures constantly change, when you build your own financial model you'll want to consider the optimal or most common long-term capital structure for the business under the current conditions.

   To arrive at your cost of debt, you must take your interest expense and multiply it by 1 minus the tax rate to adjust for the tax deductibility of interest.

4. **Select cell B5, link it to Year 1 interest, and multiply the interest by (1 – Year 1 Tax Rate) in the Income and Cash Flow tab using the formula** `='IS Cash Flow'!C20*(1-'IS Cash Flow'!B25)`.

You have determined that investors in this business and similar small businesses require a 15 percent return to own the equity.

5. **In cell C5, enter** 15% **as a hard-coded input value.**

6. **Select cell B6 and multiply the cost of capital for debt and equity by their respective percent of the capital structure and add them together to find the business's WACC with the formula** `=B4*B5+C4*C5`.

The calculated value is 10.2 percent. Check your totals against Figure 11-2.

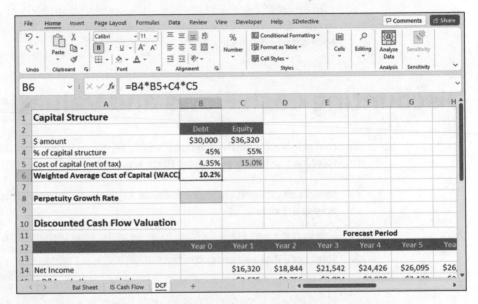

FIGURE 11-2:
Calculating the WACC.

Step 3: Finding the Terminal Value

Now you need to find the terminal value of the business at Year 7, the end of the projection period. There are many ways to estimate a terminal value of cash flows, but the most common method is using the perpetuity growth method. This uses a formula to find the value of steadily growing cash flows into perpetuity:

$$\text{Terminal value} = \frac{\text{FinalYear's FCFF} \times (1 + \text{Growth})}{(\text{WACC} - \text{Growth})}$$

This formula assumes a constant rate by which the cash flows will grow into perpetuity and values the cash flows accordingly. So far in this case study, you know the FCFF because you calculated it in Step 1. You know the WACC because you calculated it in Step 2. You don't know the perpetuity growth rate, and this is simply an assumption and should be a sustainable rate that you think the company can continue to grow forever after, usually in the range of 1 percent to 5 percent, but let's use 2 percent in this case.

Follow these steps:

1. **Return to your model and enter** 2% **in the input cell B8 on the DCF sheet.**

2. **Select cell I20 and enter the terminal value formula** =I19*(1+B8)/(B6-B8).

   You're multiplying Year 7 FCFF by (1 + Growth) and then dividing this equation by (WACC − Growth). The calculated value is $264,994. This is the terminal value and represents the value of the business in Year 7.

Discounting Cash Flows and Valuation

Now that you've found the business's FCF, terminal value, and discount rate, it's time to value the business. Follow these steps:

1. **Select cell C21 and enter the formula** =SUM(C19:C20); **copy this formula across the row.**

   This formula sums cells C19:C20 to arrive at the total cash flows to discount.

2. **Select cell B23 and enter the formula** =NPV(B6,C21:I21).

   This uses the NPV function to discount the cash flows, telling you what the series of cash flows over the seven-year future period is worth today, based on the assumed WACC. The first reference of the NPV (in B6) is your discount rate or WACC, and the second part of the formula is the total cash flows to discount.

   By discounting all the FCFF and terminal value, you have arrived at *enterprise value,* or the value of the whole business disregarding the capital structure. This value is $215,460. In order to find the value of the equity, you must add the cash the business currently has and subtract the debt the business currently owes to lenders.

3. **To add the cash, select cell B24 and link it to Year 0 Cash at Bank in the Balance Sheet tab with the formula** =`'Bal Sheet'!B6`.

4. **To add the debt, select cell B25 and enter** `=-'Bal Sheet'!B28`.

You want to show this as a negative value, so preface the formula with a minus sign. Compare your values to those in Figure 11-3.

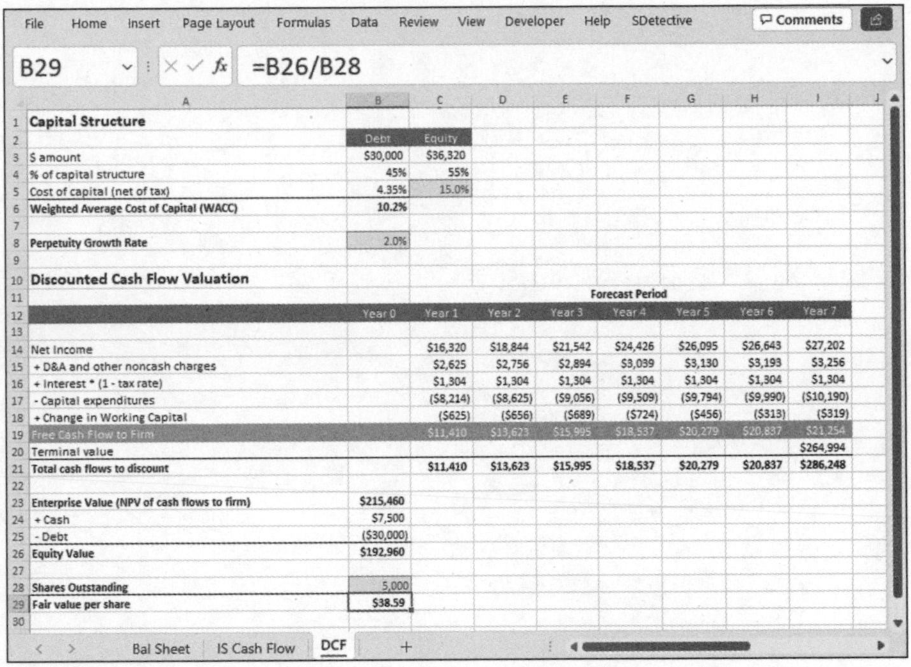

FIGURE 11-3: Completed DCF valuation model.

5. **Select cell B26 and enter the formula** `=SUM(B23:B25)`.

You should have now arrived at an equity value of $192,960. In order to find a target share price, you must divide the equity value by the number of shares outstanding. The business has 5,000 shares outstanding.

6. **Select cell B28 and enter** 5,000.

7. **Select cell B29 and enter the formula** `=B26/B28`.

The calculated value is $38.59.

Check your totals against Figure 11-3. You've now found the fair value of the business (enterprise value), its equity (equity value), and its stock price!

You can download a copy of the completed model called `File 1102.xlsx` at www. dummies.com/go/financialmodelinginexcelfd2e.

Chapter **12**

Budgeting for Capital Expenditure and Depreciation

The last two chapters offer a high-level overview of building financial models. In this chapter, you delve into more detail in one part of a financial model: the capital expenditure (CapEx).

In Chapter 10, I explain the process of purchasing assets and calculating their depreciation. For example, you purchased a coffee machine, as well as fixtures and furniture. These purchases were reflected in your cash flow statement, but you also needed to calculate their depreciation based on their useful life. You used this amount in the Income Statement and showed it on the Balance Sheet in order to show the current value of fixed assets. The way this was calculated was fairly simple — and sufficient for our purposes. Some models need to delve a little deeper, and that's what I do here.

In this chapter, I explain in more detail how to model depreciation. Here, you take a list of existing and budgeted CapEx items, convert them into a cash flow schedule, calculate the depreciation, and use the depreciated amounts to calculate the written-down value on the Balance Sheet. You also see what happens when an asset is fully depreciated and how to model this.

Getting Started

In this case study, you're charged with assembling the CapEx component for the coming year's IT budget. You've managed to pull from the fixed assets register a list of assets, the purchase price, and the purchase date. You also have a wish list of items your department wants included in the next budget. You use the information you have to model the cash flow and the depreciation.

TIP

It's always a good idea to start a modeling project with the end in mind. The outputs that you want to show in this model are the following:

>> **Output 1:** Cash required for asset purchases over the budget period (for the cash flow statement)

>> **Output 2:** Depreciation for the budget period (for the income statement)

>> **Output 3:** Written-down value of assets for the budget (for the balance sheet)

You can download the blank template, `File 1201.xlsx`, at `www.dummies.com/go/ financialmodelinginexcelfd2e`. The Calculations tab contains the data you already know and is designed for changes to be made by the user (a colleague or client who is not necessarily expected to understand how the model works) or yourself at a later date. The Assumptions tab contains assumptions you know; anything else you think of during the model-building process can be documented here as well.

The first thing you need to do is enter the time frames. Almost every model has an element of time series data, and it's important to get this right from the start. You need to decide at what level of time series detail the model should be built. (For more information on modeling time frames, see Chapter 3.) Most budget models, like this one, will be monthly. Many models are annual, such as the DCF model built in Chapter 11. Some are modeled weekly and many, such as cash flow models, are calculated on a daily basis.

In the following sections, you set up the model template with a variable time series so that the model will be reusable in the future. You also set up the titles, which also calculate dynamically as time goes by.

Making a reusable budget model template

When building the time series for this model, you can easily type in **Jan-23**, **Feb-23**, and so on into the Calculations tab, but by doing this, the model can be used only once in its current form. If you want to use it again, the following year, you'd need to update each and every date manually.

A much better idea is to enter the start date as an assumption, using a named range, and each time you use it in the model, refer to the named range. For more information about creating, using, and deleting named ranges, see Chapter 6.

Follow these steps to set up the time series for the budget template:

1. **Select the Assumptions tab and select cell B2, which contains the budget model start date.**

2. **Type** Start **in the name box in the upper-left corner, as shown in Figure 12-1.**

Now you can use this named range in your formulas as a starting point to model the time series.

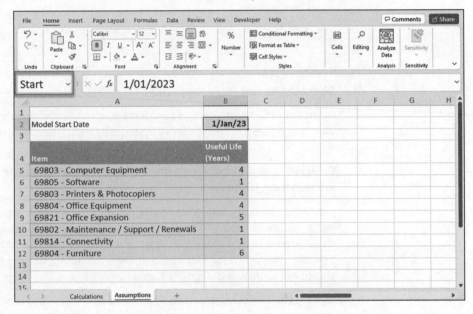

FIGURE 12-1: Creating a named range for the budget model start date.

3. **Select the Calculations tab and in cell H2, type** =Start.

The value Jan-23 appears. Note that the day of the month does not show because of the way cell H2 has been formatted.

4. **In the Font section on the Home tab, change the font color to white, as shown in Figure 12-2.**

In cell I2, you now need to add the rest of the dates. Instead of typing it in manually, you should link it to the start date now in cell H2. There are 31 days in January, so the formula =H2+31 would do the trick but copying it across would make your dates slightly inaccurate and cause problems later on. Instead, you can use an EDATE function.

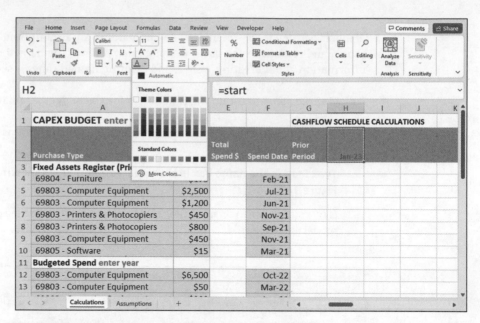

FIGURE 12-2:
Changing the
font color.

5. **Select cell I2, and enter the formula** =EDATE(H2,1)**.**

    By entering the 1 in the second part of the formula, you're given a date that is exactly one calendar month from the start date (H2). The value in cell I2 is Feb-23.

6. **Copy cell I2 all the way across the row to S2, so that you have all months entered from Jan to Dec.**

    Just for fun, go back to the Start date assumption on the Assumptions page, and enter the formula **=TODAY()**. It will show the month and year of today's date. Go back to the Calculations page, and you'll see that the budget starts from this month and runs for 12 months into the future. Use the Ctrl+Z shortcut to undo and change the start date back to Jan-23.

    While you're here, you should also add in the dates for the depreciation calculations from column Y onward.

7. **Select cell Y2.**

    Now, you could simply link this cell back to cell H2, but that would be a case of spaghetti links (see Chapter 14). It will work, but it's not good modeling practice.

8. **Copy all the cells in the range H2 to S2 across to Y2 to AJ2.**

    This will link back to the source. Now you're ready to build the budget.

Creating dynamic titles

Before you get into the modeling, take a moment to update the titles in red. It'll be helpful to show the year in the title, but you don't want to hard-code the year, because that means the template can't be reused. Instead, use the YEAR() formula coupled with the ampersand (&) to make a dynamic title:

1. **Select cell A1 and edit the formula to** ="CAPEX BUDGET "&YEAR(Start).

2. **Change the font to black if necessary.**

3. **Select cell A11, and enter the formula** ="Budgeted Spend "&YEAR(Start).

These two formulas in cell A1 and A11 will pull out the year of the start date only, and will automatically change when the start date changes. For another example of using the ampersand in dynamic text, see the example of linked dynamic text in Figure 4-5 (see Chapter 4).

Output 1: Calculating Cash Required for Budgeted Asset Purchases

Now that you've set up the layout of the model, you can start to model the numbers. The Calculations page contains all the information you need to create a cash flow schedule and calculate the depreciation. The top section you'd obtained from the fixed assets register, and the second part is the budget for the coming year.

The first thing you need to do is calculate the total line item amounts in column E. Follow these steps:

1. **Select cell E4 and enter the formula** =D4*C4.

2. **Copy the formula down the column to row 24.**

3. **Select cell E25 and press Alt+=.**

   This inserts a total.

4. **Check your totals against those in Figure 12-3.**

   Now, you can use the dates to populate the cash flow schedule. Don't worry about the prior period in column G for now — just focus on comparing the dates in the time series to the spend date in order to populate the cash flow schedule.

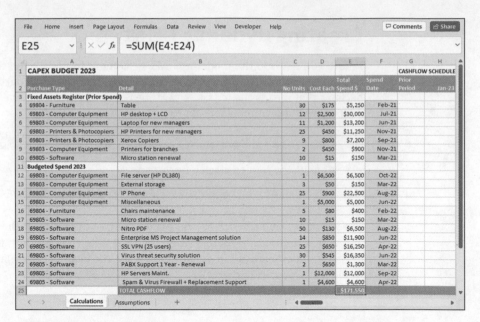

FIGURE 12-3:
Calculating total CapEx.

5. **In cell H4, enter** =IF($F4=H$2,$E4,0)**.**

   The calculated value in cell H4 is zero because the spend in row 4 occurred in the prior year, not Jan-23.

REMEMBER

   Be sure to use your mixed cell referencing (using the dollar signs) correctly. For a refresher, see Chapter 6.

6. **Copy this formula all the way across and down the range H4:S24.**

   By doing this, you're following good modeling practice by having consistent formulas in blocks of data wherever you can.

7. **Clear the zeros in cells E11 to S11 and compare your totals to Figure 12-4.**

   If the referencing has been done correctly, most of the values should be zero, with a few values showing.

   You'll notice that no values are showing for the prior period in column G. You need to add a different formula here, which shows the spend value only if the spend occurred prior to the start date of the model. Again, refer to the named range you created earlier because the start date is an arbitrary value that will change.

8. **Select cell G4 and enter** =IF(F4<=Start,E4,0)**.**

   The calculated value in cell G4 is $5,250.

9. **Copy cell G4 down the range G4:G10**

   There is no need to copy further than row 10.

10. **Copy the total in cell E25 across the range G25 to S25.**
11. **Compare your totals to Figure 12-4.**

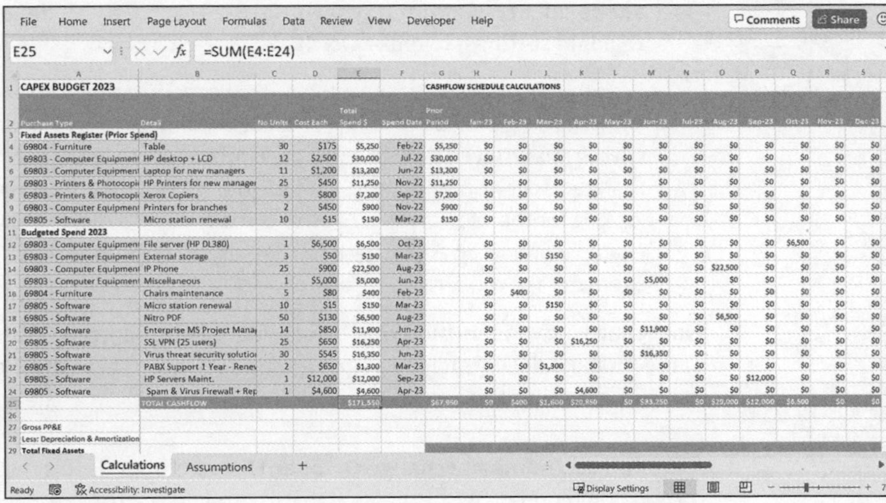

	A	B	C	D	E	F	G	H	I	J	K	L	M	N	O	P	Q	R	S
1	CAPEX BUDGET 2023						CASHFLOW SCHEDULE CALCULATIONS												
2	Purchase Type	Detail	No Units	Cost Each	Total Spend $	Spend Date	Prior Period	Jan-23	Feb-23	Mar-23	Apr-23	May-23	Jun-23	Jul-23	Aug-23	Sep-23	Oct-23	Nov-23	Dec-23
3	Fixed Assets Register (Prior Spend)																		
4	69804 - Furniture	Table	30	$175	$5,250	Feb-22	$5,250	$0	$0	$0	$0	$0	$0	$0	$0	$0	$0	$0	$0
5	69803 - Computer Equipment	HP desktop + LCD	12	$2,500	$30,000	Jul-22	$30,000	$0	$0	$0	$0	$0	$0	$0	$0	$0	$0	$0	$0
6	69803 - Computer Equipment	Laptop for new managers	11	$1,200	$13,200	Jun-22	$13,200	$0	$0	$0	$0	$0	$0	$0	$0	$0	$0	$0	$0
7	69803 - Printers & Photocopi	HP Printers for new manager	25	$450	$11,250	Nov-22	$11,250	$0	$0	$0	$0	$0	$0	$0	$0	$0	$0	$0	$0
8	69803 - Printers & Photocopi	Xerox Copiers	9	$800	$7,200	Sep-22	$7,200	$0	$0	$0	$0	$0	$0	$0	$0	$0	$0	$0	$0
9	69803 - Computer Equipment	Printers for branches	2	$450	$900	Nov-22	$900	$0	$0	$0	$0	$0	$0	$0	$0	$0	$0	$0	$0
10	69805 - Software	Micro station renewal	10	$15	$150	Mar-22	$150	$0	$0	$0	$0	$0	$0	$0	$0	$0	$0	$0	$0
11	Budgeted Spend 2023																		
12	69803 - Computer Equipment	File server (HP DL380)	1	$6,500	$6,500	Oct-23		$0	$0	$0	$0	$0	$0	$0	$0	$0	$6,500	$0	$0
13	69803 - Computer Equipment	External storage	3	$50	$150	Mar-23		$0	$0	$150	$0	$0	$0	$0	$0	$0	$0	$0	$0
14	69803 - Computer Equipment	IP Phone	25	$900	$22,500	Aug-23		$0	$0	$0	$0	$0	$0	$0	$22,500	$0	$0	$0	$0
15	69803 - Computer Equipment	Miscellaneous	1	$5,000	$5,000	Jun-23		$0	$0	$0	$0	$0	$5,000	$0	$0	$0	$0	$0	$0
16	69804 - Furniture	Chairs maintenance	5	$80	$400	Feb-23		$0	$400	$0	$0	$0	$0	$0	$0	$0	$0	$0	$0
17	69805 - Software	Micro station renewal	10	$15	$150	Mar-23		$0	$0	$150	$0	$0	$0	$0	$0	$0	$0	$0	$0
18	69805 - Software	Nitro PDF	50	$130	$6,500	Aug-23		$0	$0	$0	$0	$0	$0	$0	$6,500	$0	$0	$0	$0
19	69805 - Software	Enterprise MS Project Mana	14	$850	$11,900	Jun-23		$0	$0	$0	$0	$0	$11,900	$0	$0	$0	$0	$0	$0
20	69805 - Software	SSL VPN (25 users)	25	$650	$16,250	Apr-23		$0	$0	$0	$16,250	$0	$0	$0	$0	$0	$0	$0	$0
21	69805 - Software	Virus threat security solutio	30	$545	$16,350	Jun-23		$0	$0	$0	$0	$0	$16,350	$0	$0	$0	$0	$0	$0
22	69805 - Software	PABX Support 1 Year - Renev	2	$650	$1,300	Mar-23		$0	$0	$1,300	$0	$0	$0	$0	$0	$0	$0	$0	$0
23	69805 - Software	HP Servers Maint.	1	$12,000	$12,000	Sep-23		$0	$0	$0	$0	$0	$0	$0	$0	$12,000	$0	$0	$0
24	69805 - Software	Spam & Virus Firewall + Rep	1	$4,600	$4,600	Apr-23		$0	$0	$0	$4,600	$0	$0	$0	$0	$0	$0	$0	$0
25		TOTAL CASHFLOW			$171,550		$67,950	$0	$400	$1,600	$20,850	$0	$33,250	$0	$29,000	$12,000	$6,500	$0	$0
26																			
27	Gross PP&E																		
28	Less: Depreciation & Amortization																		
29	Total Fixed Assets																		

FIGURE 12-4: The completed cash flow schedule.

Take a moment to understand what this sheet is now telling you. You've taken the total spend for each item in column E and spread it out over the full year. The totals of each of the columns G through S should be equal to the total of column E. If they aren't, you need to figure out why.

REMEMBER

A good financial modeler is always looking for opportunities to include error checks in their financial model. Here's a good example of where you can include one. For more information about error checks, see Chapter 4.

Follow these steps:

1. **Select cell E26 and enter the formula** =E25-SUM(G25:S25).

   The calculated value will be zero because the totals are identical.

2. **If you want, use conditional formatting to color the entire cell red if the error check has been triggered.**

   If you choose to do this, select Conditional Formatting on the Home tab of the Ribbon, click Highlight Cells Rules, select More Rules, and create a new rule under Format Only Cells That Do Not Contain a Zero. Change the formatting to red fill.

   Now let's test the error check to see if it works.

3. **Select cell F12 and change the value to Oct-24 instead of Oct-23.**

The error check in cell E26 is triggered because that date is outside the range of the budget schedule and is not being picked up.

WARNING

4. **Select cell F12 again, and type in** 10/15/23 **(or** 15/10/23, **depending on your regional settings) to enter Oct 15, 2023.**

Even though the date is within the budget schedule range, the cost in row 12 still isn't being picked up! This is because the dates in row 2 are actually the *first of each month* (even though it has been formatted to show only the month and the year) so it won't pick up 15th of the month because the formula is only looking for the 1st. This kind of error is really easy to make, and it's a good example of how an error check can identify an error that's been made by a user after the model is complete.

Now that you've identified this error, you need to correct it and ensure that the same mistake doesn't happen again going forward. There are a couple of different ways of handling this:

>> **You can manually change October 15 to October 1.** This method is not recommended because, although it'll correct the error in this instance, it won't stop any users from making the same mistake again.

>> **You can insert an extra column to the right of column F, and convert each date that has been entered to the first of the month using a formula such as** =EOMONTH(F4,−1)+1. This method will work, but you'll need to make it clear to the user that any date that is entered will be converted to the 1st; otherwise, users will be under the mistaken impression that any date that is entered will have the *exact* number of days for the depreciation calculations.

>> **You can stop the user from entering incorrect data in the first place.**

My preferred solution for this problem is to stop the user from entering an incorrect value in the first place, using data validations. Follow these steps:

1. **Select the range F4 to F24 and then select Data Validation from the Data Tools section of the Data tab.**

The Data Validation dialog box appears.

2. **On the Settings tab, change the validation criteria to allow a list and use the mouse to select the range** =$H$2:$S$2, **as shown in Figure 12-5.**

3. **Click OK.**

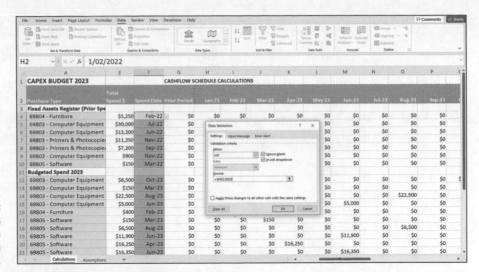

FIGURE 12-5:
Restricting errors
with a data
validation
drop-down box.

TIP

Data Validations are used for a number of different purposes in financial modeling. In this instance, they're used to restrict entry and avoid user error. They're also widely used in scenario analysis. For an example of how to do this, turn to Chapter 8.

After you've added the data validation, you need to document what you've done to show users that they can't simply enter any old data. If they try to enter an invalid date, they'll get a confusing and frustrating error message unless you explain why.

To prevent user frustration, you can add an input message to the cell so that users know what sort of data they can enter. This will also serve to document this model. For more information on using data validation input messages to document assumptions, turn to Chapter 4.

Follow these steps:

1. **Select the range F12 to F24 and then select Data Validation from the Data Tools section of the Data tab.**

   The Data Validation dialog box appears.

2. **Select the Input Message tab, enter some instructions such as those shown in Figure 12-6, and click OK.**

3. **Click one of the cells.**

   The drop-down box and input message appear.

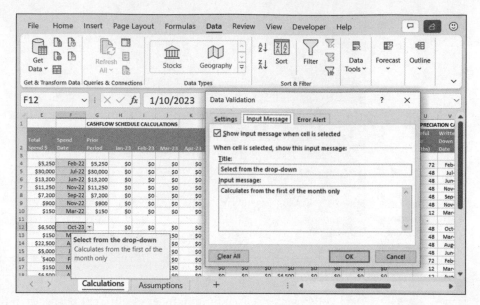

FIGURE 12-6:
Using a data
validation input
message to
document the
model.

4. **Try entering an invalid date, such as October 15, or any gobbledygook.**

   You get an error message.

   You can customize this error message on the third tab of the dialog box if you want.

TIP

This means that users cannot enter dates in past periods — which they should not be doing anyway. If you wanted to allow that functionality, you'd need to enter a list of allowable dates elsewhere in the model and link the drop-down boxes to that data instead.

REMEMBER

Because this data validation drop-down box is dynamic, the options that appear will change if the dates change. Try this out by changing the start date of the budget on the Assumptions from January 2023 to January 2024. Go back to the drop-down boxes in column F of the Calculations page, and you'll see that the options available change from dates in 2023 to 2024. When you build the model in this way, making changes in the future is straightforward.

Output 2: Calculating Budgeted Depreciation

Now that the spend has been spread out over the year for the cash flow, you can turn your attention to calculating depreciation. In order to do this, you need a few pieces of information:

>> The useful life of the asset

>> The written-down date

>> The number of months that have elapsed since purchase

Useful life

The useful life can be worked out from the class of the asset, which has already been entered on the Assumptions page. You can refer to the table using a XLOOKUP function. To review how to use this function, refer to Chapter 7.

Follow these steps to calculate the useful life:

1. **On the Calculations page in cell U4, enter the formula** =XLOOKUP(A4,'Assumptions'!$A$5:$A$12,'Assumptions'!$B$5:$B$12).

The calculated value is 6. This is the number of years the asset will last, but you need to show it in months for your depreciation calculation.

2. **Add *12 to the end of the formula in cell U4 to convert the number of years into months.**

The entire formula is now =XLOOKUP(A4, 'Assumptions'!$A$5:$A$12, 'Assumptions'!$B$5:$B$12)*12 and the calculated value is 72.

WARNING

Getting units of time mixed up in a situation like this is very easy. Be sure to label carefully. On the Assumptions page, the useful life is shown as Years in the label in cell B4 and on the Assumptions page in cell U2 the label is clearly labeled to show that the time period has been converted to months.

3. **Copy the formula down the column of data.**

An #N/A error appears in cell U11. This happens because the XLOOKUP function can't find the title in cell A11, so it returns an error.

4. **Go back to the XLOOKUP function and add a zero in the "if not found" field, as shown in Figure 12-7.**

TIP

Because you've added the *12 to the end of the formula, it's no longer a pure function, so going back to the dialog box by pressing the *fx* button to the left of the formula bar won't work. To show the dialog box, click anywhere within the XLOOKUP words on the formula bar and *then* press the *fx* button; the dialog box now appears.

5. **Copy the formula in cell U4 down the column of data again, and compare your results to Figure 12-7.**

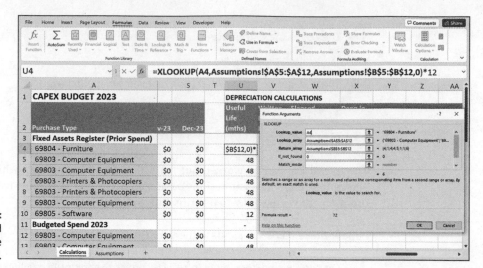

FIGURE 12-7:
The completed useful life calculation.

Written-down date

Now you know when the asset was purchased (or is supposed to be purchased) and you also know how long the asset is expected to last. With these two pieces of information, you can go ahead and calculate the date at which the asset is expected to be fully depreciated. You can use the EDATE function again just as we did earlier in this chapter to calculate the exact date at which the asset will be fully depreciated.

Follow these steps:

1. **Select cell V4 and enter the formula** =EDATE(F4,U4).

The calculated value is Feb-28.

2. **Copy the formula down the range.**

Cell V11 returns an incorrect value of Jan-00 again because there is no date value in cell F11 because of the title row. Your options are to:

- Clear the cell so that it's blank.

- Add an IF statement around the formula that will not calculate the written-down date if no date value has been entered in column F. If you choose this option, the formula in cell V4 is =IF(F4=0,"",EDATE(F4,U4)). Then copy it down the range.

WARNING

Note that a zero in the first "value if true" field will not work in this instance because a zero result in this formula will simply show as Jan-00. Therefore, a "" is necessary because that will show as a blank value. Be careful, however, when using this technique — a "" value is often treated as text by Excel and can cause some problems in calculations.

The depreciation schedule for the current year

Leave the Months Elapsed Since Purchase and Depn in Prior Period calculations aside for now, and start scheduling out the depreciation from column Y onward. What you need to do here is to show the depreciation only if the schedule date is between the spend date and the written-down date. Or in other words, only if the schedule date is greater than the spend date and less than the written-down date.

This formula is going to be more complex than what we have done so far, as it will contain a nested IF statement. Start by building the first part of the formula; show the depreciation only if the schedule is greater than the spend date. Follow these steps:

1. **Select cell Y4 and enter the formula** =IF(Y$2>$F4,$E4/$U4,0).

   You can either type the formula directly into the cell or use the Function Arguments dialog box, as shown in Figure 12-8. The calculated value will be $73.

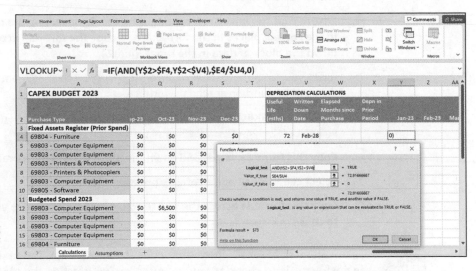

FIGURE 12-8: Using the Function Arguments dialog box to build an IF statement.

WARNING

Notice that columns B, C, and D are missing from Figure 12-8. This is because Freeze Panes has been added to this document already. Be careful when using sheets with Freeze Panes added — it's very easy to miss cells in a range when they aren't showing on the sheet.

This formula takes the cost of the item and divides it by the useful life to calculate the depreciation — but only if the asset has already been purchased. Take special care with the referencing. Be sure to put the dollar signs before the row or the column you want to fix so that we can then copy the exact same formula all the way down and across the block of data.

2. **Copy the formula across the range Y4:AJ24, and sense-check to make sure that it looks correct.**

   The depreciation should show only *after* the spend date has already elapsed on the schedule.

   Again, row 11 is causing problems, but you can deal with this later, after you've finished this formula.

   Now it's time to add in the written-down date, which is the second part of the formula, so it should show only if the spend date has elapsed *and* the written-down date has not elapsed.

3. **Go back to cell Y4 and edit the formula to** `=IF(AND(Y$2>$F4,Y$2<$V4), $E4/$U4,0)`.

   The calculated value is still $73.

4. **Ensure that the mixed referencing is correct by inserting the dollar signs in the correct places in the formula, and copy the formula across and down the block of data in the range Y4:AJ24.**

   Again, you can remove the #N/A errors in row 11 by clearing them or adding the IFERROR function around the formula.

5. **To add the IFERROR function around the formula, in cell Y4 enter** =IFERRO R(IF(AND(Y$2>$F4,Y$2<$V4),$E4/$U4,0),0).

6. **Copy this formula across and down the block of data in the range Y4:AJ24.**

7. **Select cell Y25 and add a total by pressing Alt+=.**

8. **Copy this formula across the row to column AJ and compare your totals to those in Figure 12-9.**

REMEMBER

Take a moment to sense-check this depreciation schedule. The first line of defense against error is to check as you go. After you've finished the block of data, do a spot-check on a random cell such as cell Z14. Select the cells and press F2. This will show you exactly which cells are being used in the formula because they'll be highlighted, as shown in Figure 12-9. Take a look at cell AA10. Why is it returning a zero value when the cell next to it has a value of $13? This is because the asset has reached the end of its useful life and, therefore, no depreciation should be calculated from March onward.

FIGURE 12-9: Calculating depreciation.

The formula bar shows: `=IF(AND(AA$2>$F10,AA$2<$V10),$E10/$U10,0)`

	A	S	T	U	V	W	X	Y	Z	AA	AB	AC	AD
1	CAPEX BUDGET 2023				DEPRECIATION CALCULATIONS								
2	Purchase Type	Dec-23		Useful Life (mths)	Written Down Date	Elapsed Months since Purchase	Depn in Prior Period	Jan-23	Feb-23	Mar-23	Apr-23	May-23	Jun-23
3	Fixed Assets Register (Prior Sp												
4	69804 - Furniture	$0		72	Feb-28			$73	$73	$73	$73	$73	$73
5	69803 - Computer Equipment	$0		48	Jul-26			$625	$625	$625	$625	$625	$625
6	69803 - Computer Equipment	$0		48	Jun-26			$275	$275	$275	$275	$275	$275
7	69803 - Printers & Photocopie	$0		48	Nov-26			$234	$234	$234	$234	$234	$234
8	69803 - Printers & Photocopie	$0		48	Sep-26			$150	$150	$150	$150	$150	$150
9	69803 - Computer Equipment	$0		48	Nov-26			$19	$19	$19	$19	$19	$19
10	69805 - Software	$0		12	Mar-23			$13	$13	=IF(AND(AA$2>$F10,AA$2<$V10),$E10/$U10,0)			
11	Budgeted Spend 2023												
12	69803 - Computer Equipment	$0		48	Oct-27			$0	$0	$0	$0	$0	$0
13	69803 - Computer Equipment	$0		48	Mar-27			$0	$0	$0	$3	$3	$3
14	69803 - Computer Equipment	$0		48	Aug-27			$0	$0	$0	$0	$0	$0
15	69803 - Computer Equipment	$0		48	Jun-27			$0	$0	$0	$0	$0	$0
16	69804 - Furniture	$0		72	Feb-29			$0	$0	$6	$6	$6	$6
17	69805 - Software	$0		12	Mar-24			$0	$0	$0	$13	$13	$13
18	69805 - Software	$0		12	Aug-24			$0	$0	$0	$0	$0	$0

Depreciation in prior periods

Now that you've calculated the depreciation amounts for the budget year, you can turn your attention to prior years. You need to do this for your Balance Sheet because you need to show the assets at their original purchase price, and then deduct the depreciation to arrive at the current written-down value.

First, you need to work out how many months have elapsed since asset purchase at the beginning of the budget year so that you can figure out how much depreciation to carry forward. You can do this by deducting the budget start date (January 1, 2023) from the asset's date of purchase (February 1, 2022, for the first asset). The formula =Start–F4 in cell W4 will return the value 334, which is the number of days between the two dates. To convert this number of days to months, you need to divide it by, say, 30 with the formula =(Start–F4)/30. This is probably close enough for our purposes in this model, but it would be more accurate to use a function such as YEARFRAC, which calculates the *exact* period of time between the two dates.

Follow these steps to calculate the amount of time that has elapsed since the asset was purchased:

1. **Select cell W4 and enter the formula** =YEARFRAC(Start,F4).

   The first field contains the beginning date, the second field contains the ending date of the period. This returns the number of years between the dates; you can convert to months by multiplying the result by 12.

2. **Edit the formula to** =YEARFRAC(Start,F4)*12.

3. **Copy this formula down the range W4:W10.**

Note that this formula is only relevant for assets purchased in the past, so the bottom half of the schedule can be left blank.

You can now calculate the depreciation for prior years in column X by dividing the original purchase amount by the useful life to arrive at the monthly depreciation amount. This amount is then multiplied by the number of elapsed months to work out how much depreciation has been incurred in prior years.

4. **Select cell X4 and enter the formula =(G4/U4)*W4.**

5. **Copy this formula down the range X4:X10.**

Again, note that this formula is only relevant for assets purchased in the past, so the bottom half of the schedule can be left blank.

6. **Copy the sum formula across from cell Y25 to cell X25 to calculate the total for the prior period.**

7. **Compare the totals to those in Figure 12-10.**

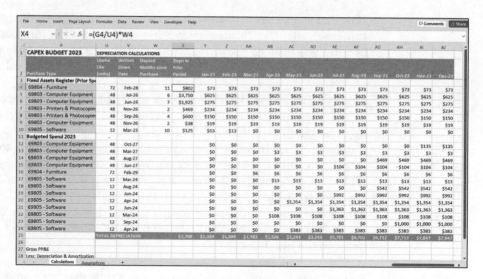

Output 3: Calculating the Written-Down Value of Assets for the Balance Sheet

For the balance sheet, you need to know how much the asset was originally purchased for, and how much has been depreciated to arrive at the written-down value. You already have all the pieces of information that you need to calculate this, and a place to enter it in row 27 of this model. Note that these assets will be called property, plant, and equipment (PP&E) on the balance sheet. For more information on how to incorporate these calculations in a full working financial model, see Chapter 10.

Follow these steps:

1. **In cell G27, enter** =G25+F27 **to calculate the total cost of the assets.**

This row is a cumulative total that will keep adding more assets as they're purchased. Note that although there is no value in cell F27, for the sake of formula consistency, you're still including it so that the formula can be copied across the range consistently.

2. **Copy this formula across the row to column S and compare your figures to those in Figure 12-11.**

3. **In cell G28, enter** =-X25+F28 **(note the minus sign after the equals sign).**

Again, you include cell F28 for consistency, even though it does not contain a value. The calculated value is –$7,708.

4. **Copy this formula across the row to column S and compare your figures to those in Figure 12-11.**

5. **Add these cells together in cell G29 with the formula** =SUM(G27:G28).

The calculated value is $60,242

6. **Copy this formula across the row to column S and compare your figures to those in Figure 12-11.**

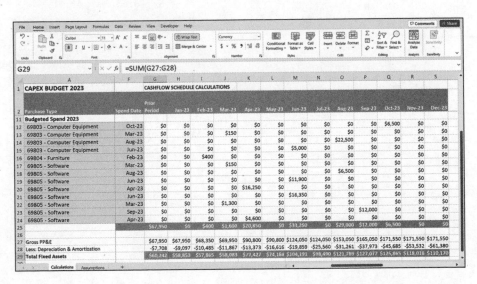

FIGURE 12-11:
The written-down value of assets calculation.

Now that you've completed this model, it can be used as a stand-alone model, or each of the completed outputs can be used as inputs for an integrated financial statements model.

You can download the completed version of this model, called `File 1202.xlsx`, at `www.dummies.com/go/financialmodelinginexcelfd2e`.

4

The Part of Tens

IN THIS PART . . .

Employ strategies to avoid errors when building and using your financial model.

Discover common pitfalls of modeling and find out how to avoid them.

Chapter **13**

Ten Strategies for Reducing Error

I f you aren't absolutely paranoid about making a mistake in your financial model, you should be! Even people with a little experience using Microsoft Excel know how easy it is to get something wrong. Both formula and logic errors are easy to make — and they're prevalent in corporate financial models. As a financial modeler, you have to be vigilant about errors as you build the model. In this chapter, I offer up ten strategies you can employ to reduce errors when building your financial models.

Using the Enter Key

The most common errors in financial models are silly formula mistakes — for example, picking up the wrong cell or missing a dollar sign in the cell referencing. Because these mistakes are the easiest ones to make, they're also the easiest to avoid.

TIP

After entering a formula in a cell, press the Enter key. Don't just click somewhere else.

There are two reasons not to click somewhere else after entering a formula.

>> **You may accidentally pick up an incorrect cell, which then autocorrects to a completely incorrect formula, as shown in Figure 13-1.**

>> **More important, when you click somewhere else after entering a formula, you're not checking what you just entered.** You need to be deliberate about what you've just done — don't just quickly move on to the next task. When you finish entering a formula, look at the result. Does it look right? Is the number what you expected?

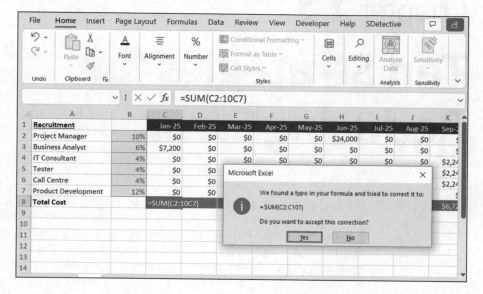

FIGURE 13-1: If you click elsewhere after entering a formula, you may accidentally pick up a cell you didn't mean to pick up.

REMEMBER

Pressing the Enter key is your number-one line of defense against errors.

Checking Your Work

A lot of modeling is trial and error. Making mistakes is okay — you just want to make sure you find your mistakes before someone else does! Silly formula mistakes are the easiest ones to make — and the most embarrassing. Fortunately, by employing good error-checking techniques as you build the model, formula errors are the easiest ones to detect and correct.

TIP

After you finish entering a formula, and after you've pressed the Enter key (see the preceding section), pause for a moment to check the result. Even if you're in a hurry. Especially if you're in a hurry. When you have to get a report out by the end of the day and the formulas are flying, that's when mistakes happen. Use a calculator or, if it's a simple sum, highlight the range you're adding, and check the total in the lower-right corner in the status bar, as shown in Figure 13-2. (The green triangle in the upper-left corner of cell C8 alerts you to the fact that something isn't quite right with this formula.)

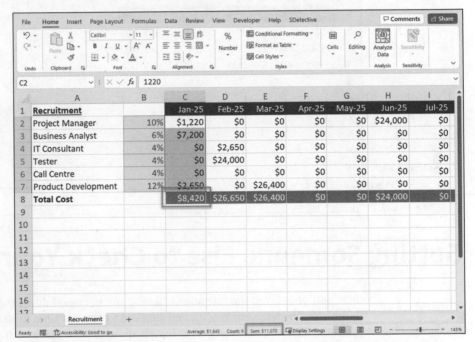

FIGURE 13-2: Checking the sum total in the status bar.

Highlighting cells and checking totals using this method is a good way of checking for errors. By checking your work as you build, you're less likely to let errors slip through the cracks.

Checking It Again

After you've checked your formula and perhaps copied it down a block of calculations, check it again! Another way to check the formula visually is to press the F2 shortcut key, which shows exactly which cells are being used in the formula (see Figure 13-3). This technique is most useful if the source cells are nearby and on the same sheet. When you've copied down all the cells in a block of data, do a spot-check with the F2 key to make sure it's picking up the correct cells.

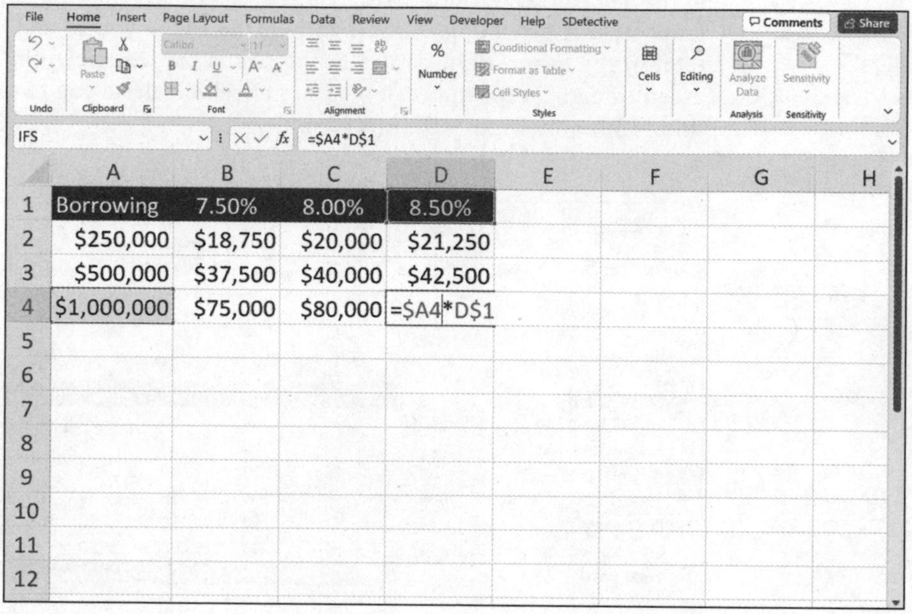

FIGURE 13-3:
Spot-check
formulas using
the F2 key.

Getting Someone Else to Check Your Work

Once you've entered the formulas, checked them, copied down the block, checked the totals, finished your model, and checked again, it's time to have someone else look at it. I highly recommend having an agreement in place with one of your colleagues where you check each other's work *before* it gets sent to senior management. There's no faster way to lose credibility than having your mistakes pointed out in public.

Why have someone else review your model? Because that other person will bring a fresh perspective. Sometimes you've looked at your model for so long that you just can't see the glaring error right in front of you. Just explaining the model's logic to someone else can also help you to see holes in the logic and ways to improve the methodology.

If the model is high profile or very important, you may want to get it audited by a model audit firm. Many organizations specialize in conducting professional model audits. This is really the only way to be absolutely confident that there are no errors and your model is working correctly.

Documenting Assumptions

A model is only as good as the accuracy of the assumptions. The phrase "garbage in, garbage out" has never been more relevant than in the context of financial modeling. Even the most beautifully built, best-designed model will be completely worthless if the input assumptions that go into it are incorrect.

Important decisions are made based on the outputs of the model, so it's absolutely critical to list clearly (and sometimes in mind-numbing detail) the assumptions that have gone into the model.

REMEMBER

Models are only as good as the data they contain, and the answer they produce should most certainly not be taken at face value. When presented with a model, a smart manager or decision maker will query all the assumptions and the way it's built.

As a financial modeler, you must ensure that all the assumptions have been validated to the best of your ability. Document clearly where the numbers came from so that there can be no possible misinterpretation of the assumptions you've used. That way, the assumptions can be revisited and possibly revised at a later date.

Documenting Methodology with a Flowchart

When you're explaining a complex process, such as one represented by your financial model, it can sometimes help to have a diagrammatic flowchart that explains the way that the numbers have been calculated in your model.

Excel doesn't create a flowchart of the model very easily, although there are add-ins that can help you do this. Without the help of add-ins, you can use SmartArt or simply cells and arrows to create a flowchart to document the inflows and outflows of your data within the model.

A flowchart isn't always necessary, but if your model contains a large number of sheets and calculations and is difficult for others to follow, a flowchart can be helpful for checking the logic. It's also useful in explaining the methodology of your model to other people.

Stress-Testing with Sensitivity Analysis

After you've finished the model, you can test to see if the calculations are working correctly by changing an input and seeing what impact that change has on the numbers. This technique of changing one single input in isolation is called *sensitivity analysis* (as opposed to *scenario analysis,* which involves changing several variables at once; see the next section).

For example, after you've finished the café model in Chapter 10, you can test that the model is working correctly by changing one of the input assumptions and seeing what effect that change has on the output of the model. Follow these steps:

1. **Set your model to the base case on the IS Cash Flow page.**

   Note that Other Costs is $29,192 and Net Income is $7,791.

2. **Go to the Assumptions sheet and change the consumables per cup in cell B17 from $0.45 to $1.00.**

3. **Stop for a moment to think about what effect you would expect this change to have on your Income Statement.**

4. **Go back to the IS Cash Flow page.**

   You'll notice that Other Costs has jumped to $45,804 and Net Income has dropped to a loss of $3,838!

You can see that the model is working correctly, because the costs are increasing, based on the consumables cost increase, and the profit has reduced, which is what you would expect. It also shows that the model is very sensitive to changes in input costs, which is an interesting insight.

Let's try another one, a little more drastic this time:

1. **Set your consumable costs back to $0.45 and make sure the model is set to the base case on the IS Cash Flow page.**

2. **Change the pricing for large and small cups of coffee from $4.00 and $3.50, respectively, to $0.**

3. **Think about what you would expect to happen in the model.**

   Revenue should be zero, right?

4. **Go back to the IS Cash Flow page and check that that is indeed what has happened.**

Although you don't actually expect the consumable costs to increase to a dollar, and you would never charge *nothing* for your coffee, stress-testing using sensitivity analysis checks both that the formulas are working correctly and that the logic is sound.

WARNING

When checking the logic and formula calculations with a sensitivity analysis, be sure to think through carefully what you expect to happen before looking at the effect your change has had on the outputs of your model. Beware of *cognitive bias*, where you only notice things that confirm what you already think.

See Chapter 8 for more on sensitivity analysis in financial modeling.

Conducting a Scenario Analysis

After you've finished all the calculations in your model, do lots and lots of sensitivity and scenario analyses. Stress-testing with sensitivity analysis (see the preceding section) will check that the inner workings of the formulas and logic of the model are correct, but how realistic are the assumptions? If the absolute worst happens, what happens to your bottom line? How sensitive is your model to changes in key assumptions? This information will help to test the accuracy and robustness of your model, as well as the soundness of the business, product, or project the model is representing.

At a minimum, a financial model should include at least the following three scenarios, or at least some version of them:

REMEMBER

» **Best case:** Set all assumptions to the highest possible value you can conceive as being achievable (even in your wildest dreams).

» **Base case:** Set all assumptions to what you *actually* think is going to happen.

Be realistic! This is not the place to be conservative in your estimates — that's for the worst-case scenario.

» **Worst case:** Set all assumptions to the lowest imaginable value that you think might happen. If everything that could possibly go wrong does go wrong, what does our model look like?

Additionally, financial models often include other scenarios to take into account possible fluctuations in inputs due to events, such as the following:

>> **Legislation:** If changes in government legislation will have an effect on the price you can charge for your product, material supply, or additional costs such as labor, then change the inputs in your model to reflect this.

>> **Foreign exchange:** If fluctuation in currency exchange rates will affect pricing or costings, change the inputs affected by foreign exchange in this scenario.

>> **Competitors:** If the introduction of a new competitor to your market would cause *margin squeeze* (meaning that you're no longer able to charge the same amount for your product), you could include a scenario that shows a decrease in price.

These are just a few generic examples of model scenarios you might use. Scenarios can often flush out anomalies in the model. Look carefully at the results of your scenario analysis. Is it what you would expect to see? Compare the output results side by side. If you increase the inflation amount from 2 percent to 3 percent, do costs increase by the same margin as if you increase it from 3 percent to 4 percent?

TIP

Compared to formula mistakes, logic errors can be more difficult to spot. Problems with logic may involve incorrect timing, inserting the wrong inputs and source data assumptions, or using pretax instead of post-tax inputs, for example. Sometimes the mistakes can be a combination of both formula and logic errors, and scenario analysis is a good way of identifying if these sorts of mistakes exist and flushing them out.

Thorough stress-testing, along with scenario and sensitivity analyses, will provide your financial model the rigor and robustness to cope with the variety of fluctuations in assumptions that are possible in the real world.

See Chapter 8 for more on scenario analysis in financial modeling.

Taking Note of Excel Error Values

As irritating as they can be, I actually *like* seeing Excel errors in my formulas, because it means that something isn't working and I can fix it. I'd much rather see an error value than a number that looks as though it's correct when it's actually completely wrong — that'll only cause problems later on in the model.

Common sources of errors are parentheses that don't match or missing fields for functions. Table 13-1 lists some error values you may get and how to fix them.

TABLE 13-1 **Common Error Values in Microsoft Excel**

Error Value	Description
#DIV/0!	You're trying to divide by zero. If the divisor is a cell reference, make sure that it isn't empty and that it doesn't have a formula with the resulting value of zero.
#NAME?	There's a name in the formula that Excel doesn't recognize. If you used a name you defined, check its spelling.
	You can avoid this error by using the F3 shortcut or selecting a name in the Name Box instead of typing it in.
#REF!	Your formula refers to a cell that no longer exists, due to a change in the worksheet. This happens if you deleted cells referred to in the formula or pasted cells onto cells referred to in the formula. You need to rebuild the formula.
#VALUE!	The function you're using is expecting a numerical value, and you've entered text, or vice versa. You can avoid this error by using the Function Arguments dialog box.
#SPILL!	This error was first introduced in Excel on Microsoft 365 and means there are cells obstructing a dynamic array.
Circular Reference	You're trying to link a formula to itself somehow. You see *Circular* followed by a cell reference in the area below the worksheet. Trace back the logic of the formula to correct the error. See Chapter 5 for more information on how to do this.

WARNING

If you're sure that the error doesn't need to be fixed, you can always suppress the Excel errors and stop them from showing by wrapping an IFERROR function around the formula. For example, if you have the formula =(B1-A1)/A1, you can suppress a potential error by adding an IFERROR around it like this: =IFERROR((B1-A1)/A1,0). If you do this, make sure that it doesn't suppress an error value that you need to know about and correct.

Instead of cringing at a horrid #VALUE! error value, or suppressing it with an IFERROR function, take notice of it instead. Figure out what's wrong, and get to the bottom of it. An Excel error value is far more helpful than the alternative, which is to have deceivingly innocent number values that are, in fact, incorrect.

TIP

If you see ###### (known as railroad tracks) in a cell, you may think there's an error. Good news! This isn't really an error at all. It just means the result is too long to fit in the cell. Just make the column wider, and — *voilà!* — the railroad tracks disappear.

Including Error Checks

A good financial modeler is always looking for opportunities to include error checks in the financial model. If you know that the sum total in the CapEx schedule should be equal to the sum of each individual item, add an error check to your calculations to check it automatically, so that the user or modeler can see at a glance if the formulas are calculating correctly. You can do this very simply by deducting one value from the other or inserting an IF function. For detailed instructions on how to build error checks, see Chapter 4.

WARNING

Note that error checks are not a substitute for good practices such as checking and auditing your formulas. Error checks are most appropriate for capturing errors a subsequent user has made. They're less likely to highlight a model-building error.

Chapter **14**

Ten Common Pitfalls to Avoid

Throughout my career as a financial modeler, I've seen countless things go horribly awry. Many of these problems can be attributed to at least one (or sometimes several) of the pitfalls I describe in this chapter. Why focus on the negative? So you can learn from the mistakes of those who've come before you! If you're aware of these potential problems, you can work to avoid them.

The Numbers Don't Add Up

"So, are we confident in these numbers?" Often, that's the first question you'll be asked when presenting a model or drawing conclusions from one. You need to be absolutely sure of any numbers you're presenting, and you need to be able to explain exactly how you came up with the results.

Confidence in the numbers comes from an intimate understanding of the process and calculations that make up the model. The audience or those you're working with will be able to detect any uncertainty on your part. Read through the strategies to reduce errors in Chapter 13. You can employ these strategies when building your model. And if you're inheriting someone else's model, error checking is even more important so you're completely confident that the numbers are right.

You're Getting #REF! Errors

#REF! errors are the worst kind of errors to get because it means that the cell(s) the formula is referring to have been deleted or that the formula is trying to reference a cell that doesn't exist. These errors are the most difficult to fix because the offending cell is no longer there, so the entire formula needs to be rebuilt. To fix this type of error, you need to go back to the beginning, assess what the formula was trying to do, and rebuild it from the ground up.

WARNING

You may be tempted to wrap an IFERROR function around the formula to suppress any error from showing at all. If you do this, you can end up masking errors that need to be corrected.

The best way to avoid having errors in your model is to *never let anyone else touch it.* In a corporate team environment, of course, this isn't practical; in fact, it defeats the purpose of building a financial model in the first place. You can prevent Excel errors from appearing in your model when others use it by restricting the model's use with data validation and protection. For more information on how to do this, turn to Chapter 6.

REMEMBER

If errors do appear, they aren't anything to stress about but the worst thing you can do is ignore or suppress them. You need to understand why they appeared, get to the bottom of the problem, and fix it.

You Have Circular References

Circular references are the result of a formula that somehow links back to itself. Generally, you should not allow a circular reference in your model. If you're building a model, the best way to avoid circular references is to simply undo what you just did as soon as the circular reference warning appears. If you've inherited a file that contains circular references (or if you didn't solve the problem in your own file when the problem first appeared), you can end up spending a lot of time trying to get them sorted out.

The most common circular reference occurs when you accidentally include a cell's reference in its own formula. For example, in Figure 14-1, I've built the formula =SUM(B3:B8) in cell B8. An error message appears immediately. If I ignore the error message by clicking OK, the formula simply won't calculate correctly. Although this might seem really obvious, it's surprising how easily these kinds of circular reference errors can be made.

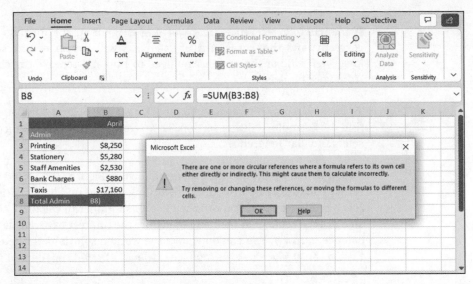

FIGURE 14-1:
A circular
reference.

Take a look at a more complex example. In Figure 14-2, I have the opening and closing balance of a cash flow forecast. In row 8, I'd like to calculate the interest income. Because I don't know the exact timing of when the cash was paid or received during the month, it's most accurate to calculate the interest income based on the average of the opening and closing balance. So, the formula in cell B8 is =AVERAGE(B5,B9)*$B$2. However, one of the inputs to cell B6 is cell B5. And one of the inputs to cell B5 is B6. And so it goes, culminating in a circular reference.

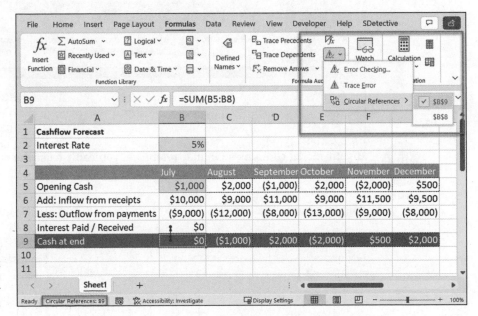

FIGURE 14-2:
A more complex
example of a
circular
reference.

If this circular reference error warning is ignored, the formula won't calculate correctly, and the words *Circular References* will appear on the status bar at the lower-left side of the screen. You need to find and remove the circular reference from your models.

TIP

To locate circular references in a model, click the Formula tab on the Ribbon, and find the Formula Auditing section. Then, from the Error Checking drop-down box, select Circular References.

Note that one solution to the problem shown in Figure 14-2 would be to get around it mathematically by inserting a "working cash at end" calculation, as shown in row 5 of Figure 14-3. You can then use this number to calculate the interest payable or receivable, and then add or deduct the interest to arrive at the ending cash balance in row 7. You can download the worked solutions to the example in `File 14-1.xlsx` at www.dummies.com/go/financialmodelinginexcelfd2e.

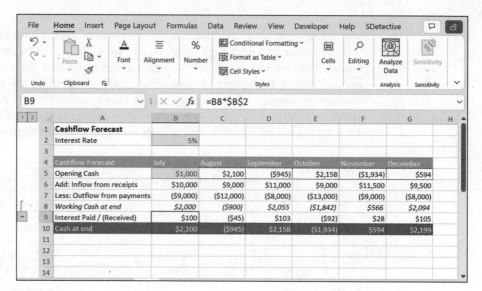

FIGURE 14-3: The solution.

REMEMBER

If your model contains a circular reference, you can't trust the calculations. You need to find and remove the circular reference from your model.

The Model Has Too Much Detail

Attention to detail is an important attribute for a successful financial modeler to have. In fact, many modelers are detail-oriented people because big-picture thinkers seldom have the patience for the intricacies and technical minutiae required for complex financial modeling. However, it's easy to lose yourself in the detail and get completely bogged down by it.

REMEMBER

When you're building a model, you need to maintain a sense of perspective and remember that a financial model is only a *representation* of reality — it's not *actual* reality.

Putting too much detail in a model — for example, calculating the *exact* number of customers without rounding to the nearest whole number or nearest hundred — creates a false impression that you know more than you really do. The model is just an *estimate* of what you think might happen. There's only one outcome you can be sure of: Whatever the output of the model, you can be sure it won't be *exactly* correct.

TIP

Think about the level of detail that's required by the users of the model. Sometimes you may need to go down to unit cost level in order to calculate revenue, but if no one will need or use these assumptions, then unless you need it for calculation, you don't need to put them in. A model that provides more detail than is required or needed can be counterproductive.

Information is powerful, and a detailed approach allows you to draw on this power. Just be careful that you aren't giving yourself extra and unnecessary work, or confusing, overloading, or misleading the model users.

The File Size Is Out of Control

TIP

When you start getting a fair amount of data in your financial model, it's pretty easy to end up with an enormous Excel file that takes a long time to calculate, making it difficult to review or share with others.

If the large file size is due to a large number of rows (say, more than 100,000), consider using the data model in Power Pivot to store the data instead. (Turn to Chapter 2 for more on this tool.)

If you find your model getting out of control (and you're using standard Excel, without the help of Power Pivot or any other add-ins), here are a few tried-and-tested tips you can use to keep that file size down:

TIP

» **Remove any unnecessary formatting.** Colors and formatting should only apply to the necessary range, not an entire row or column. Avoid manual formatting and use Styles instead.

When you're clearing cells that you're no longer using, you probably do so by selecting the cell and pressing the Delete key. This action clears the contents and formulas, but it doesn't clear the formatting. If you suspect this is a problem, you can press Ctrl+A to select all cells; then on the Home tab of the Ribbon, in the Editing section, click the Clear drop-down and select Clear Formats.

» **Make sure formulas are referencing only the range they need to (not selecting the entire row or column).** If your formulas are referencing more cells than they need to, this will use more memory. For example, use the formula =SUM(A1:A1000) to allow for additional rows instead of =SUM(A:A). Alternatively, you can format the data as a table and refer to the automatically expanding table ranges in your formula instead.

» **Remove (or at least check the size of) any logos or images that you're using.** A single JPG file inserted in a model can easily add 10MB to an Excel file size.

» **Avoid PivotTables.** PivotTables really chew up memory. If you have multiple PivotTables, make sure they're using the same data source, and not creating a whole new one.

» **Remove external links to other files.** To check if there are any external links in your model, go to the Data tab on the Ribbon and click Edit Links in the Connections section. If the Edit Links button is grayed out, that means there are no external links. If they exist, click the button and when the Edit Link dialog box appears, click Break Links to paste the data from all external links as values, and the external links will be removed. If you absolutely have to use external links, have the source file open at the same time; this will speed things up.

» **Check for redundancies in inputs and calculations.** Sometimes a model evolves, and there may be parts that are no longer used or parts where information has changed. See Chapter 5 for techniques on how to check for redundancies.

>> **Avoid volatile functions.** Some of the most commonly-used volatile functions are OFFSET, INDIRECT, RAND, NOW, TODAY, ROW, and COLUMN. Overuse of these particular functions in your model can really slow down your calculations. If you must use them, try to limit their appearance in the model. For example, =TODAY( ) is very useful for giving today's date, but instead of using it multiple times in a formula, have it in one single cell and continually reference back to that one cell for today's date.

>> **Make sure you aren't using the XLS file type.** XLSX is a much more compact file type, and you'll see a huge difference in speed and file size if you use it. XLSB is an Excel binary workbook file type that is even more compact than XLSX.

If you've tried all these tips and you're still having problems, consider switching the calculation to manual (you can do this by clicking the Formulas tab on the Ribbon, going to the Calculation section, and selecting the manual calculation option). Then press F9 only when you need to recalculate. You'll know if something needs to be calculated, because you'll see *Calculate* in the status bar.

Finally, as a last resort, a little trick is to leave one cell at the top of the column with the live link and paste all the other cells as values. Copy the cell down and recalculate when you need to refresh. This certainly isn't a preferred option, because it's time-consuming and prone to error, but that's why it's a last resort.

Your Model Is Full of "Spaghetti" Links

A link that links to a link, which then, in turn, links to another link, and so on throughout the model is called a *spaghetti link*. Spaghetti links can be confusing and difficult to follow, and they aren't good modeling practice. Wherever possible, you're always much better off linking directly to the source.

For example, in Figure 14-4, I have a model that's calculating student fees at a university. It's laid out in a repetitive, block format, which is a good way to lay out a model because it's logical and sequential. Each block leads on to the next one, which makes it easy to follow the calculations. You can take a look at the links in this file yourself by downloading File 14-1.xlsx at www.dummies.com/go/financialmodelinginexcelfd2e and selecting the sheet labeled 14-4.

At the top of each block, the dates have been laid out across the top. Linking these dates is a good idea, because it will make it easy to change if you want to reuse or update the model. However, as you can see in cell B38, I've linked the dates in row 38 to those in row 29. Row 29 is linked to row 20, which in turn is linked to row 11. Row 11 links to the top row, row 2, a perfect example of spaghetti links.

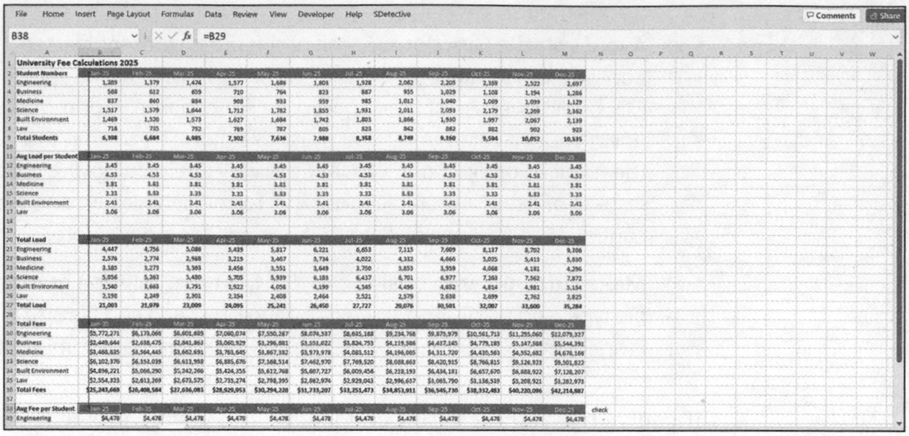

FIGURE 14-4: Spaghetti links in a model.

This works well, until I decide to remove a block. Later on, I decide that showing the average load per student separately is unnecessary, so I delete this block. This causes havoc in the model, meaning that any links subsequent to the second block become #REF! errors, because the cell they referenced has been deleted (see Figure 14-5).

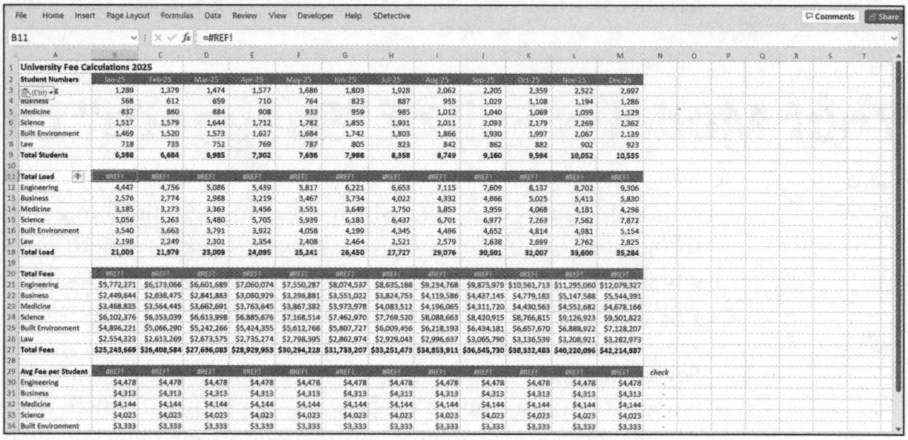

FIGURE 14-5: Deleting a block causes #REF! errors when spaghetti links are used.

Note that this hasn't happened to the list of faculty names on the side. Although these names are also repetitive and could have easily been connected, I've correctly linked them to the source instead, so they aren't affected when the second block is removed.

This is a very simple example of what can go wrong when using spaghetti links, but there are other reasons to link directly to the source. When checking or validating a model, spaghetti links make it much more time-consuming to audit the formula. If you're using trace precedents (see Chapter 5), imagine how frustrating it is to trace back multiple layers of dependencies instead of simply jumping to the original source data.

The Formulas Are Unnecessarily Long and Complicated

Keeping formulas as simple, clear, and straightforward as possible is always good practice. Remember that the model isn't only for you to use — it should be a tool that anyone in your team can pick up and understand with minimal explanation from you.

As you continue your journey as a financial modeler and learn very complicated and sophisticated Excel functions, you may be tempted to show off your Excel skills by creating fancy and complicated formulas. The problem is, this isn't very clever at all. A model should be as simple as possible but as complex as necessary.

This means you should start with a simple solution, and if that does the job, great! If you need additional functionality, you might need to add to it — but do it in a separate cell or a separate calculation block.

TIP

Deciding at what point to break a formula into separate cells is tricky because it also can make the model bigger. But as a general rule, and depending on the complexity of the functions used, don't try to do more than two or three things in a single cell. Break it down into separate rows or calculation blocks and lay it out so that it's easy to trace back and see exactly how the numbers have been calculated.

For example, this calculation to come up with student fees seems simple enough:

Student Numbers × Load per Student × Fees per Load Unit = Total Fees

But when converted to Excel, it's more difficult to follow:

```
=B3*VLOOKUP($A12,Assumptions!$A$2:$B$7,2,0)*VLOOKUP($A12,
Assumptions!$A$1:$C$7,3,0)
```

Even though the formula is only multiplying three numbers together, which is not difficult to follow, the fact that the first two numbers are derived from a VLOOKUP function makes it difficult to check and understand. The formula is much easier to follow if the calculation is laid out in separate blocks.

REMEMBER

As you're building a model, take a moment to consider the user who needs to make sense of your formulas afterward. Anyone using this model will want to check the numbers for themselves and make sure they follow how they've been calculated. A long and complicated formula may make perfect sense to you at the time, but it needs to be as clear and easy as possible for someone else to understand — and for you to come back later to figure out how the formula works again if you need to modify it.

No One Is Paying Attention to the Model

Imagine you've spent *weeks* slaving over your financial model. It flows beautifully, the numbers are perfect, and the scenarios work. Finally, the time has come to present your pride and joy at the weekly management meeting. You hand out hard copies, show the results on the projector, and launch into a detailed explanation of what the model is telling you about the business. "That's great," someone says, smiling politely.

"Thanks very much."

"What's for lunch?" someone else asks.

TIP

This kind of disinterest from those not involved in the model-building process can be disheartening, but there are a few things you can do to gain their interest:

>> **Involve them in the project if you can.** Ask their opinion on the subject and have them review the assumptions in advance of the meeting. If they're involved in the inputs and if they have a stake in the outputs, it's going to mean more to them.

>> **Show some visuals.** A boring black-and-white table with model outputs will put even the most hard-core bean counter to sleep. Spend some time making the outputs more meaningful with some charts and visual analysis.

>> **Don't just present an information dump, or bore them with unnecessary detail.**

For more ideas on how to better present model output, see Chapter 9.

You Don't Want to Let Go

If you've spent a lot of time on a financial model, designing it, building it, and making sure it works properly, handing it over to be operated by others can be stressful. After all, it's your creation, your "baby," and no one knows the workings of the model better than you. You're proud of it and you know it works well, but you're not sure someone else will appreciate it or take care of it the way you do.

It's natural to be worried about letting go of your model, but don't allow yourself to fall into this trap. Keeping a model to yourself is dangerous, and being dependent on one person — even you! — for any process is poor business practice. So, how do you share your models without putting them at risk? You need to teach the people who are going to be using the model how to use and maintain it from the start.

TIP

Instead of building your model in isolation, start building the model collaboratively. You'll be the model designer, the one responsible for the building of the model, but you should involve your team members in the process right from the start. Ask for their advice. Collaborate on design and assumptions input during the decision-making process. If you bring everyone onboard, you'll lessen the model's dependency on you, which means that other people will take ownership of it, too. And when they own it, they care about it.

There are some other benefits in sharing your model. Not only will it be better for the team, but by collaborating with your colleagues, you'll get the benefit of a fresh pair of eyes and a different perspective, which is extremely valuable. Your colleagues may be able to suggest developments and help you to improve the model or identify where there are errors or opportunities for a more efficient process.

TIP

Put together a user guide for your model. A user guide can help make the model sustainable and support its use, covering times when you aren't in the office, or after you've moved on because of the promotion you'll inevitably receive due to your superior financial modeling prowess.

Instead of selfishly keeping a model to yourself, you need to make sure that others understand and use your model. By using your model, they'll learn and improve their own modeling skills in the process. And that's something you can be proud of.

Someone Messes Up Your Model

You've finished with your model and convinced yourself to hand it over to the rest of your team to review or use on a regular basis. Then, one day, you hear the words that strike fear into the heart of every model designer: "Sorry to bother you, but the spreadsheet isn't working."

You try hard not to panic, but you can't help it: You break out in a cold sweat. You think to yourself, "I thoroughly checked that model and spent *hours* explaining and documenting how to use it. How did they manage to mess it up? That model was bullet-proof."

Despite a growing feeling of unease, you nonchalantly stroll over to your colleague's desk, trying to look calm. You take a look and, sure enough, there's definitely something wrong.

Take a deep breath and start with the process of elimination. Here are some places to start:

>> An audit trail of changes will allow you to quickly and effectively analyze the root cause of the issue: Is the problem with the data, or the model? You turn to the audit log on the front page, but it has been left blank. At handover, the users were asked to document any changes, but the last logged entry was your own.

>> Of course, you kept a clean copy of the completed model at handover, with every change that was made, so you can compare the current copy of the model with the last one you had. If you get different answers from the "broken" copy and the "clean" copy with the same inputs, comparing the two versions will get you closer to the source of the problem.

>> A review of any error checks you created when building the model will also identify the source of any obvious errors the users may have missed. Review Chapter 4 for more on error checks.

If you have multiple users, it becomes more challenging to determine who may have changed the model and whether it's a manual error, an unexpected activity, or an underlying problem in the model design. Tracing back to find the error is a process that may be a quick fix, or it could be quite complicated. Check out the tips in Chapter 5 — the techniques for reviewing your own model and an inherited model are essentially the same.

After you've checked and corrected an error, you can figure out what caused that particular error to happen. This, in turn, allows you to put in place further error proofing within your model or support structure. If you haven't done so already, make sure the model contains an audit log, a clean version, and error checks. Also, consider adding protection to the model and data validations for any inputs (for more information on how to do this, see Chapter 6). You can then decide to either correct the problem in the current version of the model or go back to the original by transferring the new data to a clean copy.

Index

Symbols and Numerics

error, 301
& (ampersand), 277
* (asterisk), 101
(Σ) Autosum button, 134, 135
$ (dollar sign), 101, 106
32-bit Excel, 27
64-bit Excel, 27

A

absolute cell reference, 101, 103–106
accessibility, checking, 83
accountancy qualification, 9
accuracy, checking models for, 85–87
Active filters feature (Inspect Document), 82
ActiveX controls feature (Inspect Document), 81
Adaptive Insights, 31, 32
adding
  data tables to bar charts, 208
  data tables to models, 198–199
  labels to line charts, 202
  scenarios, 48
  series names to line charts, 203–205
add-ins
  to Excel, 31–33
  for model building, 32
adjusting
  line charts to stacked area charts, 205–206
  pie charts to doughnut charts, 213–214
advanced functions, 170–172
Alt key, 123
Alt+= keyboard shortcut, 135
Alteryx, 31

amortization. *See* depreciation and amortization (D&A)
ampersand (&), 277
analysis, comparing types of, 174
Anaplan, 31
applying
  conditional formatting to error checks, 67–68
  formats to scenarios, 178–180
  Scenario Manager, 191–193
  scenarios, 173–193
  sensitivity analysis with data tables, 181–189
arrays, dynamic, 17
assets
  on balance sheet, 253
  calculating cash requirements for budgeted purchases of, 277–282
  calculating written-down value of for balance sheet, 288–290
  useful life of, 283–284
  written-down date for, 284
assumptions
  about, 29
  documenting, 53–59, 297
  entering, 231–234
  expense, 233
  redundant, 88
  revenue, 232
  scenario, 258–259
assumptions documentation
  building, 49
  as a key element of a financial model, 47
Assumptions worksheet, 231
asterisk (*), 101
audience, determining your, 51–52

audit tools, finding and correcting errors using, 84–94

auditing, add-ins for, 32

Autosum button (Σ), 134, 135

AVERAGE function, 139–140

B

balance sheet
  building, 252–258
  calculating written-down value of assets for, 288–290

bar charts, 206–208

base case scenario, 299

best case scenario, 299

Board, 31, 32

break-even points, calculating with goal seek, 129–130

budget model template, creating, 274–276

budgeting
  about, 31, 32, 273
  calculating budgeted depreciation, 282–288
  calculating cash required for budgeted asset purchases, 277–282
  calculating written-down value of assets for balance sheet, 288–290
  getting started with, 274–277

building
  assumptions documentation, 49
  balance sheet, 252–258
  bar charts, 207
  budget model template, 274–276
  cash flow statement, 248–252
  charts on formula-driven data, 219–220
  combo charts, 209–210
  data validation input messages, 55
  discounted cash flow (DCF) models, 263–271
  drop-down boxes, 125–126, 259–260
  drop-down boxes with data validations, 125–126
  drop-down scenarios, 175–180

dynamic formulas using links, 59–61

dynamic text, 221–224

dynamic titles, 277
  in error checks, 64–68
  financial models, 53–69
  income statement, 243–248
  integrated financial statements models, 229–262
  line charts, 202
  models, 48–49
  named ranges, 110–111
  pie charts, 211–212
  profit-and-loss (P&L) statement, 243–248
  red triangle comments, 54
  scenarios, 258–262
  Sunburst charts, 217
  Waterfall charts, 216–217

C

calculating
  break-even points with goal seek, 129–130
  budgeted depreciation, 282–288
  cash required for budgeted asset purchases, 277–282
  expenses, 238–243
  free cash flow to firm (FCFF), 265–267
  present value (PV), 264
  profit margin, 245
  revenue, 234–238
  weighted average cost of capital (WACC), 268–269
  written-down value of assets for balance sheet, 288–290

calculation cells, formatting, 68

calculation sheet, 51

calculations
  checking in existing models, 76
  defining, 50–51
  as a key element of a financial model, 47
  separating from inputs and results, 49

D

About the Author

Danielle Stein Fairhurst is a Sydney-based professional financial modeler with many years' experience as a modeling analyst. She helps her clients create meaningful financial models in the form of business cases, pricing models, and management reports. She has hands-on experience in a number of industry sectors, including telecoms, information systems, manufacturing, and financial services. She is also the author of *Using Excel for Business and Financial Modelling* (Wiley Finance) and she has been recognized by Microsoft as a Most Valuable Professional (MVP).

Danielle has regular engagements in Australia and around the world both in person and online as a speaker, course facilitator, financial modeling consultant, and analyst. Her custom-built training courses have been described by attendees as well presented, neatly structured, informative, practical, and extremely relevant to their everyday needs. She holds a Chartered Financial Modeler (CFM) qualification from the Financial Modeling Institute (FMI), a Master of Business Administration (MBA) from Macquarie Graduate School of Management (MGSM) and has taught management accounting subjects at Sydney University. Danielle is the founder of the Financial Modelling in Excel LinkedIn forum, which has more than 55,000 members worldwide and founded several Modelers' Meetup groups with thousands of members all over the globe. An advocate for women in finance, she was on the Diversity Council for the ModelOff Financial Modeling World Championships and founded the Women in Financial Modelling online community. She is on the Advisory Board of the FMI and on the judging panel for the Financial Modelling Awards.

Dedication

For Mike, as always.

Author's Acknowledgments

First, I must thank the many thousands of student modelers I've trained over the years both in face-to-face training courses and online. I've used their feedback and experiences to build, design, and improve the examples used in this book.

A number of people, including colleagues and industry experts, have assisted me with this book. Many of these people have taken the time to give me feedback and share their opinions on the subject. For their input and support, I am very grateful: Susan Wilkin, Gail Davies, Graham Eacott, Andrew Berg, Andrew Grigolyunovich, Steve Kraynak, Matt Allington, John Michaloudis, Ian Bennett, Lance Rubin, Justin Oh, Michael Alexander, Peter Bartholomew, and Johann Odou.

I'd also like to thank Tate, for his good cheer and help with graphics, and Mieke, for her constant supply of iced coffee as I wrote throughout our sweltering Sydney summer, as well as Enid for keeping me warm as I wrote during a winter visit to the UK.

Publisher's Acknowledgments

Associate Editor: Elizabeth Stilwell

Project Editor: Elizabeth Kuball

Copy Editor: Elizabeth Kuball

Technical Editor: Mike Talley

Production Editor: Tamilmani Varadharaj

Cover Image: © adempercem/Shutterstock

Leverage the power

Dummies is the global leader in the reference category and one of the most trusted and highly regarded brands in the world. No longer just focused on books, customers now have access to the dummies content they need in the format they want. Together we'll craft a solution that engages your customers, stands out from the competition, and helps you meet your goals.

Advertising & Sponsorships

Connect with an engaged audience on a powerful multimedia site, and position your message alongside expert how-to content. Dummies.com is a one-stop shop for free, online information and know-how curated by a team of experts.

- Targeted ads
- Video
- Email Marketing
- Microsites
- Sweepstakes sponsorship

20 MILLION PAGE VIEWS EVERY SINGLE MONTH

15 MILLION UNIQUE VISITORS PER MONTH

43% OF ALL VISITORS ACCESS THE SITE VIA THEIR MOBILE DEVICES

700,000 NEWSLETTER SUBSCRIPTIONS TO THE INBOXES OF

300,000 UNIQUE INDIVIDUALS EVERY WEEK

# of dummies

Custom Publishing

Reach a global audience in any language by creating a solution that will differentiate you from competitors, amplify your message, and encourage customers to make a buying decision.

- Apps
- Books
- eBooks
- Video
- Audio
- Webinars

Brand Licensing & Content

Leverage the strength of the world's most popular reference brand to reach new audiences and channels of distribution.

For more information, visit dummies.com/biz

PERSONAL ENRICHMENT

Staying Sharp
9781119187790
USA $26.00
CAN $31.99
UK £19.99

Facebook
9781119179030
USA $21.99
CAN $25.99
UK £16.99

Guitar
9781119293354
USA $24.99
CAN $29.99
UK £17.99

Investing
9781119293347
USA $22.99
CAN $27.99
UK £16.99

Beekeeping
9781119310068
USA $22.99
CAN $27.99
UK £16.99

Digital Photography
9781119235606
USA $24.99
CAN $29.99
UK £17.99

Meditation
9781119251163
USA $24.99
CAN $29.99
UK £17.99

Pregnancy
9781119235491
USA $26.99
CAN $31.99
UK £19.99

Samsung Galaxy S7
9781119279952
USA $24.99
CAN $29.99
UK £17.99

iPhone
9781119283133
USA $24.99
CAN $29.99
UK £17.99

Crocheting
9781119287117
USA $24.99
CAN $29.99
UK £16.99

Nutrition
9781119130246
USA $22.99
CAN $27.99
UK £16.99

PROFESSIONAL DEVELOPMENT

Windows 10
9781119311041
USA $24.99
CAN $29.99
UK £17.99

AutoCAD
9781119255796
USA $39.99
CAN $47.99
UK £27.99

Excel 2016
9781119293439
USA $26.99
CAN $31.99
UK £19.99

QuickBooks 2017
9781119281467
USA $26.99
CAN $31.99
UK £19.99

macOS Sierra
9781119280651
USA $29.99
CAN $35.99
UK £21.99

LinkedIn
9781119251132
USA $24.99
CAN $29.99
UK £17.99

Windows 10
9781119310563
USA $34.00
CAN $41.99
UK £24.99

SharePoint 2016
9781119181705
USA $29.99
CAN $35.99
UK £21.99

Fundamental Analysis
9781119263593
USA $26.99
CAN $31.99
UK £19.99

Networking
9781119257769
USA $29.99
CAN $35.99
UK £21.99

Office 2016
9781119293477
USA $26.99
CAN $31.99
UK £19.99

Office 365
9781119265313
USA $24.99
CAN $29.99
UK £17.99

Salesforce.com
9781119239314
USA $29.99
CAN $35.99
UK £21.99

Coding
9781119293323
USA $29.99
CAN $35.99
UK £21.99

dummies.com

dummies
A Wiley Brand

Learning Made Easy

ACADEMIC

Algebra I dummies

Mary Jane Sterling

9781119293576
USA $19.99
CAN $23.99
UK £15.99

Basic Math & Pre-Algebra dummies

Mark Zegarelli

9781119293637
USA $19.99
CAN $23.99
UK £15.99

Calculus dummies

Mark Ryan

9781119293491
USA $19.99
CAN $23.99
UK £15.99

Chemistry dummies

John T. Moore, EdD

9781119293460
USA $19.99
CAN $23.99
UK £15.99

Physics I dummies

Steven Holzner, PhD

9781119293590
USA $19.99
CAN $23.99
UK £15.99

1,001 Practice Questions
SAT dummies

Ron Woldoff

9781119215844
USA $26.99
CAN $31.99
UK £19.99

Organic Chemistry I dummies

Arthur Winter

9781119293378
USA $22.99
CAN $27.99
UK £16.99

Statistics dummies

Deborah J. Rumsey, PhD

9781119293521
USA $19.99
CAN $23.99
UK £15.99

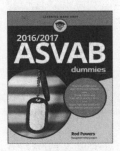

2016/2017
ASVAB dummies

Rod Powers

9781119239178
USA $18.99
CAN $22.99
UK £14.99

1,001 Practice Questions
Praxis Core dummies

Carla Kirkland
Chan Cleveland

9781119263883
USA $26.99
CAN $31.99
UK £19.99

Available Everywhere Books Are Sold

dummies.com

Small books for big imaginations

GETTING STARTED WITH Coding

Get Creative with Code!

Camille McCue, PhD

9781119177173
USA $9.99
CAN $9.99
UK £8.99

MODDING Minecraft™

Build Your Own Minecraft Mods!

Sarah Guthals, PhD
Stephen Foster, PhD
Lindsey Handley, PhD

9781119177272
USA $9.99
CAN $9.99
UK £8.99

MAKING YouTube® VIDEOS

Star in Your Own Video!

Nick Willoughby

9781119177241
USA $9.99
CAN $9.99
UK £8.99

DESIGNING Digital Games

Create Games with Scratch™!

Derek Breen

9781119177210
USA $9.99
CAN $9.99
UK £8.99

GETTING STARTED WITH Raspberry Pi®

Program Your Raspberry Pi!

Richard Wentk

9781119262657
USA $9.99
CAN $9.99
UK £6.99

EXPERIMENTING WITH Science

Think, Test, and Learn!

Olivia J. Mullins, PhD

9781119291336
USA $9.99
CAN $9.99
UK £6.99

CREATING Digital Animations

Animate Stories with Scratch™!

Derek Breen

9781119233527
USA $9.99
CAN $9.99
UK £6.99

GETTING STARTED WITH Engineering

Think Like an Engineer!

Camille McCue, PhD

9781119291220
USA $9.99
CAN $9.99
UK £6.99

WRITING Computer Code

Learn the Language of Computers!

Chris Minnick and Eva Holland

9781119177302
USA $9.99
CAN $9.99
UK £8.99

Unleash Their Creativity